In Pursuit of Dietrich Bonhoeffer

The last picture of Bonhoeffer, taken while he was in prison.

In Pursuit of
Dietrich Bonhoeffer

BY WILLIAM KUHNS

With a Foreword by Eberhard Bethge

Pflaum Press *Dayton, Ohio 1967*

First Printing, 1967

Library of Congress Catalog Card Number: 67-29763

Printed in the United States of America

to my mother and father

It all depends on whether or not the fragment of our life reveals the plan and material of the whole. There are fragments which are only good to be thrown away, and others which are important for centuries to come because their fulfillment can only be a divine work. If our life, however remotely, reflects such a fragment . . . we shall not have to bewail our fragmentary life, but, on the contrary, rejoice in it.

Letter from Tegel Prison
February 23, 1944

Acknowledgments

The author gratefully acknowledges permission from the following publishers to reproduce copyrighted material: Macmillan of New York, S. C. M. Press of London and Christian Kaiser Verlag of Munich for Bonhoeffer's *Letters and Papers from Prison;* Macmillan of New York and S. C .M. Press of London for Bonhoeffer's *Ethics* and his *Cost of Discipleship;* Harper & Row of New York and S. C. M. Press of London for *Theology and Church* by Karl Barth; Harper & Row of New York and William Collins Sons & Co. of London for Bonhoeffer's *Act and Being, Christ the Center, The Communion of Saints, No Rusty Swords,* and *The Way to Freedom,* also for *I Knew Dietrich Bonhoeffer,* edited by Wolf-Dieter Zimmermann and Ronald Gregor Smith; Harper & Row of New York for Bonhoeffer's *Life Together;* and Fortress Press of Philadelphia for *Preface to Bonhoeffer,* translated by John D. Godsey.

Foreword

It is with great appreciation that I have read this book, the first on Dietrich Bonhoeffer written by a Roman Catholic.

William Kuhns presents a genuine picture of the life and the intentions of this strongly Lutheran theologian and martyr. As a treatment by a Roman Catholic, the book draws its understanding largely from Bonhoeffer's ecclesiology, an aspect of his thought clearly outlined in the earlier writings, but tantalizingly unfinished in the later works.

I believe that the chief virtue of the book lies in its ability to maintain a basic unity in presenting a man whose life has moved through such contradictory periods of history and whose thought is so rich and varied. The difficulties inherent in Bonhoeffer's background and position have not hindered the author in presenting in their full weight Bonhoeffer's proposals for a non-religious interpretation of the Christian message. Here Bonhoeffer's ideas point the way for powerful new forms of Christianity. Here likewise Mr. Kuhns, in a way flowing out of Bonhoeffer's own conceptions, points to the most exciting challenge for the ecumenical movement: namely, the common task of spelling out in secular language what Christ wants spoken in our time. This challenge, of proclaiming Him in deeds and words which are not cheap but which are steeped in a newly found relation to Christ, may well be *the* Christian demand of our time. For this discovery can only stem from the churches' common and humble partaking in Christ's sufferings today—and tomorrow.

EBERHARD BETHGE

The more exclusively we acknowledge and confess Christ as our Lord, the more fully the wide range of his dominion will be disclosed to us.

Bonhoeffer, Ethics

Preface

The name of Dietrich Bonhoeffer needs little introduction. His emergence as a focal theological figure for the thought and efforts of our time—from civil rights to a theology celebrating the "death of God"—has been rapid and unmistakable. Martin E. Marty, editor of *The Christian Century,* has said that the theological world can be divided into two camps: "those who acknowledge their debt to Bonhoeffer, and those who are indebted but who obscure the traces to their sources."

Bonhoeffer died at the relatively young age of thirty-nine, hanged by the Gestapo in the Nazi concentration camp at Flossenbürg. What about the man has made his name appear at the head of almost every fresh theological venture of the last eight years? Why has he stimulated more interest among Catholics than any other Protestant theologian of the century? What has given his name an almost unchallenged prestige among younger Catholics and Protestants? His writings are incredibly broken, and the work which sparked the furor (his prison letters) is more a collection of half-formed ideas than a comprehensive theological statement.

In terms of Bonhoeffer's thought, the answers are not entirely obvious. Admittedly, Bonhoeffer's critique of religion and his work of hailing the "world come of age" have ushered in a new era of theology—an era given its style by such books as Bishop Robinson's *Honest to God* and Harvey Cox's *The Secular City*. But the devotion and the renewed belief that Bonhoeffer has inspired suggest that he achieved more than can be recorded in a volume on theology.

Perhaps no single truth is so striking about Bonhoeffer as his personal synthesis of life and theology. In few important thinkers of recent years, whether in theology, literature, or science, has there been such a creative interplay between thought and action. Although Bonhoeffer's theology can hardly be considered a commentary upon his activities, the impact of historical forces and personal struggles is readily apparent in his work. Hitler's catastrophic abuse of power, the apathy of the Germans when confronted by an agonizing crisis, the thwarted attempts of the renegade Confessing Church to preach the gospel undefiled by nationalism: these were among the forces that molded in Bonhoeffer a completely fresh outlook on the Church and the outline to a Christianity stripped of its "religious premise."

In attempting to describe the development and culmination of Bonhoeffer's thought, therefore, I have incorporated a biographical account of his life. The balance of life and thought which he achieved makes any serious attempt to understand his ideas inaccessible without some history of the man. For a much better, more complete understanding of the man and the forces he surmounted, a reading of the definitive biography by Bonhoeffer's close friend Eberhard Bethge is essential. Pastor Bethge lived and travelled with Bonhoeffer from 1935 until Bonhoeffer's imprisonment in April, 1943. The famous prison letters were written by Bonhoeffer to Bethge. It is Pastor Bethge whom we can thank for the preservation and publication of the *Ethics,* the prison writings, and the four volumes of the partially translated *Gesammelte Schriften* (Collected Papers). The appearance of Bethge's biography in English will be of inestimable service to theology and to the efforts of Christians everywhere.

In approaching Bonhoeffer's thought in this book, I have attempted to follow the major avenues of thought present in his writings. The treatment, compared with his original writing, is precariously brief and can serve as little more than an introduction. The stream of development which runs the gamut of his writings has been emphasized only because I believe it is crucial for an understanding of Bonhoeffer's entire meaning in the incomplete *Ethics* and prison letters.

Coming to Bonhoeffer as a Roman Catholic, I realize there are a number of inescapable limitations to my interpretation of his thought. I have tried as much as possible to surmount the obstacles and give a reliable description of his life and theology. I am convinced that few other Protestant theologians have spoken as meaningfully to Catholic minds and hearts as Bonhoeffer has, especially in his insights into the nature of the Church as community. Consequently, I do not see how Bonhoeffer poses any major obstacle to understanding among Catholics. On the contrary, he offers one of the most fertile sources for ecumenical guidelines to be found in recent theology.

This book would have been unlikely, and at moments impossible, without the assistance and encouragement of a number of people, too many to be listed here. To Dr. James Nelson, of the United Theological Seminary in Dayton; to Rev. John Kelly, of the University of Dayton: many thanks for their persevering help with the theology—and my frequent mistreatment of it. The index is the unflinching and incredibly dedicated effort of Brother Donald Wigal, S.M., of Bergamo in Dayton. Many grateful thanks to Pastor Bethge and his wife Renate for their warm and personal assistance in developing a plausible portrait of Dietrich Bonhoeffer the man. Also thanks to critic-poet John W. Jones for his surgical work on some serious abuses of language. But thanks finally to the person who has labored and suffered more with the book than anyone, my indomitable typist, Miss Karen Zekowski.

W. K.

Contents

Contents

In Pursuit of Dietrich Bonhoeffer

History, like nature, develops an excess of force to attain a necessary but modest goal. History adopts extravagant measures to preserve mankind and mobilizes immense forces to bring home to man one single, essential truth. We see and regret what seems to us a mad disproportion between senseless sacrifice and moderate success, but we should never underestimate even the most modest achievement. It is like the one chestnut among a thousand, which quietly puts forth roots into the ground and in its turn bears fruit.

From a letter written by Klaus Bonhoeffer
to his children from prison in 1943

1. *The Awakening of a Theologian*

Dietrich Bonhoeffer was born in Breslau, Germany, on February 4, 1906. His father, an eminent psychiatrist, practiced in Breslau until 1912, when he became the head of the Breslau University Hospital. Dietrich's mother, a lively, articulate woman, had descended from a leading aristocratic German family. Her father, Karl Alfred von Hase, had been chaplain and preacher to Kaiser Wilhelm. When the emperor discovered that his chaplain disagreed with his political stand, he pressured von Hase into resigning. Karl Alfred's father, the distinguished church historian, Karl August von Hase, had himself been imprisoned for his dangerously liberal views. Already in Bonhoeffer's ancestry there lay a tradition of Christian-based civil courage.

Dietrich spent his first six years in Breslau. A sensitive, happy child, he grew in an atmosphere of a warm and deeply secure family life. His twin sister, Sabine, has described the five-year-old Dietrich:

Dietrich with a shock of flaxen hair framing his tanned face, hot from romping about and trying to ward off the midges, seeking shelter in the shady corner but reluctant to obey the nursemaid's summons to come in because he is still so wrapped up in his game and oblivious of heat and thirst.[1]

The Bonhoeffer family was by any standards a large one. Besides his twin Sabine, Dietrich had six brothers and sisters: Karl Friedrich, the oldest; Klaus, who later died for his resistance work in the Second War; Walter, who was killed on the front in the First World War; Ursula, Christine, and Susanne. Apart from Susanne, Dietrich and Sabine were the youngest. Consequently, Dietrich was never considered the most likely to make the family name famous; he was always one of the "youngest three."

In 1912 the Bonhoeffers moved to Berlin, into a large house on Wargenheimsstrasse, in the Grunewald District. Here the father's intensive involvement with the university, and the family's proximity to the extraordinary cultural life afforded by Berlin, struck a new influence into the lives of the children. With neighbors such as famed theologian Adolf von Harnack and frequent guests like sociologist Alfred Weber, Dietrich grew in an atmosphere sharpened by intelligence and scholarship.

Dietrich began school at seven, attending the Friedrichs-Werder Gymnasium. At first he was frightened by the daily walk to school, which demanded crossing a long bridge. He overcame it, as he overcame other early fears, through the help of his brothers and sisters. Within a year he was an avid reader. At the age of eight he became fascinated with the making of music, and learned, at first largely by himself, to play the piano quite well. An ambition he harbored for several months, to be a musician, gradually faded as he realized that he hadn't quite that much talent.

One of Dietrich's great early loves was sports. Beside the summer home in the eastern Hartz Mountains was a large field, where in the evenings the local children would join the Bonhoeffer children in a ball game. Dietrich played fiercely, though with total honesty. He was admirably built for rugged sports and could handle himself in any game. With a sturdy, almost stout frame, he always—from boyhood till his death—looked more like an athlete than a student or scholar. Sabine recounts the time in which Dietrich once in a test of strength took the surprised governess and swung her onto the radiator.

The summer visits to the Hartz Mountains were welcomed enthusiastically by all the Bonhoeffer children. Although usually neither the father nor the mother could afford to break away from their Berlin involvements for the entire summer, the children would be accompanied to the second home by Fräulein Horn, their governess, and two assistants. In the mountains the children felt a freedom and excitement impossible in the stricter patterns of suburban Berlin. A common activity was the search for mushrooms, at which Dietrich became quite adept—and remained so all his life. In the evening the family would play games or sing folk songs, or simply watch the magnificent settling of the dusk over the mountains.

It would seem at a glance that there was nothing particularly exceptional about Dietrich's childhood; yet the closer one looks, the more exceptional his early family life becomes: exceptional because the parents were two outstanding people firmly dedicated to rearing strong children; exceptional because so many of Bonhoeffer's later convictions (his insistence upon community, his conception of authority, his demand for a fully human life) resound the experience of his childhood. Bonhoeffer lived in a family that provided an intense and beautiful setting for growth, a chance to take an optimistic outlook on the world, and the continued insistence upon self-discipline and emotional maturity.

Karl Bonhoeffer, the father, was a quiet-tempered, reserved man, yet one capable of immense understanding and sympathy. Built with a delicateness and precision further expressed in the precision of his speech and gestures, Dietrich's father impressed everyone who knew him by his simplicity and restraint. As a father, he endeavored constantly to develop the values in his children that he thought most essential: an openness and naturalness that could meet the world daily without cringing; a constant preoccupation with the feelings of others; a sturdy self-discipline and a critical knowledge of one's limitations; a total rejection of all that was false, trivial, or crude—cliches, foolishness, or any lack of earnestness in speech or expression. Despite his temperamental seriousness, Karl was capable of a liveliness and love for fun that seemed almost uncharacteristic. Once at a masquerade party he dressed as a janitor; his children were delighted that none of his assistants at the hospital recognized him—and Karl kept up the joke.

Paula von Hase Bonhoeffer differed widely from her husband. She was livelier, filled with an exuberance and a penchant for initiating projects and activities. The Bonhoeffer home was always humming with activity: whether with preparations for another party, the meeting of an important civic group, or the arrangements for one of the large family get-togethers. An excellent organizer, Paula always had the household fully in command. She loved teaching; she had, indeed, begged as a girl to be trained for teaching. It was her artistic bent which kept the Bonhoeffer family keenly interested in music, arts, and literature. Saturday evenings, a small orchestra comprising Dietrich and several brothers would play Beethoven or Bach favorites, to which she would sing.

Both Karl and Paula Bonhoeffer gave themselves to the task of rearing their children with rare zeal and competence. They looked upon the family as their world, bound by ties they considered sacred and eternal. And while admitting the final freedom of their children to make their own life choices, the mother and father both attempted constantly to instill the values and the way of thinking which would enable their sons and daughters to become responsible, respected Germans.

Dietrich's elder brothers differed from him in several ways. Karl Friedrich, who later became a biochemist, was the eldest son; his fascination with science impressed Dietrich and was perhaps one of the early reasons for Dietrich's determination to turn to theology—as an effort to commit himself likewise to an academic discipline. Walter, the second eldest son, also followed the scientific bent of the father: a courageous and outspoken young man, Walter died at the front in World War I. His death, profoundly felt in the Bonhoeffer household for years, impelled Dietrich to a kind of nationalistic craze in his late teens. Klaus later helped Bonhoeffer in the resistance. The two next girls in line—Ursula and Christine—also helped Dietrich become part of the resistance. Ursula married Reudiger Schleicher; their daughter Renate eventually became Eberhard Bethge's wife. Christine, the sharpest of the Bonhoeffer girls, was later intimately involved in the plot to kill Hitler; she was married to Hans von Dohnanyi, one of the architects of the *Abwehr* resistance circle.

As a child, Dietrich was closest of course to his twin sister Sabine. At night in bed the two children shared long solemn talks about death and eternal life. Sabine has described those evenings poignantly:

> After evening prayers and singing (which was always shared by our mother when she was at home), we lay awake a long time and tried to imagine what eternal life and being dead were like. We endeavored every evening to get a little nearer to eternity by concentrating on the word "eternity" and excluding any other thought. It seemed very long and gruesome, and after some time of intense concentration we often felt dizzy. For a long time we clung to the self-imposed exercise. We were very attached to one another and each wanted to be the last to say good night to the other; this went on endlessly and often we struggled out of our sleep to do so.[2]

Dietrich was eight when the War came. He felt something of its catastrophic proportions, but nothing like what he would feel in the mid-twenties, when the extent of the cultural eruption caused by the War would become apparent. He was twelve when his brother Walter—six years older—enlisted to fight at the Western front. Dietrich spent hours practicing the song, "Now at the last, we say God speed on your journey," and the evening before Walter left sang it to him with great ceremony. Two weeks later Walter was fatally wounded. Mrs. Bonhoeffer, stung by her son's death, seemed for the first time in her life broken in spirit. It was months before she came to be her recognizable self. Dietrich, like his brothers and sisters, was chastened by his brother's death, and came through it to recognize the inestimable horror of the War, and of war itself.

After the War, Dietrich took an increasing interest in the larger issues which were always a passionate concern in the Bonhoeffer household. The scientific tenor set by the father and followed by the brothers contrasted with Dietrich's developing fascination with philosophy and religion. He read the works of men like Dilthey and Simmel, Dostoevski and Soloviev; but Nietzsche was the most important. He would trade the books on science which he received as gifts with Susanne, for more reflective, philosophical works. Although the scientific spirit, and an accompanying agnosticism, dominated the Bonhoeffer household, Dietrich decided at the age of fourteen to enter theology. Part of his decision stemmed from his fascination with philosophy and a new-found interest in the Bible from a confirmation class he was attending. Part of the decision stemmed from a desire to match the capacities of his older brothers in a field where he felt a Bonhoeffer should become involved.

The decision to become a pastor came as a blow to his family, especially to his father. In Germany, Lutheran pastors generally come from lower and middle class families; Bonhoeffer's ancestry, although marked with theologians, distinguished his family as upper class. Years later, when Dietrich was struggling to clarify the Church's autonomy under Hitler's regime, his father wrote:

> When I heard that you intended to enter the pastorate as a boy, I thought that this was not the way that you should go, confining yourself to a corner of life. I thought at the time that such a removed and unreal existence as a pastor as I knew it from my uncle was too small; it was a pity that you would do that. Now, seeing the Church in a crisis that I never thought would be possible, I see that what you have chosen was very right.[3]

In 1923 Dietrich entered Tübingen University, where he studied briefly under such theologians as Karl Heim and Adolf Schlatter. Here his sharpness and agility of mind, already developed through frequent discussions with his father and brothers, took shape. Here Bonhoeffer began to see that the problems posed in a conversation or a course may well not be the problem, which one really wishes to grapple with—and consequently Dietrich grew in his characteristic effort of pursuing questions into more penetrating realms.

The summer after Tübingen, Dietrich spent one of the most exciting, and perhaps invaluable, vacations of his life, touring North Africa and Italy. For a young German student of the period immediately following World War I, the West—England, France, even America—held little fascination. The great enchantment came from the south: Rome, Athens, the Mediterranean. Dietrich had already studied these places in the classical history so much a part of the curriculum at the gymnasiums; now they became real and accessible, and, accompanied by his brother Klaus, Dietrich took full advantage of the opportunity to visit them for months.

Nothing on the vacation was so impressive as Rome. Here a new appreciation of the Church came to him. He admired the magnificent, towering churches; the opulent, awesome liturgy; the overwhelming sense of a universality which contrasted sharply with the provincialism of German churches. In his diary he described how profoundly moved he was by the confessions of faithful in the large churches, by the Palm Sunday High Mass at St. Peter's. He remarked once that the experience of these grandeurs, and the noticeably intense response of Catholics, helped him to "understand a little bit of the term 'Church.' "[4]

Indeed, Rome was far more to Bonhoeffer than a traveller's experience; to judge from the comments in his diary, and later, not infrequent remarks about his weeks in Rome, an entirely new understanding of the nature of the Church sprang from his experience here. He had never recognized that "Church" meant a reality far more profound, and more deeply felt, than the experience of German parishes, or German theology, could ever suggest. Above all, Bonhoeffer came to recognize that the Protestant churches lacked a vast dimension which Rome deeply affirmed: a vivid sense of the integrity and unity of Christ's Church. He said often to later students that it was healthy to have the temptation at one time to become a Roman Catholic. The students often were shocked, but they generally hadn't seen what Bonhoeffer so clearly saw in Rome.

The original impetus of Bonhoeffer's original theology is clearly a search for the contemporary meaning of the Church. His two theses deal directly with this question, and his later writings rest consistently upon it. Whatever influence Rome had upon Bonhoeffer's preoccupation with the Church can never be known exactly. Yet later mentions of the Church suggest that Rome stimulated much thought in this direction. Bonhoeffer saw in the Roman Church a warmth, an awesomeness, and an appeal absent in, but somehow necessary for, Protestantism.

Upon returning to Germany from Italy, Dietrich took up theological studies at the famed University of Berlin. Here a different world met the eighteen-year-old boy, challenged him, and to a notable extent, shaped him.

When Bonhoeffer stepped into the university, the ravages of World War I showed in a grim, unsettling way. The faculty was old, and their ideas stemmed from the 19th century and remained with the 19th century. The great theologians of only a generation earlier had been reduced to shadows, continuing a mode of thought which had been obliterated at the battlefields of Verdun and Belleau Woods. The aging, stooped Adolf von Harnack was perhaps the best example: the most brilliant and prolific theologian of modern times continued to teach exactly as he had before 1914, untouched by the grave threat the War posed to his vast synthesis of doctrine and history.

The University of Berlin was the greatest heir to a long tradition of theology, dating back to Friedrich Schleiermacher (1768-1834). "Liberal theology," also called "modernist theology," began with a major assumption, that a relevant, meaningful theology must proceed from man and move toward God. The history of liberal theology reveals not a clear body of doctrines but a temper of thought in which experience is held as the most valid criterion for religious inquiry.

The roots and heart of liberal theology lay in the 19th century. Friedrich Schleiermacher, the "father of liberal theology," was a firm idealist. He began with the question, "What does faith mean?" and concluded that religious experience ("a sense for the infinite") could be the only guide. Followers of Schleiermacher gave his initial impetus new and often startling directions, though always keeping with the original appeal to experience. Two thinkers especially influential upon Bonhoeffer were important offshoots of Schleiermacher: Albrecht Ritschl and Ernst Troeltsch.

Albrecht Ritschl (1822-1889) continued Schleiermacher's quest for a religious understanding which was relevant to modern man. Ritschl attempted to mediate between biblical and modernist thought, at a time when both the biblical scholars and the liberal theologians were disagreeing violently. Although Ritschl failed in his effort, later theologians who attempted a theology of mediation were greatly indebted to him. Bonhoeffer followed the path set by Ritschl, and his debt to Ritschl is apparent throughout this works.

Ernst Troeltsch (1865-1923) influenced Bonhoeffer in a different way. Troeltsch saw the greatest threat to Christianity in the upswing of the social sciences, and attempted single-handed to relate the Church to the sociological work of several decades. His study of the Church, emphasizing the corporate and institutional character of Christianity, provided one of the polar elements of Bonhoeffer's doctoral thesis, *The Communion of Saints.*

Bonhoeffer did not study under Troeltsch, but he was deeply impressed by Troeltsch's effort and some of his conclusions. The men under whom Bonhoeffer did study affected him in other ways. Karl Holl, the scholar who had succeeded in drawing fresh attention to Martin Luther, made quite an impression upon Bonhoeffer. In a seminar with Holl, Bonhoeffer came "to love Luther above anyone else," as Bonhoeffer's biographer Eberhard Bethge writes. Bonhoeffer was unhappy with Holl's emphasis on Luther's doctrine of conscience, and, partly in reaction, came to concern himself almost entirely with Luther's conception of the Church.

Bonhoeffer always felt that one of the greatest influences upon him at Berlin was the intellectual honesty of the magnificent old scholar, Adolf von Harnack. When Harnack died in 1930, Bonhoeffer was chosen to speak at the memorial service. He said of the historian:

He became our teacher. He approached us as the true teacher approaches his pupil. In our research he came to our side, but in his superior judgment he towered over us. The hours of hard work in early church history, for which in his last years he gathered us together in his home, led us to know him in his unswerving quest for truth and clarity. Empty phrases were foreign to the spirit of his seminar. Everything had to be clear at any price. That did not mean that questions of a most inward and most personal nature were out of place. They would find in him an ever ready listener and counsellor who was concerned with nothing but the truth of the answer. But it became clear to us through him that truth is born only of freedom.[5]

Bonhoeffer grew to see in Harnack's theories a great synthesis which admittedly had collapsed. Yet the young theologian never challenged Harnack, but constantly learned from him.

"I think of myself," wrote Dietrich almost twenty years later from his prison cell, "as a 'modern' theologian who still carries within himself the inheritance of liberal theology and is obliged to raise the questions with which it was concerned." [6] The University of Berlin convinced Bonhoeffer that the Church existed in the world, and to some extent one had to understand the world if he wished to understand the Church. But by its failures Bonhoeffer also became convinced that the Church consisted of something more than the expression of men's religious yearnings.

Liberal theology may have given Bonhoeffer the questions he would face, but his debt to this tradition was essentially a negative one. For instead of following the direction set by Ritschl, Troeltsch, and Harnack, Bonhoeffer turned to the dialectical theology of Karl Barth and committed himself firmly to Barth's revelation-centered theology.

Bonhoeffer never studied under the Swiss theologian; indeed, he never met him until his return from the United States in 1931. Yet during his years at Berlin, he read whatever he could of this new "theology of the Word of God" and was immensely impressed, if also deeply disturbed by its uprooting of the entire liberal tradition.

The publication of the second edition of Barth's *Epistle to the Romans,* by returning with unflinching loyalty to the Word of God, decimated theological thought on the continent. Following the great upheaval of the War, Karl Barth and many others like him had found their assumptions about the Church and Christian life violently shaken. Barth has himself described this confusion leading him to "grab a rope," the Epistle to the Romans, which had been a constant source of renewal to the Reformers. When the rope proved to be the bell rope, and Barth suddenly heard the bell pealing loudly, what could he do, he said, but continue?

To many, that bell rang the death-knell of liberal theology. For the movement grew quickly and attracted the younger generation of ministers and students. The dormant thinker Kierkegaard became widely read; new theologians sprang up and followed Barth—men like Paul Tillich, Emil Brunner, and Edward Thurneysen. Barth worked on a periodical, *Zwischen die Zeiten* ("Between the Times"), which became the voice of the new movement.

The years that this "revelation theology" came fully to life were the years of Bonhoeffer's study at the University of Berlin. The faculty was adamant about keeping the influence of this threatening movement out of the university. Yet a number of students, Bonhoeffer among them, carefully read and discussed every new work. After a while, it became clear that the greatest influence upon a large number of the theology students was the school of the Word of God, and not the modernist thought in which they had been trained.

Bonhoeffer later was to make a not inconsiderable number of reservations about Barth's dogmatic interpretation of Scripture. Yet he remained faithful to the major Barthian themes: the centrality of Christ, the entirely *given* character of revelation, and especially man's responsibility to listen to the true God, and not to fashion his own version of God. In a letter from Tegel prison in May, 1944, Bonhoeffer said that "Barth was the first theologian to begin the criticism of religion, and that remains his really great merit." [7] The distinction between religion and man's attempt to speak to God and revelation as God speaking to man was a crucial one in Barth's thought. In his later critique of religion, Bonhoeffer was indebted to Barth for the distinction, although he carried the notion much further than Barth had.

The complete effect of Barth upon his young disciple can be seen only as Bonhoeffer's writings progress. But even more sharply, Barth's influence upon the young theologian is revealed in Bonhoeffer's response to the Church crisis in Nazi Germany. While so many pastors reared in liberal theology quickly and unquestioningly fell into Hitler's hands, the group of pastors influenced by Barth, including Bonhoeffer, formed the core of a resisting Church, which fought vigorously for its autonomy.

Barth's theology was an extreme theology, admitting no truth for the Church beyond what can be gleaned from revelation. Reacting so strongly against liberal theology, it ignored the questions which attracted liberal theology. Yet it was these questions—the relation of God's Word to man's world, the Church and history, the Christian in a post-Christian world—which disturbed Bonhoeffer. Seeing that revelation theology failed to address these problems, Bonhoeffer decided to make the attempt. As a result, nothing is so striking in Bonhoeffer's early theology as the effort of reconciliation between Barthian and liberal thought.

By the time Bonhoeffer graduated from the university in 1927, the tensions which would dominate his life thought were already present. The concern of the pre-war liberal theology—Christianity as a meaningful experience of modern man—was a distressing problem for Bonhoeffer. Yet the concern of post-war, revelation theology—that God's Word is God's, and man must listen or destroy the Christian truth—came to be Bonhoeffer's predominant conviction. Out of this conflict came the overriding belief that God's Word is of itself relevant, deeply meaningful, and totally contemporary. Instead of "reconciling" revelation and the worldly relevance of the Christian message, Bonhoeffer saw revelation as intrinsically concrete; it remained the Church's responsibility to explore this concrete character in each new situation. What Bethge has called the "concrete nature" is the key to Bonhoeffer's earliest thought and the springboard to his later notions of Church and world, incarnational ethics and "religionless Christianity."

In 1927 Bonhoeffer presented *The Communion of Saints* to the faculty at the University of Berlin. Here the major tensions of his student years coalesced; here the young theologian—he was only twenty-one when he wrote it—began an effort which would take the remainder of his life to complete. However ambitious or pretentious *The Communion of Saints* may have been, it was for Bonhoeffer a distillation of the ideas with which he had struggled in his early years. It was likewise a pacemaker. The themes of *The Communion of Saints*—the Church as community, its revealed and concrete nature, its subsequent commitment to the world—were themes which Bonhoeffer would pursue and find ultimately fruitful.

It would be good to begin a dogmatic treatise for once not with the doctrine of God but with the doctrine of the Church, in order to make clear the inner logic of dogmatic construction.

The Communion of Saints

2. *The Communion of Saints*

Dietrich Bonhoeffer's doctoral thesis, entitled *The Communion of Saints,* or *Sanctorum Communio,* is hardly likely to attract a large reading audience today. It attracted a small audience when published in 1928, and much for the same reasons. The tone and language of the book are typical of the style predominant in German theology: an abstruse and ponderous prose which demands more plodding effort than agility of mind. Yet it must be recalled that *The Communion of Saints* was not intended for a wide audience; Bonhoeffer wrote it to impress a small group of professors. That the work confronts a major question of recent theology as seriously as it does is to its credit. That, in Karl Barth's words, it makes this confrontation in a way "far more instructive and stimulating and illuminating" [1] than most similar works is further to its credit. For Bonhoeffer was attempting nothing less than a fusion of sociology and dogmatics—in effect, a reconciliation of liberal theology and the theology of the Word of God.

The Communion of Saints may have been a work inspired

more by a student's ambition and intellectual daring than by a realistic appraisal of the enormous problems involved. Yet it is of seminal importance in the growth of Dietrich Bonhoeffer's thought. No other work concentrates so intensely upon the nature of the Church, Bonhoeffer's invariable theological theme. The effort undergirding the work indicates already Bonhoeffer's greatest concern: bringing the firmness of revelation theology to bear on the urgent questions of liberal theology, questions of the Church and the world. And apart from *Life Together,* in no other work does Bonhoeffer better explain the structure of the Church as community, an integral concept in all his thinking on the Church.

The actual thesis of the book can be inferred from the subtitle: *A Dogmatic Inquiry into the Sociology of the Church.* In a perceptive criticism of the thesis, Peter Berger has suggested that the key question is, "How can the Church, as the communion of saints, exist empirically as a social institution?" [2] Professor Berger has underestimated Bonhoeffer's attempt. Bonhoeffer was never satisfied to explain how a tension exists; he was convinced that each major tension demands a modified definition. The central question of *The Communion of Saints* might better be worded, "What *is* the Church, that it can exist as the communion of saints and, empirically, as a social reality?" Bonhoeffer does not simply ask about the relation between dogmatics and sociology in understanding the Church. Rather, dogmatics and sociology in hand, he hopes to search out a new understanding of the Church.

Ernst Troeltsch had made the attempt to relate dogmatics and sociology in a theology of the Church forty years earlier. But Troeltsch's effort had failed; without a resolute commitment to revelation, his theology had foundered and finally given over to sociology. Bonhoeffer took precautions to avoid the same error. As he wrote in explaining his method of approach:

> But to avoid misunderstanding it should be noted that the present work on *The Communion of Saints* is theological rather than sociological. Its place is within Christian dogmatics, and the insights of social philosophy and sociology are drawn into the serv-

ice of dogmatics. We wish to understand the structure, from the standpoint of social philosophy and sociology, of the reality of the Church of Christ which is given in the revelation in Christ. But the nature of the Church can be understood only from within, *cum ira et studio,* and never from a disinterested standpoint.[3]

The final point is the decisive one. Here Bonhoeffer eschews any possibility of understanding the Church without a prior belief in its major premise—that it has been established and revealed by Christ, the Son of God.

The structure of *The Communion of Saints*—there is no need to go into a long summary—begins with a statement of purpose and a definition of social philosophy and sociology. The distinction Bonhoeffer makes is a tenuous one; and Bonhoeffer's lack of an appreciation for a rigidly empirical sociology results in a sociology operating on a high level of abstraction. With this sociology as representative of the discipline, Bonhoeffer attempts to relate Christian concepts to the person and community. The book progresses with a study of "the primal state and the problem of community"—what Bonhoeffer claims is at the foundation of community existence. With an understanding of community (both dogmatic and sociological), Bonhoeffer studies the impact of sin on the community, and the return of the whole community in the communion of saints, the Church. It is this final section, on the Church as the *sanctorum communio,* which deserves further attention. For here Bonhoeffer presents such a cogent idea of the Church that Karl Barth, in reading it, would later describe the book as a "theological miracle." [4]

The direction of Bonhoeffer's thought up to the section on the Church is clear. He is attempting to reconcile a sociology of the Church with the dogmatic belief in the Church. In his long section on the Church he combines these elements into a theology of the Church distinctly his own.

"The Church is God's new purpose for man," Bonhoeffer states at the opening of his long section on ecclesiology.[5] But what is that purpose? How is it known? What is its empirical structure in this world, if any? These questions touch on the identity of the Church—and it is this question which ultimately Bonhoeffer must answer.

The dialectical structure of Bonhoeffer's argument sets the problem in polar terms.

In the concept of the Church there is a collision between two lines of thought; between the idea that the Church is founded by God, and that nevertheless, like every other kind of community, it is an empirical community.[6]

The dichotomy recalls Luther's distinction between the "visible" and the "invisible" Church. Indeed, Bonhoeffer follows faithfully Luther's thought on the Church. It is possible to see his effort to unite the "revealed" and the "empirical" as an effort, actually, to challenge the cleavage of the visible and invisible Church rooted deeply in Protestant tradition.

Luther's original position was that the Church is essentially invisible; its members are united in a spiritual community by bonds of faith. But the Church takes on visible expression; and here one must be careful, for according to Luther, an ecclesiastical institution need not always express the actual, invisible Church. Luther's original notion of an "invisible Church" (he was hesitant in using the term) did not involve the radical split which was to follow; he meant, simply, the hidden character of faith within the visible structures.

When later interpretations of "visible" and "invisible" aspects of one Church became "invisible Church" over against "visible Church," the route was opened for unlimited splintering of "visible churches." The rest is history.

Bonhoeffer's approach to the question involves a fresh approach to revelation. In Barth's theology revelation was emphasized for its otherness, God's gracious extending of his Word to man—the All pouring Himself out to the nothing. While he agreed with this view of revelation, Bonhoeffer took a new point of emphasis: this revelation must be in our world, clothed in human flesh and speaking human language; it must, as originally, be incarnated.

The application of Bonhoeffer's notion of revelation applied to the Church is clear: to believe only in an invisible Church is not to believe in the Church at all:

But what does "believing in the Church" mean? We do not believe in an invisible Church, not in the kingdom of God existing in the Church as *coetus electorum* (the womb of the elite); but we believe that God has made the actual empirical Church, in which the Word and the sacraments are administered, into his community, that it is the Body of Christ, that is, the presence of Christ in the world, and that according to the promise God's spirit becomes effective in it.[7]

He goes even further, certainly straining doctrines of Luther and Barth, if not overtaking them; "thus we believe in the means of grace within the empirical Church and hence in the holy congregation created by them."[8]

In effect, Bonhoeffer is justifying a sociological method by a theology of revelation which declares that to be revealed, the Church must exist in earthly forms, institutions which partake of the frailty and failure of the world. Here lies the central thrust of *The Communion of Saints,* and the mainspring to much of the later, far more original theology.

Emerging from this premise of concrete revelation is a stimulating image: "Christ existing as community" (or "Christ existing as the Church"—Bonhoeffer uses the terms interchangeably). The Pauline identification of Christ with his Church is important here: "Christ is really present only in the Church. The Church is in him and he is in the Church, and 'to be in Christ' is the same as 'to be in the Church.' "[9] From this step Bonhoeffer emphasizes the presence of Christ in the Church through time as a continuing revelation. So actually, a more appropriate term might be "Christ revealed as the Church," or "Christ revealed as community."

The implications here are rich; and in exploring many of them, Bonhoeffer uncovers some of the most fertile ground in *The Communion of Saints.* At one point he makes the statement:

It is only by beginning with the Church as a community of persons that the Protestant forms of baptism, confirmation, withdrawal, the gathering of the congregation and Church rules can be understood; only from this standpoint can one understand the structure of the objective spirit of the Church, as it is embodied in fixed forms.[10]

The return to Luther again is apparent; but so is the step taken beyond Luther. For Bonhoeffer does not speak of "community" in a general, all-encompassing way. His meaning is precise. He begins by making Tönnies' classic distinction between *Gemeinschaft* (community) and *Gesellschaft* (society). And drawing upon Max Scheler, he comments that real communities are generally life communities, "not because the whole of life necessarily runs its life in them, but because man can live in them in the form proper to his vital personal being." [11] His concept of community was also heavily influenced by Hegel: in a community the "objective spirit" takes on a personal character, and this in turn becomes a "collective will." Essentially Bonhoeffer's final concept of community is one of a living group of people becoming, in more than a metaphorical way, a single body, and a single person.

Bonhoeffer does not restrict his thought on community to a structural definition. In a chapter entitled "The Holy Spirit and the Church of Jesus Christ—The Actualization of the Essential Church," he describes vividly the meaning of true Christian community and its penetrating demand:

In this state, established by Christ, of being "with one another," which is shared by the Church and its members, the being "for one another" is also given. This active "being for one another" can be defined from two standpoints: Christ is the measure and standard of our conduct, and our conduct is that of a member of the body of Christ, that is, of one equipped with the strength of Christ's love, in which each man can and will become Christ for his fellowman.[12]

Bonhoeffer's conviction that the Church's existence hinged on men living in true community would grow, and find later expression in his little book, *Life Together*. Already from a doctrinal viewpoint it is present, and it figures decisively in Bonhoeffer's answer to the question, "What is the Church?"

At the conclusion of *The Communion of Saints,* Bonhoeffer makes a statement which would become prophetic of his own life and of the future Church in Germany:

> Our age is not poor in experiences, but in faith. Only faith can create true experience of the Church, so we think it more important for our age to be led into belief in the Church of God, than to have experiences squeezed from it which as such are no help at all, but which, when there is faith in the *sanctorum communio,* are produced of their own accord.[13]

Besides showing the incidental role of experience in the Church, such a statement witnesses its author's uncommon insight into the nature and peculiar difficulties of the Church.

Any careful assessment of Bonhoeffer's doctoral thesis is bound to reveal certain inherent weaknesses, which admittedly slacken the force of his argument. Bonhoeffer's dependence on a sociology operating on such a high level of abstraction that it seems "social philosophy," his use of Hegel's terms in constructing his thesis, his failure to distinguish between the Christian and the sociological sources: these have seriously weakened the initial effort—to establish a dogmatics of the empirically known Church.

However, for a man twenty-one years old the accomplishment is remarkable. Bonhoeffer attempted to answer an enormous question, "What is the Church?" And although his sociology has been invalidated by later, more empirical studies, Bonhoeffer's theological effort remains an important work on the concrete Church. The tension of working with two theological starting points enabled him to discuss revelation without abandoning his commitment to the world. Consequently his stress on the "concrete" or "worldly" character of revelation gave Barthian theology a new foothold in the Church. This stress on the concrete would grow in Bonhoeffer's thought; indeed, it is a stable underpinning for the structure of thought found in the *Ethics* and the prison letters.

The final result of *The Communion of Saints* lies then, not in the work itself or in its impact upon ecclesiology in the

1930's (it probably had none), but in providing a theological basis from which Bonhoeffer could progress. The seeds for such growth are present: the dependence upon, yet the reach beyond Luther's theology; the concern for revelation's innate concrete and human character; the recognition of the Church's nature as community.

During the 1930's and the 1940's theologians took a fresh interest in the theology of the Church. No concern became so vital and was met by theologians with such a sense of urgency. Two powerful forces contributed to this new concern: the arm of Hitler in Germany, which was effectively crushing the German Churches; and the ecumenical movement, which had entered its international—and for that reason critical—stage. During the remainder of his life Bonhoeffer would be plunged in both currents, more than most theologians of his time. Already the direction of his thought was clear; the struggles of the university years had given Bonhoeffer his theological mandate. However, involvement in the Nazi crisis and the turbulent ecumenical movement made fresh demands upon him, and forced a clearer, further understanding of the Church—a doctrine which would emerge only after 1940 in the unfinished *Ethics*. If his final development carried a "concrete Church" far beyond what he might originally have expected—all the way to a "religionless Christianity"—it must be admitted that such a conclusion was possible only because the beginnings had been set in *The Communion of Saints*.

The 'Church' therefore has not the meaning of a human community to which Christ is or is not self-super-added, nor of a union among such as individually seek or think to have Christ and wish to cultivate this common 'possession'; no, it is a communion created by Christ and founded upon him, one in which Christ reveals himself as the new man—or rather, the new humanity himself.

Act and Being

3. *Act and Being*

When he graduated from the University of Berlin, Bonhoeffer was young, only twenty-one years old. He was also free, unencumbered by the commitments of a ministry to the Church under Hitler and to his ecumenical activities, which were soon to come. Bonhoeffer took advantage of that freedom, and tasted Europe; he likewise soon became convinced that the great need sensed at that time in Europe was for peace. In 1941 he wrote a letter to a young man about these years, a letter which is worth quoting at length:

You are now having your own experiences, and they are completely different from the ones I had when I was your age. I really believe that a great deal depends on what one experiences in his twenties, and above all on how he experiences it. For me those were the years around 1926. My studies were about over; it was possible to study and work in complete freedom; you could travel and see something of Europe. Europe was then gradually recovering once more from the poverty, the divisions, and the hatred which the World War had brought with it. Germany was beginning to earn again a place in the world through work, science, and spirit. Old prejudices of the people against one another were giving way to a hope that was rising among the peoples of the West for a better, more fruitful life together in a spirit of peace. The best forces of the peoples were striving to achieve the peace—which to be sure was from the start greatly threatened. One sensed something like an accidental task, even mission, in the world. One worked and thought he knew what he was working for. Circles were formed that were serious and knew themselves to be intellectually responsible.[1]

Bonhoeffer took part in these forces, and the "mission" which could be sensed in the world attracted few young men as powerfully as it attracted him. His ministry in Spain brought out this sense of mission effectively. On February 15, 1928, Dietrich left home for a year as assistant curate to a German parish in Barcelona. The German colony there numbered about six thousand, but Bonhoeffer was astonished to discover how few of these were actually regular churchgoers. Their number was slightly over fifty.

Barcelona was his first break from the academic life in several years, and Bonhoeffer appreciated a life free of the intellectual concerns so overwhelming at the university. In a letter to his friend Helmut Rössler he wrote:

> You know something about the work that I am doing, from my first letter; it is quite a remarkable experience for one to see work and life really coming together—a synthesis which we all looked for in our student days, but hardly managed to find; really to live *one* life and not two, or rather half a life. It gives the work value and the worker an objectivity, a recognition of his own limitations, such as can only be gained in real life.[2]

From this point of view, the Spanish interlude proved to be invaluable. As Bonhoeffer wrote, again to Rössler:

> I'm getting to know new people every day; here one meets people as they are, away from the masquerade of the "Christian world," people with passions, criminal types, little people with little ambitions, little desires and little sins, all in all people who feel homeless in both senses of the word, who loosen up if one talks to them in a friendly way, real people; I can only say that I have

gained the impression that it is just these people who are much more under grace than under wrath, and that it is the Christian world which is more under wrath than under grace.[3]

During the year Bonhoeffer read a great deal. One author, Albert Schweitzer, struck him forcefully; after reading his works, Bonhoeffer came to speculate frequently on the future of Christianity in Europe. The Lutheran problem of power—the belief that exercising power is sinful, yet necessary in the name of responsibility—brought him to read a number of books on Eastern religions, especially on Buddhism and Hinduism. Because of his deep feelings about world peace, the question of power was a continuously disturbing one for Bonhoeffer, and he looked constantly to the East—especially to Gandhi—for a Christian alternative.

During his stay in Barcelona, Bonhoeffer took a fresh interest in Christian ethics. His work in an empty parish helped convince him that most of the Church's ethical teachings were far too ethereal and unrealistic. The Church would recurrently utter a vacuous principle, without specific application. In notes entitled, "What is a Christian Ethic?" Bonhoeffer wrote:

> Ethics is a matter of earth and of blood, but also of him who made both; the trouble arises from this duality. There can be ethics only in the framework of history, in the concrete situation, at the moment of the divine call, the moment of being addressed, of the claim made by the concrete need and the situation for decision, of the claim which I have to answer, for which I have to make myself responsible. Thus there cannot be ethics in a vacuum, as a principle; there cannot be good and evil as general ideas, but only as qualities of will making a decision. . . . But through this freedom from the law, from principle, the Christian must enter into the complexity of the world; he cannot make up his mind a priori, but only when he himself has become involved in the emergency and knows himself called by God.[4]

The notes recall Nietzsche; indeed, in the notes Bonhoeffer draws upon Nietzsche's favorite figure, the giant Antaeus. While vastly stronger than any man, Antaeus could easily be overcome as soon as he lost contact with the earth. The notes also anticipate Bonhoeffer's future ethical thought, developed more systematically and extensively, but again following man into the world and pleading for his moral life within that world.

Bonhoeffer returned to Berlin early in 1929. Before he could lecture, it was necessary for him to present his *Habilitationsschrift,* a dissertation admitting him to the faculty. After consulting with Reinhold Seeberg, his advisor, Bonhoeffer decided to work with the philosophical assumptions underlying the new "theologies of the Word of God"—those of Barth, Brunner, Bultmann, Tillich, and Gogarten. Like *The Communion of Saints,* the new work, originally entitled *Akt und Sein* (*Act and Being*), is forbidding in its profuse, heavily academic style. Especially forbidding is the subtitle: "Transcendental Philosophy and Ontology in Systematic Theology."

The premise on which Bonhoeffer wrote the book is the premise on which he wrote almost all his works: for the Word of God truly to be a revelation, it must take on the language and the style of the world. Here this premise is applied to the difficult area of theological methodology. If a theologian studies the Word in a systematic way, he must depend on the structural support of a humanly constructed philosophy. Bonhoeffer does not challenge the use of philosophy, but he insists that a theologian be highly conscious, and fiercely critical, of his own philosophical tools. *Act and Being* studies the failures entailed by theologians who uncritically adapt either of the two major philosophical assumptions "act" or "being."

Briefly, Bonhoeffer tries to reduce the philosophical assumptions of the theologians to an idea of God as revealed in His acting or in His being. The first, "act theology," is the fundamental biblical mode of thought: God shows himself to man in events, and calls man in moments of crisis to make decisions. In this theology man cannot "know" God with great certainty; he can only listen in the moments of revelation. Bonhoeffer looks to Karl Barth as the great "act" theologian; and he identifies Emmanuel Kant as its philosophical source. "Being theology," on the other hand, is philosophical in nature, rather than biblical. Bonhoeffer draws his description from the prominent philosopher Martin Heidegger, who that same year published his major work, *Sein und Zeit* (*Being and Time*). In "being theology" the approach is firmly objective; man *can* know God, and he can rest confident in his knowledge. The major "being" theologian is regarded as Paul Tillich, who developed a theology approaching God as "the ground of our being."

In *The Communion of Saints* Bonhoeffer attempted a reconciliation of two major theological traditions. In *Act and Being* he is attempting a mediation of even greater scope: to relate two philosophical modes of thought which underlie all of the new theologies. As Franklin Sherman has noted, the debate between the two realms of thinking built upon these assumptions is still a serious theological question.[5] Is God known in the events in which he acts in the world, or is he known as Being-Itself and New Being, to use Paul Tillich's phrases? Is the Church an event, happening again and again in man's response to the Gospel; or is it an organized institution with continuity in time and space?

Bonhoeffer's point of synthesis may be jarring to the theologians of either camp. Revelation, he states, does not lie in a static residuum of a past occurrence; nor can revelation be conceived as "the ever-free, pure and non-objective act which at certain times impinges on the existence of individuals." [6] Revelation—and here Bonhoeffer drives his argument home—"is the being of the community or persons, constituted and embraced by the person of Christ." [7]

The attempt, like that of *The Communion of Saints,* is a daring one. Only in the Church—and the Church carefully defined as personal community—is there a unity of act and being. Its dependence upon the Christian's act of faith gives the Church a character of act. Yet by its very establishment and continuing presence in the world the Church has a being, which is God's revelation of His life.

The attempt typifies Bonhoeffer's early thought: only in the *concrete Church* can revelation come through to man entirely. Theology, Bonhoeffer suggests, tends often to obscure and dilute revelation. And unless the Church, with its inborn tension of revelation as act *and* being, provides the center for all theological work, no one will truly understand God's Word. "The Christian community is God's final revelation: God as 'Christ existing as community,' ordained for the rest of time until the end of the world and the return of Christ." [8]

At the heart of *Act and Being* lies the equation of revelation with the Church. "The distinction between thinking of revelation individualistically and thinking of it in relation to community is fundamental." [9] The doctrine has firm roots in St. Paul, though Bonhoeffer does not draw upon the Pauline writings to support his argument. Bonhoeffer is concerned that the Church recognize its responsibility to reveal Christ—and that it make any necessary changes to meet that responsibility. He insists that one character of the Church is critical for the Church in revealing Christ: its life of community.

Bonhoeffer's emphasis on the Church as community revealing Christ suggests that he is more interested in exploring the nature of the Church than in pursuing the original argument of his book. Indeed, an immediate criticism of the work is its constant leaping between the levels of theology and philosophy without clearly indicating which is which. Yet despite the overdrawn description of the Church, *Act and Being* is significant for what it reveals of Bonhoeffer's thought at the time: his criticism of Barth, his refined notion of revelation, and the first indications of many of his later ideas.

Especially interesting is Bonhoeffer's criticism of the man who had influenced his thinking so profoundly: Karl Barth. Although a year later, in America, Bonhoeffer would vigorously defend Barth's theology, in *Act and Being* he challenges Barth on some very decisive points.

Bonhoeffer categorizes Barth as an "act theologian." In his earlier writings Barth denounced the intrusion of philosophy—man's reconstruction of God's Word—into theology. Bonhoeffer's first criticism is put to Barth simply: how can the theologian, who must depend on the philosopher for his vocabulary and concepts, discredit philosophy? The consequence for such a theologian is that he *is* in fact dependent upon a philosopher, but refuses to admit that dependence. As a result, he is incapable of being critical of the influence. Emmanuel Kant's impact upon Barth's theology may not be all that Bonhoeffer claims. Yet Barth's non-rational basis of belief and his concentration upon the act of belief clearly bear the imprint of Kantian philosophy. Above all, however, the overwhelming danger in Kantian thought—that we come to understand thoroughly our act of knowing but lose certainty about the existence and nature of whatever is "known"—becomes evident in Barth's theology. And Barth, either ignoring or discarding the Kantian influence, makes no effort to clarify the problem of real existence.

Apparently, the danger to which Barth has succumbed in describing a God inaccessible to our thought is of great concern to Bonhoeffer. Indeed, the young man's emphasis on the concrete or worldly character of revelation can well be seen as a corrective for Barth's excessive view of God and His Word. "God is not free from man," Bonhoeffer remarks in his criticism of Barth, "but for man. Christ is the Word of the freedom of God. God is 'there', which is to say: not in eternal non-objectivity, but—let us say it with all due caution—'haveable', graspable in his Word within the Church." [10]

Barth was probably not influenced by such criticism; his later theology, however, does move away from the stand he took during the 1920's and toward a more objective theology. As with many of his insights in his two theses, Bonhoeffer's major contribution is to the progress of his own thought. The articulation of Barth's danger assisted him in modifying his Barthian notion of revelation and in clarifying his own theological stand.

The movement in Bonhoeffer's concept of revelation seen in *Act and Being* has real importance in the perspective of his later work. To equate the Christian community with the revelation of Christ was certainly a radical stroke, despite its strong biblical origins. Although revelation had been the dominant theme of the Word of God theologians during the 1920's, Bonhoeffer is here taking a step beyond *The Communion of Saints,* and several steps beyond these theologians, in regarding the Church itself *as* the revealed Word of God.

"Revelation . . . happens within the communion; it demands primarily a Christian sociology of its own." [11] Bonhoeffer had already begun that sociology in *The Communion of Saints,* and it is unfortunate that he never continued to develop it. The emphasis Bonhoeffer places on the social nature of the Church, and of revelation's dependence on a vibrant communion (as distinct from an institution), opens a new field for the study of the Church and Christian ethics. Bonhoeffer's later identification of "religion" with inwardness and the sin-sick soul bears out this earlier thinking. Indeed, in an outline for a book prepared shortly before his death, Bonhoeffer restated his conviction of the Church's role as revelation, if in fresh terms:

> The Church is her true self only when she exists for humanity. . . . she must take her part in the social life of the world, not lording it over men, but helping and serving them. She must tell men, whatever their calling, whatever it means to live in Christ, to exist for others. . . . She must not underestimate the importance of human example, which has its origin in the humanity of Jesus, and which is so important in the teaching of St. Paul. It is not abstract argument, but concrete example which gives her word emphasis and power.[12]

Actually, the seed of many of Bonhoeffer's mature ideas—responsibility, community, the Church in the world, the criticism of a "religious premise"—can be found in *Act and Being.* "It is only from the person of Christ," writes Bonhoeffer, for example, "that other persons acquire for man the character of personhood." [13] This statement anticipates a notion central to the *Ethics:* that man becomes wholly man only through conforming to Christ.

As a thesis, arguing in its own right the unity of revelation as act and being in the Church, Bonhoeffer's *Act and Being* lies open to some severe criticism. Bonhoeffer's use of philosophy and theology would tend to dissatisfy both philosophers and theologians who do not agree with his premises. Likewise, many of his generalizations about "act" theologians and "being" theologians could be challenged. But an even more vulnerable area is Bonhoeffer's attempted point of synthesis. If the Church is all that he says it is, "Christ existing as community," where does the Church make such an impression upon the world—or even upon Christians? Admittedly, *Act and Being* is highly theoretical. But Bonhoeffer's idealism keeps his treatment on a plane which often bears scant resemblance to the situation which men experience.

Despite its failures, however, *Act and Being* makes an important stride forward in Bonhoeffer's growth as a theologian. It certainly marks the end of a purely academic—and perhaps for this reason, intensely idealistic—conception of the Church. From this point on, the events and demands of Bonhoeffer's life would leave little room for undisturbed academic work, and would just as effectively discourage him from desiring such work. The issues that grew out of the Nazi crisis and the ecumenical struggle forced confrontation; any other alternative was cowardice and betrayal.

Indeed, following *Act and Being,* any attempt to separate Bonhoeffer's life from his thought would be impossible. The academic life had ended. And gone with it, seemingly, was the liberty to construct a theology without interferences. It is a tribute to Bonhoeffer's open and perceptive mind that he could find in these "interferences" the critical questions facing contemporary theology. And it is a tribute to his conjunction of involvement and thought that the frenzied activities of these years would result, not in a diminishing of his theological mind, but in an incredible expansion, making it large enough to embrace the secular world.

. . . It is quite a remarkable experience for one to see work and life really coming together—a synthesis which we all looked for in our student days, but hardly managed to find; really to live one *life and not two, or rather, half a life.*

Letter of 7 August, 1928 to Helmut Rössler

4. *The Beginning Ministry*

The years between Bonhoeffer's graduation from the University and his commitment to the special seminary in Finkenwalde were among the most uncertain years of his life. The academic life as such was over—a life which, despite its freedoms and opportunities, we can infer from Bonhoeffer's letters stifled and constrained him. A year spent in America on a fellowship convinced Bonhoeffer of his potential as a theologian; but the critical social problems of Berlin in the early thirties—depression, nationalism, a Church sagging from within —impressed him with the need for committed and dynamic pastors, men who would speak of Christ in the midst of a world unwilling to be shaped by Christ.

America, in which Bonhoeffer spent the academic year of 1930-31, acted as a watershed. The young man who sailed to New York in September with a keen determination to raise and face substantive theological questions returned, sensing deeply his responsibility to the Church on a level where theology could never be completely adequate. The summer in Barcelona had already suggested to him the dimensions of pastoral attention. But America—and especially its Negro dilemma, in which Bonhoeffer became concerned—helped him to see that a life spent in the lecture halls at the University of Berlin could well be an escape from the real confrontation of being a Christian in his time.

Two months before leaving for New York, Bonhoeffer delivered his inaugural lecture to the University of Berlin faculty: "The Question about Man in Contemporary Philosophy and Theology." Like his earlier theses, the address approached a serious philosophical-theological question with the effort of arriving at conclusions with immediate pastoral implications. At the climax of the lecture, Bonhoeffer looked, as he had in *Act and Being,* to the Church. On the final page of the partially remaining text is the statement:

> The Church is the hidden Christ among us. Now therefore man is never alone, but he exists only through the community, which brings him Christ, which incorporates him in itself, takes him into its life. Man in Christ is man in community; where he exists in community.[1]

Community was to dominate Bonhoeffer's thinking on the Church for years: indeed, it would serve as a critical point of reference for many of his concepts and decisions over the coming period of struggle.

The Sloan Fellowship, which Bonhoeffer had been awarded, stipulated an academic year at Union Theological Seminary, in upper Manhattan. The Church Consistory in Germany granted Dietrich the leave, and in September he sailed to New York.

The year, if discouraging from a scholarly point of view, was nevertheless provocative and instructive. Bonhoeffer found the theology taught at the seminary vapid and stifling; compared with his experience of Barth's revelation theology—and even the liberal theology taught by the Berlin professors—the seminary's version of liberal theology (Barthian thought had yet made little impact in America) was weak and flaccid. Within weeks after the courses and seminars had begun, Dietrich admitted to a new-made friend, Paul Lehmann, that he hardly hoped to learn much theology that year. It would be more of an effort to learn America.

Dietrich did learn America. Over the semester vacation, he managed to borrow an Oldsmobile, and with Paul Lehmann and two other friends—Erwin Sutz of Switzerland, and the French pacifist, Jean Lasserre—he toured the United States, dipping at one point into Mexico. His most vital contact with America, however, came through a Negro student at Union whom Dietrich came to know: Frank Fisher. Fisher introduced Dietrich to Harlem—not a mile from the seminary campus—and through Harlem, to a moral dilemma which Dietrich recognized as critical and severe. On Sundays he and Frank would visit Harlem, meeting Negroes, and striking up conversations. Dietrich read a number of books by Negroes, especially novels, and remarked enthusiastically about them in letters to his grandmother. Eventually he came to learn a number of Negro spirituals, which he intensely admired; later he would take many back with him to Germany. In a paper written in 1939 he remarked that the solution to the Negro dilemma "is one of the decisive future tasks of the white churches." [2] The failure and widespread apathy of Americans in this area disturbed him.

If he did not learn much theology, Dietrich nevertheless attempted to introduce the Americans to Barth. Here he was at least partially successful. A small number of students like Paul Lehmann recognized the bankrupt condition of American theology, and were fascinated by the dialectical theology described by Bonhoeffer. In a seminar led by John Baille on the relation between cosmology, philosophy, and theology, Dietrich pressed energetically the need to draw upon Barth as a starting point. In his presentation to the seminar entitled "The Theology of Crisis," he stated:

Coming to a man like Karl Barth after half a year of consideration of the problem of relation between cosmology, philosophy and theology, I confess that I do not see any other possible way for you to get into real contact with his thinking than by forgetting at least for this one hour everything you have learned before concerning this problem . . . Here we stand on an entirely different and new point of departure to the whole problem. We stand in the tradition of Paul, Luther, Kierkegaard, in the tradition of genuine Christian thinking.[3]

Whatever effect Bonhoeffer had upon the theological climate of Union Seminary, he certainly impressed teachers and fellow students with his grasp of theological questions. In the seminars he was constantly attempting to redefine questions and ferret out the central problems, convinced often that the questions raised were only ruses distracting from the real issues. Years later Reinhold Niebuhr would recall him as a "brilliant and theologically sophisticated young man."[4] Paul Lehmann, the American student who came to know Dietrich best, remembers him as a young man displaying a rare agility of mind and a constant openness to unfamiliar experiences. Warm despite an initial appearance of cool aloofness, gifted with a rich sense of humor despite his intense intellectual work, Dietrich seemed at once most un-German and typically Germanic. His fine blond hair, his stiff heel-clicking head-bobbing handshake, his passion to excel: these were the most evident, and most German, characteristics. But Lehmann has noted another set of characteristics: his fascination with ideas completely out of his range (Dietrich read the pragmatist William James with real fervor); his natural, unstooping relationship with fellow students. "Dietrich," Lehmann wrote, "manifested a contagious freedom, openness and integrity in relating to all sorts and conditions of men, to people as *human* beings. This was the exact and concrete counterpart of his incisive and critical dealing with ideas."[5]

If Bonhoeffer's response to America was wholehearted and energetic—and everything he attacked was—his response to the Church in America was nevertheless dim. He found the sermons preached in America to be intellectually and spiritually vacuous. The seminary, which he enjoyed, he later criticized for a sterility of intellectual life on the part of students—resulting largely, he suggested, from such American customs as a common dormitory. What disturbed Dietrich above all, however, was the absence of an inner drive toward doctrinal truth. Theology in America lacked passion, concern, fury: it was a task necessary for a time, but certainly nothing like the intense effort which it had been for Bonhoeffer, and for men like Barth before him, in Europe. The torpor that surrounded theology in America made Bonhoeffer extremely critical of the American churches. In a letter to his friend Rössler he stated, "The vast work of the American missions is hollow within; the mother church itself is really dying." [6]

It is difficult to estimate America's influence upon the young theologian. He later admitted, in a letter to Eberhard Bethge from his prison cell, that the impact was a profound one. "I don't believe I have changed very much, except at two periods of my life, the first under the first conscious impact of Papa's personality, and the second when I was abroad." [7] The time of his American visit corresponds to a general broadening of outlook inevitable for anyone stepping from a highly charged intellectual atmosphere into the active ministry. Bonhoeffer's later ecumenical drive, his work to create a warm human community in the seminary he would one day operate at Finkenwalde, his growing awareness of the pastoral relationships among churches as being a major ecumenical need: these are probably the fruits, largely, of his year in America.

Among the friends he made in America, Dietrich came to know Jean Lasserre, the noted French pacifist, quite well. At the time Lasserre was, like Dietrich, a European student in theology coming to Union as a Sloan Fellow. Initially Dietrich sensed very little in common with Lasserre; the memory of the War, and especially of the Versailles Treaty, still burned in the young German's mind, and Lasserre was an avowed pacifist, besides being a Frenchman. But two things about Lasserre struck Bonhoeffer and made a lasting imprint. For one, Lasserre was a theologian of greater seriousness and acumen than his American counterparts, and his theology, even at that stage, centered on the search for the meaning of the peace enjoined by Christ. But even more: Lasserre was visibly committed to following Christ in a way Dietrich had never experienced before.

In one of his most important prison letters, Dietrich would later refer to Lasserre:

I remember talking to a young French pastor at America thirteen years ago. We were discussing what our real purpose was in life. He said he would like to become a saint. I think it is quite likely he did become one. At the time I was very much impressed, though I disagreed with him, and said I should prefer to have faith, or words to that effect. For a long time I did not realize how far we were apart. I thought I could acquire faith by trying to live a holy life, or something like it.[8]

Although Dietrich never encountered Lasserre after the year in America, there can be no doubt that this Frenchman heightened Bonhoeffer's sensitivity to Christ's call, and perhaps opened the way that led to *The Cost of Discipleship*. And although Bonhoeffer would never become a confirmed pacifist in the sense that Lasserre already was, Christ's injunction for peace took on for him a new meaning and a grave seriousness after his meeting with Lasserre. This new insight would later play a large part in Bonhoeffer's opposition to the Nazi regime in Germany.

At the end of his stay in America, Dietrich found himself seriously considering returning to Germany via India, to observe Gandhi and to learn more of the Hindu religion. India betokened something to Bonhoeffer; his letters suggest that he felt it had some great secret essential for reviving Christianity in Europe. "A mighty land," he wrote of the country to Rössler. "I should like to see if perhaps the one great solution comes from India; for otherwise it all seems to be over, and the death throes of Christianity seem upon us." [9] What specifically attracted him was Gandhi. These were the years of Gandhi's heroic struggles to achieve liberation of India through nonviolent resistance. As with other Europeans, Bonhoeffer came to see in Gandhi, the saintly Hindu, a reflection of Christ incriminating the mediocrity of the western Church. "If we cannot see in our personal lives that Christ was here," Dietrich wrote, "then we want to see it at least in India." [10] The journey to India collapsed after Dietrich and Lasserre tried unsuccessfully to find a steamer bound for India. Bonhoeffer decided to return the same way to Berlin.

Dietrich decided that, before taking up his new assignment, he would make two important visits. Through his student colleague at Union Seminary, Erwin Sutz, Dietrich was able to visit Karl Barth at his home at Bonn. And in September he was to attend the World Alliance Conference for Promoting International Friendship through the Churches, being held in Cambridge.

Bonhoeffer had long wished to meet the man most important in shaping his thought, and, to that extent, his life. He had never studied under Barth, never had the opportunity to hear Barth lecture. Now he traveled to Bonn with expectations that were never let down. The story is told that Bonhoeffer (who had corresponded earlier with Barth) met him personally by interjecting a curious statement of Luther from the floor during a lecture: "The curse of the godless man can sound more pleasant in God's ears than the hallelujah of the pious." Delighted, Barth immediately looked around, asking the students, "Who threw that in?"

Dietrich's letters to Erwin Sutz from the two weeks spent at Bonn revealed the young man's immense respect and reverence for Barth. In one letter written slightly after a week at Bonn, Bonhoeffer said, "I don't think that I have ever regretted anything that I have failed to do in my theological past as much as the fact that I did not come here earlier." [11] Most impressive is his description of Karl Barth the man, contrasted with the great mind of Barth, which so far was all Bonhoeffer had encountered.

> But it is important and surprising in the best way to see how Barth stands over and beyond his books. There is with him an openness, a readiness for any objection which should hit the mark, and along with this such concentration and impetuous insistence on the point, whether it is made arrogantly or modestly, dogmatically or completely uncertainly, and not only when it serves his own theology. I am coming to understand more and more why Barth's writings are so tremendously difficult to understand. I have been impressed even more by discussions with him than by his writings

and his lectures. For he is really all there. I have never seen anything like it before and wouldn't have believed it possible.[12]

It is questionable whether Bonhoeffer ever felt a kinship with any man more profoundly than that which he felt with Barth. Not that he agreed with everything Barth said, or even that he would never move from his original standpoint within Barth's thought on revelation. Bonhoeffer would move, eventually, into a different perspective of thought, from which he could criticize Barth's "positivism of revelation." The two men differed in their backgrounds: Barth began as a Swiss pastor who moved into dogmatics; Bonhoeffer began as a highly trained theologian. Barth's overriding transcendental concern—to keep God beyond man's reach—almost contradicted Bonhoeffer's insistence on concrete revelation. Yet the two men sensed at once a unity and a sympathy both mutual and profound. They found each other fascinating discussion partners. Once, in a letter to Barth written weeks after the days in Bonn, Dietrich frankly admitted what inspiration the Swiss theologian had been for him:

Please excuse me if I was a burden to you in August with my perhaps too obstinate and—as you once said—"godless" questions. But at the same time I would like you to know that I know no one who can free me from these persistent questions as you can, and that I have to talk to you like that because I feel with you, it is hard to say why, in a strange way quite certain that the way in which you see things is somehow right. When I am talking with you, I am brought right up against the thing itself, whereas before I was only continually circling round it in the distance, and that is for me a quite unmistakable sign that here I've somehow got to the point.[13]

"I don't look forward to going home," Bonhoeffer wrote glumly to Sutz late in July. No wonder. The idyllic atmosphere of Barth's home, the evening discussions that trailed deep into morning, the long intervals for reading and writing bore little resemblance to the hectic life awaiting Bonhoeffer in Berlin. Worse, Germany of August, 1931, was overrun with economic and political headaches. Seven million men were unemployed;

the government was unstable and ill-equipped, if also too encumbered by its clumsy weight, to handle the crisis. Parliament had been sapped of its power by political bungling; the Reich Chancellor, Heinrich Brüning, held much of the power, but he conflicted with too many major political figures. The powerful propaganda machine created by Hitler was gradually unseating major rival parties from the Reichstag, the German Parliament; in the 1930 election Hitler's National Socialists (Nazis) leaped from 12 to 107 members. No less unsettling was the fiery nationalism, kindled largely by the resentment toward the Versailles Treaty. During these years the nationalist fervor raged through the German populace with all the fury of a religious awakening.

Bonhoeffer recognized the crisis, even before he stepped into it. During the weeks at Bonn he read several books on economics, hoping to make some efforts to curb the serious problems he would face after his return from the Cambridge Conferences in the fall. He wrote:

> The outlook is really exceptionally grim. There is in fact no one who can see ahead even a little way. People generally, however, are under the very definite impression that they are standing at a tremendous turning point in world history . . . Seven million unemployed, that is fifteen or twenty million people hungry; I don't know how Germany or the individual will survive it. Economic experts tell me that it looks as though we are being driven at a tremendous rate towards a goal which no one knows and no one can avoid.[14]

On October 4, 1931, Bonhoeffer delivered the Harvest Festival Sermon, which also reflected this mood; but it likewise reflected Bonhoeffer's courageous call to a deep love of God, even in the midst of depression. The scriptural text for the sermon is indicative of Bonhoeffer's underlying confidence over this period: "For them goodness is better than life" (Ps. 63. 3).

The harsh challenges facing Germany do not seem to have discouraged Bonhoeffer's activity; if anything, they stimulated him to more and more of it. Upon attending the Cambridge Conference in September, Bonhoeffer became one of three secretaries in the Youth Commission. In October he began ministering as the student chaplain at the Technical Institute (like a high school) in Charlottenburg, a section of Berlin. He began that fall to teach at the University of Berlin, offering courses in "Systematic Theology of the Twentieth Century," and a seminar in "The Idea of Philosophy and Protestant Theology."

As a young university professor, Dietrich absorbed, attracted, and excited his students. As one of his early students later observed: "What fascinated me in this man from the very beginning was the way he saw things; he 'turned them round,' away from where they were stored for everyday use, to the place God had ordained for them. . . . To tell the genuine from the unreal question was of the greatest importance for theology." [15] In his lectures Dietrich spoke in his quick, clipped voice: a very concentrated, yet cool and reporter-like dispassion. He felt that the teacher-student chasm, fostered by the university's lecture system, hindered the type of thinking he wanted to instill. He suggested that a small group meet outside the ordinary classes. He and the students met once a week in the room of Wolf-Dieter Zimmermann, in the northeastern sector of Berlin. Here, in a crowded room, a dozen or so young men would sit together and discuss Christology, the nature of a sacrament, Barth's revelation theology, the implications of recent political developments for the Church. "That winter 1932-33," Zimmermann has written, "did not produce anything, but it taught all of us to 'theologize.' " [16] After the long theoretical discussions, the group would move to a beer cellar at the Alexander Platz.

Bonhoeffer impressed his students with his far-flung reading, and his sharp, articulate mind, but above all with his simple and honest humanity. Zimmermann recounts an episode in which Bonhoeffer and a group of students were spending a spring weekend at his shack near Bernau; Dietrich had planned to spend the time catching up on his readings in Christology. He kept groaning as he read, "Oh, it is difficult." Once at dusk, beside a lake, Zimmermann mentioned the impressive sight of the sun across the waters. Dietrich looked up for a brief moment, said, "Imposing," and continued reading. His habits were unusual to his students; but they accepted them, out of an admiration for the man. Another incident recounted by Zimmermann suggests how Bonhoeffer continually surprised his students by his unique way of looking at things. "Once," wrote Zimmermann, "while talking of books, I asked him whether he owned a certain book: 'Yes, you can have it.' I refused, protesting in alarm, because I dared not carry off a book from a professor, whereupon he said: 'What on earth is your idea of property?' "[17]

Probably the most rewarding effort of the beginning years, however, was a confirmation class of forty boys from Wedding district north of Berlin, an area afflicted most acutely with the economic and social plight of the depression. Another teacher had found the large class unruly and unmanageable, and gladly turned it over to Bonhoeffer. Dietrich began teaching the boys in November. At Christmas he wrote to Sutz describing the work:

At the beginning the young men behaved like mad things, so that for the first time I had real problems of discipline. But what helped most was telling them quite simple biblical stuff with great emphasis, particularly eschatological passages. Now there is absolute quiet, the young men see to that themselves, so I need no longer fear the fate of my predecessor whom they quite literally worried to death. Recently I was out with some of them for two days; another group is coming tomorrow. We've enjoyed being together.[18]

In the letter Bonhoeffer went on to describe the home visits which he was paying to the families of each boy:

I'm looking forward to this time immensely. That is real work. Their home conditions are generally indescribable: poverty, disorder, immorality. And yet the children are still open; I am often amazed how a young person does not completely come to grief under such conditions; and of course one is always asking oneself how one would react to such surroundings. There must be a great—and I think also a moral—power of resistance in these people.[19]

Besides his visits to their homes, Bonhoeffer moved into a room in the Wedding district and kept the door open. The students came for meals, games, discussions, and Bible readings. In a letter written shortly before the end of the semester, Dietrich expressed some of the agitation and confusion that his work with the young men had created:

It sometimes seems to me that all our work comes to grief on the care of souls. To think of those excruciating hours or minutes when I or the other person try to begin a pastoral conversation, and how haltingly and lamely it goes on! And in the background there are always the ghastly home conditions, about which one really cannot say anything. . . . In short it is a very troubled chapter, and I sometimes try to console myself by thinking that this sort of pastoral care is something which just wasn't there before. But perhaps it is really the end of our Christianity that we fail here. We have learned to preach again, at least a little bit, but the care of souls? [20]

Nowhere in his early work did Bonhoeffer sense the urgency of pastoral work as he did with his confirmation class. And probably no other experience flung him so profoundly into the doubt that would hang for years: the uncertainty whether to commit his life to theology, or to the active ministry. Here, too, was probably lodged an early realization of the futility of so many of the older religious practices, what would later become the assault on "religion" as an obfuscation of true Christianity.

Dietrich was surprisingly successful with the boys. His background, so aristocratic and removed, had certainly not prepared him to grapple with forty Wedding adolescents. One of his students, Richard Rother, later described Dietrich's rapport with the class:

He was so composed that it was easy for him to guide us; he made us familiar with the catechism in quite a new way, making it alive for us by telling us of many personal experiences. Our class was hardly ever restless, because all of us were keen to have enough time to hear what he had to say to us. Once one of us boys unpacked his sandwiches in the middle of class and started eating. This was nothing unusual in the north of Berlin. Pastor Bonhoeffer said nothing at first. Then he looked at him, calmly and kindly, but long and intensely, without saying a word. In embarrassment, the boy put his sandwich away. The attempt to annoy our pastor had come to nothing through his composure and kindness—and perhaps through his understanding for boyish tomfoolery.[21]

The forty boys were all confirmed in March. Bonhoeffer remained in contact with many of them, and throughout his lifetime letters never stopped coming from the boys, testifying to the influence he had been for them.

Over this period the demands of a vital ministry kept Bonhoeffer from advancing rapidly in his theology. The insistence upon a concrete, "graspable" revelation grew. Dietrich's pastoral work convinced him as never before that the Incarnation contained the Church's working principle for its daily life. As he wrote to Rössler, "Invisibility as a theological doctrine will never get us anywhere. . .Being thrown back again and again upon the invisible God is senseless. No one can take it any longer." [22] A new recognition emerged, a much more realistic understanding of the Church:

> The Church is a union of religiously inclined, interested men, strangely fond of displaying their religiosity in their form of "Church." They belong today mostly to a level of society whose prominent characteristic might be regarded, not as a particularly lively spirituality or a special creative power, but at best as a certain comfort in their own righteousness.[23]

One reason for the slackened theological development at this time was Bonhoeffer's gradual movement from systematic theology toward biblical exegesis. Bonhoeffer had never been enthusiastic about recent biblical scholarship, notably the finding of linguists and archaeologists. Yet his convictions about revelation and the needs of a pastoral ministry led to a biblical-centered approach to theology. During the 1930's he produced a number of commentaries, most of them originating as lecture series: "Creation and Fall" (1932), "King David" (1935), "Temptation" (1938), and many shorter pieces. If his biblical works are not accurate scientific efforts to locate original meanings, they do reflect the earnest attempt to find the contemporary meaning of God's Word.

The early months of Bonhoeffer's ministry—in both America and Berlin—gave the young pastor a strong taste of the need Christians and non-Christians felt for a spiritual reality in which they could believe. More forcefully, however, Dietrich discovered over these months the abysmal distance between the Church as it worshipped and spoke and claimed to believe, and those innumerable people who could see nothing in the Church to attract them. The tension was a painful one, and as a lecturer to many of the men who would become pastors shortly, Bonhoeffer could see the roots of an uninspired congregation in the thought and attitudes shared by most of the theologians and clergy.

But these discoveries only marked the beginning. It was evident to anyone very perceptive in 1932 that the rampant nationalism in Germany, combined with the economic and political turmoil, would probably lead to a critical testing period for the German people. Bonhoeffer, sensing a coming challenge, had no idea what demands and responsibilities would be asked of him in the end. But he did perceive the immensity of what was coming. And he saw, with a brutal clarity, how ready—or unready—the German churches were to enter loyally into the future struggles. In the summer of 1932, six months before the installation of Adolf Hitler as Germany's Chancellor, he stated:

> Should we be surprised if again days come for our Church in which the blood of martyrs will be demanded? If some of us really should have the faith and the honor and the loyalty to shed this blood, then indeed it will not be the innocent and shining blood of the first witnesses . . . Our blood will be heavily burdened with our deep guilt; the guilt of the unprofitable servants.[24]

The question is a very simple one: Just how do you conceive your kingdom of God on earth?
"Thy Kingdom Come," Address given November 19, 1932.

5. *The Confessing Church Struggle*

Two of the most powerful forces to hit the Church in the twentieth century were its battle with Nazi power and the ecumencial movement. Bonhoeffer felt the full impact of each force, and for ten years was caught between them. Each struggle made unyielding demands upon his energy and moral resources. Both proved decisive in shaping the final, mature theology of the 1940's. Yet Bonhoeffer was in no sense submerged by his involvement in the two struggles. His efforts sprang not from circumstances, but from the needs of the Church as he saw and interpreted them. His letters and sermons reveal a clear mind attempting to determine the basis on which a Confessing Church, bolting from the Nazi-controlled Church, should act. His theological writings of this period, scant as they are, reflect a lucid, calm intelligence, though one at times intensely disturbed.

The questions which arose in these years, first in the practical sphere of the Church's survival, then in theory, were fundamental: the Church's future in Germany, the Church's relation to the state, the authority and responsibility of an ecumenical council of churches. Bonhoeffer's earlier theological training and especially his intense effort to come to grips with a meaningful doctrine of the Church gave him solid preparation for the work ahead. It is amazing that in the midst of the long struggles, Bonhoeffer could continuously pursue the one goal: God's Word today. In a letter written in 1936 to a seminarian, Bonhoeffer could honestly state: "In all speaking and acting in the Church I am concerned with the primacy, with the sole honor and truth of the Word of God." [1]

The Church struggle was an effort of the churches to remain independent and to keep to their work of preaching the Word. Bonhoeffer saw the conflict coming with the very installation of Adolf Hitler as Chancellor on January 30, 1933. Two days later Bonhoeffer gave a radio address on "Changes in the Conception of the Leader of the Younger Generation," in which he warned that a fixation to the person rather than the office would lead to idolatry. The radio message was cut short, and from the outset Bonhoeffer was labelled an enemy of the Third Reich.

On April 7, the Aryan Clauses were issued, forbidding anyone of Jewish origins or anyone married to a Jew from holding any office in the state. The prohibition extended to the Church, and was only the beginning of a long series of encroachments designed to usurp the power of the Church.

The General Church elections were held July 23, and these plainly forecasted the coming struggle. The "German Christians," those clergy and laymen who took a racist view of the German Church and sided with Hitler, gained 70% of the votes. Early in September the Prussian General Synod, an important organ of the Church hierarchy, agreed to the Aryan Clauses. Only weeks later, Hitler insured that an election would make Army Chaplain Ludwig Müller, an ardent German Christian *Reichsbischof*, the major governing figure in the German Evangelical Church.

The control of the Church by German Christians was not all that disturbed men like Bonhoeffer. It was becoming clear that Hitler intended to bend the Church to his purposes, or cripple it if it refused to bend. Pastors were discouraged from speaking out against early Nazi abuses; the government abetted ecclesiastical authorities who were sympathetic with the nationalist fervor of the regime. Eventually churchmen like Pastor Schneider who voiced serious disapproval with the government were sent to prison camps or moved to rural parishes.

Opposition from within the Church to Hitler's encroachments was not long in coming. Once the more perceptive and committed Church leaders saw the direction events were taking, they formed a synod, which created the Pastors Emergency League. Originally numbering 2,000 pastors, this League provided a temporary basis for later, more highly organized resistance.

On January 3 and 4, in 1934, the Barmen Synod met; here the central figures of the Pastors Emergency League issued a declaration stating the errors which had been introduced into the Church. Karl Barth and Dietrich were responsible for framing the declaration; its first and second articles recall Barth's thought:

> Jesus Christ, as he is testified to us in the Holy Scripture, is the one Word of God, whom we are to hear, whom we are to trust and obey in life and in death.
>
> We repudiate the false teaching that the Church can and must recognize yet other happenings and powers, images and truths as divine revelation alongside this one Word of God, as a source of her preaching. . . .
>
> We repudiate the false teaching that there are areas of our life in which we belong not to Jesus Christ but to another lord, areas in which we do not need justification and sanctification through him.[2]

As the Confessing Church grew, building upon the Barmen Declaration as its statement of origin and purpose, Pastor Martin Niemöller, the courageous and outspoken critic of the Nazi abuses, gradually took control.

The Confessing Church was an active resistance movement attempting to re-establish the Church in all its fidelity to God's Word. Eventually the Confessing Church declared the German Church, from which it was splitting further every week, heretical and no longer the Church of Christ.

From its inception the Confessing Church faced mighty odds. *Reichsbischof* Müller, determined to wipe out the opposition, came to require all pastors to take an oath of loyalty to Hitler as absolute leader of the German people. Further steps were taken, and eventually the conflict became sharply drawn, not simply between two churches who both claimed the authority of the Gospel, but between the Confessing Church and the totalitarian regime.

Yet despite the convictions and heroic efforts of numerous pastors and Church members, the Confessing Church gradually deteriorated after 1935. By the later 1930's it was too weak to offer any serious frontal opposition.

Dietrich Bonhoeffer took part in the growth and battles of the Confessing Church from its birth. His uncertainty about the action needed can be seen in a letter he wrote to Karl Barth in September, 1933:

> What is the consequence for us if the Church really is not just an individual congregation in any one place? How do things stand with the solidarity of the Pastorate? When is there any possibility of leaving the Church? There can be no doubt at all that the *status confessio* has arrived; what we are by no means clear about is how the *confessio* is most appropriately expressed today.[3]

What Bonhoeffer and others meant by *confessio* in those months before the Barmen Declaration was a "witnessing community." The Confessing Church was to witness to the German people the truth of Christ's Word, impaired by the Nazi image of man.

In the midst of the early struggles, Dietrich Bonhoeffer sensed as never before a disturbing confusion and uncertainty about his future. The earlier conflict—whether to become a theologian or a pastor—persisted. In an important letter to his eldest brother, Karl Friedrich, Dietrich wrote early in 1933:

> It is queer how hard one finds it to make up his mind. . . . Simply looking at one's own faculties and wondering whether they lie in this or any other field is completely useless. One's knowledge of oneself is inevitably poor. The question is that of combining the

function of parson with that of university teaching. For I think that I mustn't give the work of teaching up. Klaus [a brother] says "no." Reudiger [a brother-in-law] says "yes." The others have not said a word—and neither have I.[4]

But added to this inner turmoil was another conflict: centering in the condition of the Church in Germany in the summer of 1933. Dietrich could see that the kind of pastoral work he wanted to commit himself to—intense, free, exploratory—was becoming increasingly impossible in Berlin, and, for that matter, throughout Germany. The same problem held him from teaching fulltime at the university: there the stifling atmosphere among the faculty and the oppression of creative theological thought made a professorship unthinkable. Bonhoeffer found that in conscience he could not dedicate himself to a Church dominated by German Christians.

The decision to accept a pastorate in England came out of this struggle, and for Bonhoeffer the decision was a distinct relief. The lectures he had given at the university that summer of 1933 on Christology would prove to be his last experience of teaching there. In October Dietrich packed, and with his close Jewish Lutheran friend, Franz Hildebrant, sailed for London.

Bonhoeffer was immediately criticized for the move, most incisively by Karl Barth:

I do not think of regarding your departure for England as anything but a necessary personal interlude. . . . What is all this about "going away," "the quietness of pastoral work," etc., at a moment when you are just wanted in Germany. You, who know as I do that the opposition in Berlin and the opposition of the Church in Germany as a whole stands inwardly on such weak feet! [5]

Barth was understandably angry. But Dietrich firmly believed he needed the chance to act as a pastor; and besides, he was coming to see his stay in England as a fertile opportunity for helping the Confessing Church. In exchange for salary and living quarters, Pastor Hildebrant accepted much of Bonhoeffer's parish work, freeing Dietrich to act as a foreign emissary of the Confessing Church. For the Confessing Church, struggling desperately for fidelity to God's Word in the midst of Germany's infatuation with a nationalistic spirit, needed someone to represent its efforts honestly to the outside world.

Dietrich contacted a number of the men he had met in the ecumenical movement, and eventually met Dr. George K.A. Bell, one of the movement's major figures. Dr. Bell, the Bishop of Chichester, was at that time Chairman of an International Christian Commission for Refugees, aiding the Jewish emigrants from Germany. Dr. Bell was an influential figure during those years, not only in his own organization, the Universal Christian Council for Life and Work, but in several others. Until the opening of the War, Bonhoeffer urged Dr. Bell to represent the German Church crisis to the ecumenical gatherings and figures with whom he was so influential. During his stay in England, Dietrich met with the Bishop frequently, and through him came into much closer touch with the Life and Work Movement, as well as with other major ecumenical ventures.

While Bonhoeffer was in London, the Confessional Church went through its strongest period of resistance. With the Barmen Declaration of late May, 1934, the Confessing Church declared itself to be the true Church of Christ, genuinely proclaiming God's Word. That summer, members of the Confessing Church, including Bonhoeffer, decided on the touchy question of regarding the Confessing Church as a free church, such as the Quakers or Anabaptists. The decision was negative. Bonhoeffer described the state of the Confessing Church in a letter at this time:

> There is not the claim or even the wish to be a Free Church besides the Reichskirche, but there is the claim to be the only theologically and legally legitimate Evangelical Church in Germany, and accordingly you cannot expect this Church to set up a new constitution, since it is based on the very constitution which the Reichskirche has neglected.[6]

Bonhoeffer performed a great service to both the Confessing Church and the outside churches by interpreting the Church struggle to the world beyond Germany. Hitler had carefully selected men to provide the rest of Europe with a specially prepared version of what was happening in Germany. International conferences, such as Life and Work, were attended by representatives of the German Church. Confessing leaders were discouraged from attending. Bonhoeffer had been involved in the Pastors Emergency League before leaving for London, and he knew Niemöller. His visits to various conferences and meetings in Germany sometimes numbered two a month. He would sometimes telephone Niemöller as frequently as once a night for weeks. Consequently, he was able to portray the real struggle to the churches not only in England, but throughout the rest of the world. Bishop Bell, who became the leading figure in relating the ecumenical movement to the German situation, depended largely on Bonhoeffer for his information and contacts.

The time in England, then, was not uneventful. Indeed, Bonhoeffer took advantage of the freedom he would have been denied in Berlin by becoming profoundly involved in ecumenical work and attempting to persuade the ecumenical churches to pressure Hitler for the autonomy of the Church. Bonhoeffer continued as Secretary of the Youth Commission in Life and Work, and in the summer of 1934, at the Life and Work Conference in Fano, Denmark, he was elected a co-opted member to the Universal Christian Council for Life and Work.

During his stay in London, the role of the Church in Germany in the face of war became Bonhoeffer's abiding concern. Every day the threat of Germany's attack on weaker nations seemed more imminent, and the question of the Church's responsibility in the face of such a threat agonized Bonhoeffer. Dietrich met C. F. Andrews, the close personal friend of Mahatma Gandhi, and his biographer. Through long conversations with Andrews, Bonhoeffer again renewed his desire for a visit to India to meet Gandhi and study his methods of nonviolent resistance with the idea of applying them in Germany. Bishop Bell wrote to Gandhi and arranged for a meeting with Bonhoeffer and plans were made for a two or three month stay in early 1935. Before Dietrich could work out preparations, though, a call came asking him to undertake the illegal training of seminarians for the Confessing Church. It was a painful decision. Bonhoeffer certainly wanted to return to Germany, but with some tactic—nonviolent resistance, he had hoped—which would equip the Confessing Church for a more effective stand against the Nazis. The seminary task was without doubt a risk, and a grave one. Bonhoeffer's decision was almost inevitable, however; he would return to Germany.

On April 26, 1935, Bonhoeffer met his first seminary class at Zingst, a village on the Baltic Sea. The seminary involved theological study, but was essentially a preparatory period for men already trained in theology and almost ready to enter the ministry. The situation at Zingst was too primitive, however; Bonhoeffer soon moved to Finkenwalde, on the Baltic near Stettin. Here the living quarters were more comfortable and the atmosphere conducive to the work.

From Finkenwalde, Bonhoeffer continued his work in the Confessing Church. He also wrote, a practice he had lacked time for in England. His themes became increasingly biblical; no seminarian left Finkenwalde unimpressed with Bonhoeffer's commitment to the Word of God.

Any effort to interpret the development in Bonhoeffer's theology of the Church over the years 1932-36 must necessarily be incomplete. Never in his life did Bonhoeffer provide a graduated systematic theology. Yet few of his writings exist in such a fragmentary state as the sermons and lectures of these years. The themes and questions are clear: the unity of the Church and the churches, the role of the Church in a totalitarian state, Church and state, the source of authority in the Church, the Church's responsibility in the persecution of the Jews. But Bonhoeffer's writings on these questions are not always completely unified and organized, if only because most of his writings were addresses and sermons, which were conditioned by the organization or congregation to which they were directed.

There is no question of the mainstay in all of Bonhoeffer's theological thinking of this period. The second resolution of the Ecumenical Youth Conference, which Bonhoeffer had an important hand in framing, expressed it lucidly: "The essential task of the Church is to proclaim the Word of God. Therefore the Church can never be a function—even if it be the highest function—of the people." [7]

A firsthand glance at these years is enough to ascertain the importance of the question of Church and state in Bonhoeffer's theology. Some commentators have suggested that this question dominated Bonhoeffer's thinking of the period. Actually, his move to England kept him from facing the question head-on, as Niemöller and other Confessing Church leaders had to face it. The questions Bonhoeffer faced were more subtle, less direct: what is the responsibility of the state toward the Church? What ordinarily, should be the function of the Church in society—and what in a time of crisis?

One important point which should be taken into consideration here is Bonhoeffer's temperament and pacifist beliefs. The state with which Bonhoeffer struggled was preparing to enter into war, and was already warring on the Jews and the churches. For a long while Bonhoeffer firmly believed that the Church could not act against the state, no matter what the state's offenses. The fact that he later took part in the resistance movement to kill Hitler shows how drastically his thought would change.

In his approach to Church and state, Bonhoeffer was more deeply affected by Luther than by any other man or tradition. Luther had reacted violently to the Church's interference in the state; as such, he had taught a subjugation of the Church to the temporal authority of the state. The Church was to be promoted, fostered, and to an extent, controlled by the state. The authorities, he insisted, should be kept separate. "One should not mix these two authorities," he wrote, "the temporal and the spiritual, the courthouse and the Church; otherwise the one devours the other and both perish, as happened under the papacy." [8] Luther insisted that the Church could not transgress its own boundaries when there came to be question of involvement in the state, even if the state were tyrannical and unjust. "As humbly as I conduct myself when God sends me a sickness," he said, "so humbly should I conduct myself toward evil government."[9] The outcome was a conception of the state which could rule over the Church in all temporal concerns.

The history of the Lutheran Church in Germany continued Luther's view. Although (up to 1933) it was a history remarkably free of tyrannical governments, it was likewise one without any tradition of rebellion. Luther's doctrine and the Lutheran Church—not to mention aspects of the Germanic temperament itself—had been a suitable training ground for submission. The only step needed was for someone to harness that submission. Hitler accomplished this task well.

The earliest clear statement of Bonhoeffer's views on Church and state comes from a lecture given November 19, 1932, only a few months after the National Socialists had won enough election seats to control parliament. The lecture was entitled "Thy Kingdom Come," and was Bonhoeffer's attempt to describe just what we are asking for in this phrase of the Lord's Prayer. The Kingdom, wrote Bonhoeffer, comes to us on earth and is present in a twofold form: as the final kingdom of the miraculous resurrection that breaks through all earthly kingdoms; and as the kingdom of order that affirms and preserves the earth with its laws, community, and history. In other words, the kingdom of God comes in the combination of Church and state. Yet the tension persists; the Church, as miracle, appears to break through all order, whereas order continues in preparation for the miracle. "The kingdom of God exists in our world exclusively in the duality of Church and state."[10]

Bonhoeffer goes further by attempting to describe how the kingdom of God is present in Church and in state. In the Church, the kingdom is present "insofar as the Church bears witness to the miracle of God. The function of the Church is to witness to the resurrection of Christ from the dead."[11] The state does not properly witness, but preserves life that the Church can exercise its witness: "The state acknowledges and maintains the order of the preservation of life . . . and [exercises] its authority here in preventing the destruction of life."[12]

What then is the proper relationship between Church and

state? Bonhoeffer's words reflect Luther: "The Church limits the state, just as the state limits the Church, and each must remain conscious of this mutual limitation. Furthermore, each must bear the tension of coexistence, which in this world must never be a coalescence."[13] Bonhoeffer makes an interesting point in his conclusion: at the end, both Church and state will exist no longer; but there will be only the Lord as Creator, the crucified and resurrected one.

In 1932 Bonhoeffer also developed his doctrine of *Erhaltungsordnungen,* or orders of preservation. Here a break from Luther's original doctrine is more apparent, although the reference to Church and state is implied. Bonhoeffer described the orders of preservation as God's continuing action in the fallen world, an action which promises the coming of a new creation. Any order which becomes closed and hardened to God's Word must eventually be destroyed. The Church must ask the question: Which orders can most quickly stop this sickness leading the world to death and hold the world open for the Gospel? It is on this basis that any order must be judged.

Bonhoeffer never applied this doctrine, with its heavy christological emphasis, to the state; it would have been worthwhile to follow his conclusions. Later, in his *Ethics,* he would develop a similar doctrinal approach, which he called the four mandates. In the mandates the state is placed under the judgment of the Church.

As the Nazi Party took control of Germany and began to crush the German Church, Bonhoeffer sensed with growing apprehension the impotence of the traditional Church-state doctrine. His efforts to provide a more active base for the Church during these years were tentative and exploratory, without a lengthy theological rationale. In an essay entitled "What Is the Church?" he suggested that the Church has two words to speak to the state: the first under ordinary conditions, the second in a time of crisis. The first word is for the state to recognize its limitations and finitude. Bonhoeffer acknowledges that the existence of a second word is disputed; yet he suggests an active political responsibility and decision. The same notion is touched upon, again briefly, in the second resolution of the Youth Commission of Life and Work, which Bonhoeffer helped draft: "The Church, which may not enter the political struggle, must nevertheless enjoin its members to study social questions with the ultimate aim of action." [14]

During this period Bonhoeffer, like many of his confreres, never did succeed in formulating a successful Church-state theory appropriate for approaching the situation in Germany. Bonhoeffer, if anyone, recognized the need for a fresh doctrinal interpretation. As he said in another context, "The rusty swords of the old world are powerless to combat the evils of today." [15] Indeed, Bonhoeffer's later efforts to provide a clear doctrinal basis for Church-state relations can be seen in the *Ethics;* however, even this attempt was not completely satisfactory. The problem, as Bonhoeffer gradually came to see, was much larger than Church and state; it involved the condition of man in the modern world, and the nature of the Church's relationship to that world. Only in handling these two questions would Bonhoeffer ever supply the basis for a viable Church-state theology.

During these years, Bonhoeffer's notion of the Church slowly became more spiritual and less worldly. At first sight, the movement seems a theological regression. But Bonhoeffer was left with little choice. The German Church had made nationalism a must for Christian faith, and Teutonic blood a deeper bond than spiritual brotherhood. (One particularly enthusiastic curate read the following "Bible passage" at a meeting of Christians: "In the beginning was the Nation, and the Nation was with God, and the Nation was God, and the same was in the beginning with God. . . ." [16] No one in the audience, including a bishop, seemed disturbed.)

Bonhoeffer reacted to the degradation of the German Church by emphasizing with all his power the true origin of the Church in Christ. The day of the decisive Church elections (July 23, 1933) Bonhoeffer spoke vigorously in a sermon: "But it is not we who build. He builds the Church. No man builds the Church but Christ alone. Whoever is minded to build the Church is surely well on his way to destroying it; for he will build a temple to idols without wishing or knowing it. We must confess—He builds." [17] The emphasis is typical of Bonhoeffer ever since he had been under the influence of Barth's thought; here, however, he makes little explicit effort to insist upon the concrete nature of the Church. Instead, he speaks now of a "hidden Church"—which "appears as the powerless defenseless gospel of the resurrection, of the miracle." [18] As he stated in the summer of 1933 to his Christology class:

> With this humiliated One, the Church goes its own way of humiliation. It cannot reach out for a visible authorization of its way, since He, at every point, refuses this. As the humiliated Church it must look with neither vain complacency to itself, as if its humility were a visible proof that Christ is present. Humiliation is not a proof to which one can draw attention. There is no law or principle which the Church must follow. There is only this fact of humility, which is God's way with the Church.[19]

The Church is Christ, stated Bonhoeffer elsewhere, in the hiddenness of history. Actually, the concrete emphasis, the insistence on the *world* as the locus of the Church, is still present in Bonhoeffer's thought, but with a fresh perspective. The earth may be cursed, but into the cursed land Christ has come, building his Church in the land's hidden recesses. "Indeed," Bonhoeffer wrote, "it is this hiddenness which really constitutes the curse . . . not that it bears thistles and thorns, but that it conceals God's countenance, so that even the deepest furrows of the earth do not unveil for us the hidden God." [20]

The theme was an appropriate one; certainly it spoke to the men who were struggling to keep the Confessing Church alive in those days. Yet in many ways, a doctrine of "hiddenness" was insufficient, for it begged the fundamental question of the Church's existence in Germany. Gradually Bonhoeffer recognized that it was not enough to speak of a "hidden Church"; the line had to be drawn more tightly, with no doubts remaining. Bonhoeffer had a number of opportunities to challenge German Christians and those who remained cautiously indecisive; he took advantage of them all. He fought for a long time in the struggle defending the statement, "Whoever knowingly separates himself from the Confessing Church in Germany separates himself from salvation." Later he directed fierce words at the pastors in the Confessing Church who neglected the Church's basic mission by getting too involved in Church politics. Bonhoeffer's words leave no doubt: the Church struggle as he saw it was either-or, and each month sharpened the contrast. It is significant that by the time he was operating the seminary at Finkenwalde, Bonhoeffer had left behind him many of the theoretical problems of the Church and was concentrating upon the basic problem of the Christian's commitment to God in the world.

During these years, a fresh theological problem emerged, one which would demand Bonhoeffer's complete attention in the later writings. The question of Church and world was never a major concern with Luther; and although liberal theology prided itself on exploring the relationship, Bonhoeffer had never agreed with the approach taken by this school. The question became urgent during the Nazi regime: how should the Church respond to Jewish persecution, the nation's preparation for an aggressive war, the intoxication of the people with a dangerous leader? Bonhoeffer realized that a major reason for the failure of the Confessing Church in Germany was its lack of a theological doctrine of Church and world. Worse: the absence of such a doctrine forced upon the Church an unreal notion of itself which was, as Bonhoeffer later suggested in his prison letters, essentially self-destructive.

The search for an adequate Church-world doctrine was never more than a weak, preliminary one until Bonhoeffer began work on the *Ethics*. Yet his writings of the period between 1932 and 1936 show a recurring questioning of the relationship, and a circling effort to define the problem.

The most important writing in this regard is "Thy Kingdom Come," the November, 1932, address. Here Bonhoeffer sets forth a positive concept of the world—but positive only because Christ has come into it. "It is to this cursed earth that Christ has come . . . the kingdom of Christ is a kingdom that, coming from above, is sunk down into the cursed ground." [21] Bonhoeffer's real concern, however, is the role of the Church in the world, just as it will be later in his final works. To pray the Lord's Prayer, Bonhoeffer states, demands a deep concern for the world: "The hour in which the Church today prays for the kingdom is one that forces the Church, for good or ill, to identify itself completely with the children of the earth and of the world. He wrote in a paper, "What Is the Church?"

This prayer is prayed solely by the congregation of the children of the earth, who refuse to separate themselves from the world and who have no special proposals to offer for its improvement. The people of this community also do not consider themselves superior to the world, but persevere together in the midst of the world, in its depth, in its trivialities and bondages.[23]

The ideas are provocative; they clearly bear the seeds of the *Ethics* and the theological excursions in the prison works. Another outlook, which Bonhoeffer would develop in his *Ethics,* is the manner in which the Church *is* the world and belongs to the world. He wrote in a paper, "What Is the Church?"

The Church is a bit of the qualified world, qualified by God's revealing, gracious Word, which, completely surrendered and handed over to the world, secures the world for God and does not give up. The Church is the presence of God in the world. Really in the world, really the presence of God. The Church is not a consecrated sanctuary, but the world, called by God to God; therefore there is only *one* Church in all the world.[24]

The later developments in Bonhoeffer's thought, then, can already be glimpsed: a negation of Christianity as fleeing to another world, the Church's concrete responsibility to the people of this world, the Church's existence as a community within the world, the Church as *being* the world, that part of the world drawn to God. Here an important question might be raised: Without the upheaval of National Socialism and the conflict in the churches, would Bonhoeffer have developed his Church-world relationship of the *Ethics,* and the religionless Christianity of his prison letters? The question is all the more significant as critics charge Bonhoeffer's thought with the restriction of being valid only in the extraordinary situation from which it emerged.

Of course, the question can never be completely answered. To what extent is an environment responsible for any man's thought? There are clues, however, which suggest that had Bonhoeffer only pursued his early lines of thought, he would have reached many conclusions similar to "religionless Christianity" and his Church-world doctrine. The most evident clue would be the anticipation of these conclusions in Bonhoeffer's academic and early writings. Another would be his constant effort to give the Confessing Church struggle a theological context—and not let the struggle overshadow its theology. This effort can be seen to a remarkable extent in Bonhoeffer's response to the Jewish question, a response admirable for a theologian, if disappointing for a responsible German pastor.

There can be little question that Bonhoeffer, along with innumerable other Church leaders, failed to respond in a fully vigorous, courageous way to the waves of Jewish persecution instigated by Hitler. It should be noted, however, that upon the publication of the Aryan Clauses in April of 1933—the announcement of an outright racist state—the first outcry to come from the Lutheran Church was a speech delivered only days later by Dietrich Bonhoeffer.

In "The Church and the Jewish Question," Bonhoeffer acknowledged the problem by posing two questions: What is the Church's attitude to the action of the state? And what should the Church do as a result of it? The opening paragraph of the discussion may seem disconcerting to us today, yet it must be remembered that Bonhoeffer's theological background was severely limited on this point:

> Without a doubt, the Church of the Reformation has no right to address the state directly in its specifically political actions. It has neither to praise nor to censure the laws of the state, but must rather affirm the state to be God's order of preservation in a godless world; it has to recognize the state's ordinances, good or bad as they appear from a humanitarian point of view. . . . The action of the state remains free from the Church's intervention.[25]

Bonhoeffer continues, in words that seem to open wider the gates at Buchenwald and Flossenbürg:

Without doubt the Jewish question is one of the historical problems which our state must deal with, and without doubt the state is justified in adopting new methods here. It remains the concern of humanitarian associations and individual Christians who feel themselves called to the task, to remind the state of the moral side of any of its measures, i.e., on occasions to accuse the state of offences against morality. . . . The true Church of Christ, however . . . will never intervene in the state in such a way as to criticize its history-making actions, from the standpoint of some humanitarian ideal.[26]

These paragraphs leave Bonhoeffer open to serious misunderstanding. It must be recalled that the position of the Jews in Germany had always been precarious, to say the least: Luther himself was noted for his disdainful attitude toward the Jewish race. As such, the early stages of Hitler's persecution did not appear to most Aryans as anything especially disturbing. The very effort of preparing a paper on the question indicates that Bonhoeffer was disturbed—although for theological reasons, rather than from indignation at the injustices being foisted upon the Jews. (Bonhoeffer was disturbed at the persecution in a basically human way. Yet he revealed his own mild anti-Semitism in stating. "The Church of Christ has never lost sight of the thought that the 'chosen people,' who nailed the redeemer of the world to the cross, must bear the curse for its action through a long history of suffering.")[27]

What is most remarkable about the paper, however, is not its failure to denounce violently the Nazi government for its action, but rather Bonhoeffer's attempt to clarify the doctrinal responsibility of the Church in the face of such a crisis. The Church, he stated, can act in three possible ways toward the state: it can ask the state whether its actions are "legitimate and in accordance with its character as state, i.e., it can throw the state back upon its responsibilities."[28] Secondly, the Church can aid the victims of action taken by the state. This alternative was exemplified in the relief program for Jewish refugees set up by the ecumenical commissions working together. The third possibility—surely the one to be demanded least often—is "not just to bandage the victims under the wheel, but to put a spoke in the wheel itself." [29] Action of this type would be directly political, and the Church should resort to it only if the state brings about too much or too little order.

Bonhoeffer admitted that the exclusion of Jews from public office and many public places did not necessitate the third decision—whereas the exclusion of baptized Jews from Church services did. In this later case, Bonhoeffer was firm: "What is at stake . . . is rather the task of Christian preaching to say: here is the Church, where Jew and German stand together under the Word of God; here is the proof whether a Church is still the Church or not." [30]

As a leading Church figure, Bonhoeffer is open to severe criticism in his response to the outburst of Jewish persecution. Yet nationalism and the sense of Teutonic superiority had reached an epidemic stage in 1933. Bonhoeffer was one of the few to keep his head, and to have acted quickly, if quietly, in the midst of the furor. (Even the brilliant and heroic Pastor Niemöller was an enthusiastic supporter of Hitler for many years, and believed in many of the myths whipped up by the Nazi propaganda machine.)

Bonhoeffer's statement on the Church and the Jews assures at least one thing: his conviction that the Church should face real problems, no matter how embarrassing and painful. It was a concern shared at this juncture by very few of his fellow pastors, so many of whom clustered together to "save the Church" while forgetting the people that made the Church worth saving.

In all, the period from 1932 to 1936 was a hectic one theologically. Its demands upon Bonhoeffer wrenched him from a theoretical approach to theology and forced upon him questions which gave wider berth to his developing thought. Exploratory notions of Church and state, the hidden Church, the Church's responsibilities to the world emerged, forecasting the later shape of his theology. Above all, however, the period had the effect of an initiation upon Dietrich. Despite the persistence of doubts, despite the continual longing to pull away from it all and work quietly on theology, Bonhoeffer was pulled into the grip of a conflict which would demand active involvement and constant theological effort. What above all enabled him to move successfully through that conflict was his unfailing effort to identify the Church's real needs, and to relate to those needs the Person of Christ as He is known today.

Socialism has succeeded in setting itself up on an international basis not because the German worker knows the French and the English worker, but because they have a common ideal. Similarly, Christians too will only learn to think internationally when they have a great, common message. We need today more than anything else in the ecumenical movement the one great reconciling message.

"A Theological Basis for the World Alliance?"
delivered July 26, 1932, in Czechoslovakia

6. *The Ecumenical Movement*

"The really disquieting problem of ecumenical work," Bonhoeffer wrote in 1932, "is not the relationship between organism and organization but that between truth and untruth in the preaching of the different churches." [1] The comment typifies the critical tenor of Bonhoeffer's ecumenical thought. Just as he saw efforts to proliferate interchurch organizations as irrelevant to the real ecumenical task, so he carefully appraised doctrinal differences and the statements issued by the World Alliance and other ecumenical groups.

Not that he questioned the ecumenical movement itself. Upon returning from the World Alliance meeting in 1931, he introduced a report with the statement, "The work of the World Alliance is progressing slowly but surely, and the urgency of this work must be impressed upon everyone." Bonhoeffer was committed to a unification of the churches as few Germans were—especially after 1934, when he saw that a statement made by the ecumenical Church was needed to support the Confessing Church.

Bonhoeffer's thought on Church unity and the authority to be vested in an ecumenical Church council (such as the World Alliance) hardly resembles the hearty "We're with you!" writings on Church unity so common during the 1930's. Indeed, Bonhoeffer's ideas on Church unity and authority are subtle, at times carefully evasive. He rebelled at answers which swept over the entangled problems of centuries of division and splintering of churches. Where he could provide no clear answers of his own, he probed new possibilities, without, however, developing new doctrinal statements. The result is a period of thought on the Church and its unity which is far more exploratory than affirmative.

Dietrich Bonhoeffer was an apt candidate for ecumenical involvement. He had travelled to North Africa, Spain, throughout America, Cuba, Mexico, and was adept in several languages. Then there were his two treatises on the Church, which in many respects provided the outline to deeply ecumenical theology. His only real restraint was the prevailing attitude toward international church work so prevalent in Germany during the 1930's.

Bonhoeffer was aware how particularly severe the climate in Germany against ecumenical work had become. The high crest of nationalism, holding aloft a snobbish Lutheran ministry, wrote ecumenism off as disloyalty. "They disown the German fate and perplex the conscience at home and abroad," stated two important churchmen. Nonetheless, Bonhoeffer stepped into the movement fully conscious of what he was doing, and within a few years he fashioned for himself an indispensable position in the movement.

The ecumenical movement encompassed several organizations which stemmed from the important World Missionary Conference in Edinburgh in 1910. The most immediate group to spring from the 1910 Conference was the Faith and Order movement, an organization concerned with the study of comparative doctrines. In 1927 at Lausanne the first and major Faith and Order conference was held, which stressed the nature of the Church, its message to the world, and its integral unity.

The Faith and Order movement was strongly an Anglican effort, centering on doctrinal issues which were the keynotes of Anglican theology.

However, a Nordic ecumenical venture—and the one which highly influenced Bonhoeffer in his approach to ecumenical work—was the World Alliance for Promoting International Friendship through the Churches. Archbishop Nathan Söderblom, primate of the Church of Sweden, had attempted for years to unite the churches before the War as a means of allaying the conflict. Throughout the War he continued to work with the churches in hopes of finding ways to end the holocaust. In October of 1919, Söderblom was finally able to convoke sixty delegates at Oud Wassenaar near the Hague in Holland. Here the participants took up the controversial questions of war guilt and the Church's responsibility and failure in the War. Out of this conference grew an amazing spirit of trust and mutual understanding, which in the year following history's most brutal war, came as a surprise to all the participants. The World Alliance grew as a Christian confederation, and its concern continued to be peace and the Church's responsibility for world peace.

Developing from the World Alliance and closely parallel in many respects to Faith and Order was a third movement, Life and Work. Söderblom's major hope had always been for an international council of churches on the scale of Faith and Order, only concerned with common action rather than doctrinal discussion. The first world conference for Life and Work was held at Stockholm in 1925. The outline covered by the conference suggests the direction that Life and Work hoped to take:

(1) The Church's duty in the light of God's plan for the world.
(2) The Church and economic and industrial problems.
(3) The Church and social and moral problems.
(4) The Church and international relations.
(5) The Church and education.
(6) Cooperation between churches.

The stated purpose of the movement was "to perpetuate and strengthen the fellowship between churches in the application of Christian ethics to the social problems of modern life." Doctrinal issues, of course, arose; yet the major impetus of the Conference, namely Christian action, kept Life and Work vital, and in many respects the most significant ecumenical movement of the 1920's. It was Life and Work which Dr. G.K.A. Bell, the Bishop of Chichester, headed after 1934 and which attracted many of Bonhoeffer's efforts.

Bonhoeffer's letters make it fairly clear that he felt the World Alliance to be the most meaningful ecumenical effort, mainly because its goal was not posed as a doctrinally dubious "Church unity," but an effective concern for the peace enjoined by Christ. Throughout his work with the World Alliance, Bonhoeffer came to see world peace as a far more urgent and realistic goal for the united churches than "unity." Indeed, he spoke often against the shallow efforts to pose a doctrinal unity where in reality the obstacles to unity were innumerable. Truth, Bonhoeffer came to realize, was a far more reliable standard for ecumenical work than "unity."

"The Churches in the World Alliance," he stated to the Youth Peace Conference in 1932, "have no common recognition of the truth. . . . We may not play with the truth, or else it will destroy us." [2] He searched out doctrinal differences relentlessly, not from a factious frame of mind but from a carefully attained perspective of ecumenical goals. To Bonhoeffer the ecumenical struggle was not a matter of "dialogue" in the talkative, compliant sense, nor of an easy concession of doctrinal conflicts for a cheap unity; it was the search for integral Christian truth.

Clear-headed and sure of his goals, Bonhoeffer entered the ecumenical struggle with the Cambridge World Alliance Conference in 1931. In his report of the Conference, Bonhoeffer highlighted two tensions which arose, and which followed him in all his ecumenical work. "We saw a common need and a common duty . . . in the lack of a great basic theological understanding of our work," [3] he said. Ecumenical work, especially once it reached the stage of common resolutions and action, demanded a new theological outlook, one which could bridge doctrinal differences. Bonhoeffer's conscious awareness of this need stimulated him, no doubt, in his search for the grounds of a concrete command issued by the churches together.

The second tension had to do with this concrete command: "The fact that the churches have composed yet another resolution will simply be ignored in wide circles in this country, unless they do something now." [4] Bonhoeffer, for all his sensitivity to doctrinal foundations, knew that fruitful ecumenical relations could issue only in action. The action needed most, he believed, was peace—but a real peace, the *pax Christi,* not simply an absence of international war. At the Berlin Youth Conference, Bonhoeffer recorded in his report a question which must have struck him forcefully:

> Is the Church a place where Christ is "preached" without anything really happening in that place, or does this witness of the Church mean that Christ himself is present and effective in the witness (the Church as the Body of Christ, and an extension of the Incarnation)? [5]

The questions Bonhoeffer put to himself these years centered in the tension of authority and command of the churches acting together. The extension of an older strain of thought—the concrete character of revelation, and of the Church—is here most apparent.

Partly as a result of his insistence on the concrete command, partly because of Bonhoeffer's careful doctrinal inspections, the question of Church unity was never adequately answered—or for that matter formulated—by Bonhoeffer during this period. It does seem strange that the major idea of a movement would never be taken up directly by such a leading advocate. When he came to the question, usually at the close of his speeches and papers, Bonhoeffer would state flatly, "I know of no solution here." His earlier theology had stressed Church unity, but not in consideration of the nagging problems Bonhoeffer saw now: conflicting theological traditions, shifting conceptions of the

Church, serious cultural differences, and absence of clear-sighted purposes. Without doubt, Bonhoeffer believed in one Church, holy and catholic, guided by the Spirit. However, he did not know how to relate the varying churches to this one Church, or interpret them as part of it. He was certain that no Church could be true to Christ if it created its own laws and style. As he wrote in 1937:

> Life together under the Word will remain sound and healthy only where it does not form itself into a movement, an order, a society, a *collegium pietatis,* but rather where it understands itself as being a part of the one, holy, catholic, Christian Church, where it shares actively and passively in the sufferings and struggles and promises of the whole Church.[6]

In a sense, Church unity was unimportant for Bonhoeffer. It was like ultimate sanctity, an ideal which Christians accept, but leave to God's work and God's good time. What was important was the action of the churches right away, where it was needed: in establishing and protecting peace. Here unity had to be presumed as much as struggled for; here the problem was as much of making acts of faith as it was of struggling for a lucid theology. But above all—and this point cannot be ignored—the problem was one of attaining effective action. Only in terms of this goal of action does Bonhoeffer's developing thought in the ecumenical movement make sense.

The complexity of the issues and the lack of systematic writings on ecumenism make Bonhoeffer's ideas in this area especially difficult to follow. Several of his addresses do lend themselves to a study of his theology on the movement, and probably the most fruitful approach to his ecumenical thought would be a careful look at these few addresses.

The first document available from Bonhoeffer on the ecumenical movement is his report on the World Alliance Conference in Cambridge, which he wrote for *Theologische Blätter,* a popular journal. The theme of the conference was, as Bonhoeffer stated, the disarmament question. The stand of the conference was firm:

The honor of the nations now arming and the course of justice were at stake . . . . Thus the conference was able to send out a unanimous message to the churches of the world, stating that, in its view, war as a means of settling international disputes was contrary to the spirit ("mind and method!") of Christ and his Church.[7]

In this report Bonhoeffer already located the two tensions which ran simultaneously through the history of the movement: the need for an ecumenical theology, and the need for common, purposeful action. Here, likewise, he made a statement regarding the need for more than a general resolution:

"Christian principles"—applied art—are most dangerous to true Christianity precisely at such conferences and yet they must be expressed as long as men simply do not know any more, in which case, of course, it would be a good thing to admit that openly.[8]

The need for an effort which stretches beyond a mere statement of the ideal—in other words, the need for concrete action, in whatever way is most feasible and effective—is already apparent. Bonhoeffer included in the report, in a tone of strong personal endorsement, that the Youth Conference (a group within the World Alliance) *hesitated* on sending out a resolution: "There was too strong a feeling that the attempt must first be made to see new relationships afresh and that high-flown statements were not a good beginning." [9] It is significant that Bonhoeffer, who helped arrive at the decision to hold back in the resolution, that week was elected the Youth Conference co-secretary for Germany and Central Europe.

A year later, in July, 1932, Bonhoeffer presented what is probably the most important of his papers in the ecumenical movement, "A Theological Basis for the World Alliance." The occasion was the Youth Peace Conference in Czechoslovakia. The opportunity was perfect; Bonhoeffer had been asked to provide his own theological formulation of purposes for the World Alliance for Promoting International Friendship through the Churches. Nowhere else would he have the freedom to explore his own ground as here. And nowhere else would he find an audience as young and as willing to accept new ideas.

His opening words are, "There is still no theology of the ecumenical movement." More than ever conscious of the need, Bonhoeffer sets out to explain the importance of such a theology. "As often as the Church of Christ has reached a new understanding of its nature it has produced a new theology, appropriate to this self-understanding." [10] The implication for the ecumenical movement was there; Bonhoeffer is not long in stating it. If the movement does not succeed in producing a new theology, "it is nothing but a new and up-to-date improvement in Church organization." [11] Bonhoeffer goes on to charge the absence of this new theology with making ecumenical thought "powerless and meaningless."

The thought is direct and ruthless. But Bonhoeffer is leading somewhere, and soon he indicates the direction.

> But what is it that has emerged time and again with rudimentary force at the international youth conferences of recent times? . . . It is the recognition of the deep helplessness that there is precisely in those questions which should be the *basis* of our being together.[12]

The questions then facing a new theology are: "What is Christianity? What is the relationship between the forms of modern life and the Christian message?" The failure to answer these questions in a commonly meaningful way has spelled the failure of the ecumenical thought. "We ask for a responsible theology of the ecumenical movement for the sake of the truth and certainty of our cause." [13]

The introduction shows clearly the size of the question Bonhoeffer is facing. Yet he attempts to outline "some of the basic theological questions," using, of course, his own themes and constructs. The first question rings of the need for a concrete revelation. "With whose authority does the Church speak when it declares this claim of Christ to the whole world?" [14] Bonhoeffer has already established an ecumenical right for the World Alliance: if Christ's claim is to the whole world, then churches should associate to express this claim better. And these churches can rightly express His claim—for "the Church is the presence of Christ on earth, the Church is *Christus praesens.* For this reason alone the Church has authority." [15]

At this point Bonhoeffer suddenly turns to a development both startling and persuasive:

Because of the *Christus praesens,* the word of the Church here and now must be a valid, binding word. Someone can only speak to me with authority if a word from the deepest knowledge of my humanity encounters me here and now in all my reality. Any other word is impotent. *The Word of the Church to the world must therefore encounter the world in all its present reality from the deepest knowledge of the world, if it is to be authoritative.*[16] (italics added)

Bonhoeffer had earlier mentioned the need for knowledge of the world, especially in sections of *The Communion of Saints.* Here, however, this knowledge takes on the character of a sacramental attribute of the command. Indeed, further on Bonhoeffer states, "What the sacrament is for the preaching of the Gospel, the knowledge of firm reality is for the preaching of the sacrament. *Reality is the sacrament of command.*" [17]

Sacramental in what sense? It must be recalled that in Lutheran theology the sacrament stood as a parallel to the Word, another aspect of God's gracious revelation—rather than a unique order in which the natural is infused with the supernatural. Here Bonhoeffer is using the word "sacrament" in an effort to return to the Thomistic notion of the natural receiving the supernatural—or in Lutheran terms, *finitum capax infiniti* (the finite containing the infinite). For the Church's command to be valid, it must be a concrete command—meaning one that is spoken from a thorough understanding of the situation. The Church, Bonhoeffer implies, has the responsibility to learn social, economic, political conditions, and to learn them well before it speaks. But when it speaks, God's Word is being uttered, and God's authority has been invoked. Such an approach gives the Church a powerful mandate, and charges it with an awesome responsibility.

But Bonhoeffer pursues the questioning further. With what certainty can the Church preach the commandment of God?

With the certainty of the Gospel? "Can the Church say 'We need a socialist ordering of economics,' or 'Do not engage in war' with the same certainty as it can say 'Thy sins be forgiven thee'?"[18] Both Gospel and commandment have authority only when spoken in a concrete way; that is evident. Otherwise, as Bonhoeffer states, "things remain in the sphere of what is generally known, human, impotent."[19] The crucial problem is where to locate the principle of concreteness in the Gospel, and in the commandment. Building upon Luther's dictum that the Word of God should be above all heard, Bonhoeffer suggests that the Gospel becomes concrete in the hearers—whereas the commandment becomes concrete in those who preach it. The implications are obvious:

> The preacher must therefore be concerned so to incorporate the contemporary situation in his shaping of the commandment itself relevant to the real situation. It cannot be, "War is evil—but rather, 'Fight this war,' or 'Don't fight this war.' "[20]

"A commandment," Bonhoeffer states emphatically, "must be definite, otherwise it is not a commandment."[21] The danger of building upon principles is the danger of building upon sand; only concrete, definitive commands can mark the true Church of Christ.

Such a theological basis for an ecumenical alliance of churches hardly seems directed toward unity, but rather toward a sound doctrinal basis for common study of the problems of peace and firm commands to achieve peace. The objection is a valid one; Bonhoeffer's foremost concern in the ecumenical movement surely was not Church unity, or at least organizational and cultural unity. That his "ecumenical theology" would turn into a "theology of the concrete command" shows his real concern with the movement. Yet, in relation to other theologians at the time who were attempting an immediate but ineffective Church unity, Bonhoeffer's direction seems remarkably realistic. Church unity was a final goal, and one which presumably could not be approached directly. To offer the World Alliance a secure theology for its search to understand the world situation and declare specifically what the churches should teach, was indeed a limited goal. Yet it might have been a far wiser approach than attempting to provide a theological synthesis embracing every problem and yet achieving nothing.

The remainder of Bonhoeffer's speech dealt with exploring and clarifying the fundamental point of the concrete command. Bonhoeffer did not evade the obvious question. "God's commandment for us today is the order of international peace,"[22] he stated. This was, after all, the original purpose of the World Alliance under Söderblom.

Unfortunately, Bonhoeffer never provided another theological explanation of the ecumenical movement's goals as clearly outlined in his own thought as this World Alliance speech. His *Ethics* does take up the responsibility for complete knowledge and concrete action, though not in the domain of Church preaching.

Two minor papers can be seen as following this effort to construct a theology of ecumenical work—both of them, interestingly enough, stressing the need for a theological basis for such work. Bonhoeffer's report of the Berlin Youth Conference in April, 1932, was written for *Die Eiche*. Bonhoeffer reported there on two speeches, "The Church and the Churches" and "The Church and the Nations," as well as the controversy stimulated by the speeches. The problems which arose indicate the focal tensions of ecumenical work at the time: the united Church's responsibility to act, the nature of Church unity; the problem (raised by Bonhoeffer) of doctrinal truth; the natural world and its relationship to the revealed Church. The report was all too brief for the vivid and unconcluded arguments which arose. It does show what Bonhoeffer was involved in.

In his speech to the World Alliance Conference at Fanö, Denmark, in 1934, Bonhoeffer applied his own insistence on a concrete command. His talk was on peace, and amounted to an effort to convince the delegates that peace could be achieved only through the united churches working together. "How does peace come about?" Bonhoeffer asks.

> Through economic insurance? Through rearmament? Hardly; here peace has been confused with safety. There is no way to peace along the way of safety. For peace must be dared. It is the great venture. It can never be safe. . . . "Who can take the risk of peace?" The individual Christian cannot do it. When all around are silent, he can indeed raise his voice and bear witness, but the powers of this world stride over him without a word.[23]

Such individual pacifism may be heroic, but it is never effective. Nor can the individual Church, suffocated by the nation which limits it, achieve peace. "Only Christ over all the world can speak out so that the world, though it gnash its teeth, will have heart." [24] The words were spoken in the spirit of Nathan Söderblom, and reveal an optimism and hopefulness rarely seen in Bonhoeffer during this period.

Bonhoeffer would later state of the Fanö conference that here "the ecumenical movement entered on a new era. It caught sight of its commission as a Church at a quite definite point, and that is its permanent significance." [25]

Bonhoeffer's lengthy paper, "The Confessing Church and the Ecumenical Movement," was written in 1935. Few non-Germans would have agreed completely with the thesis of the paper. There Bonhoeffer claimed that the ecumenical movement was undergoing the same "identity crisis" that the Confessing Church had undergone. And the success of the ecumenical movement, he maintained, hinged on the way in which it followed the path taken by the Confessing Church.

The paper contains numerous odd insights on the historical intervention of the two forces; it is a paper which Bonhoeffer was clearly in an excellent position to prepare. "In this encounter," he stated forthrightly in the paper, "the ecumenical movement and the Confessing Church ask each other the reason for their existence." [26] The statement is historically accurate: the plea of the Confessing Church for recognition by the ecumenical movement forced a period of introspection on the movement—just as the movement's questions to the Confessing Church demanded fresh thinking by the Confessing leaders on its nature as a Church. From an historical point of view, the document is valuable; however, it does little to suggest or further Bonhoeffer's own thought.

What does give an excellent idea of Bonhoeffer's emerging thought at this time are his letters pleading with Dr. Bell (of Life and Work) and Leonard Hodgson (of Faith and Order) to intervene in Hitler's control of the German Church. The situation of the Church in Germany had become critical by late 1934. Bonhoeffer was convinced that if the Church were free to preach what it should, the Nazi regime could be stopped, or at least retarded. He was likewise convinced that the pressure of the European and British churches in strong and unequivocal statements could intimidate Hitler into letting go of the churches. (It was no secret that Hitler thought the Protestants "insignificant little people, submissive as dogs"—an attitude which Bonhoeffer hoped would work to the churches' advantage.)

Bonhoeffer's initial effort—during the period when he was in Britain—was to convince the ecumenical leaders that the Confessing Church could not be treated alongside the German Church. What was at stake was the ecumenical movement's recognition that the renegade Confessing Church *was* the Church of Christ in Germany. Late in 1933, Bonhoeffer wrote to Dr. Bell:

> It seems to me that the responsibility of the ecumenic work has perhaps never been so far-reaching as in the present moment. If the ecumenical Churches would keep silent during those days, I am afraid that all the trust put into it by the minority would be destroyed. . . . We must not leave alone those men who fight—humanly speaking—an almost hopeless struggle.[27]

In a letter a few months later, the plea was stronger:

> There is really a moment now as perhaps never before in Germany in which our faith in the ecumenic task of the churches can be shaken and destroyed completely or strengthened and renewed in a surprisingly new way. And it is you, my Lord Bishop, on whom it depends whether this moment shall be used. . . . Please, do not be

silent now! I beg to ask you once more to consider the possibility of an ecumenic delegation and ultimatum.[28]

The Bishop of Chichester was slow to move—not that he didn't want to, but simply because securing a statement from the churches of innumerable European nations verging on such a touchy political-ecclesiastical matter was not easily done.

In a letter that August to Bishop Ammundsen, Chairman of the Minorities Commission of the World Alliance, Bonhoeffer anticipated that Fanö Conference in stating:

I feel that a resolution ought to be framed. All evasion is useless. And if the World Alliance in Germany is then dissolved—well and good. At least we will have borne witness that we were at fault. Better that than to go on vegetating in this untruthful way. Only complete truth and truthfulness will help us now.[29]

No Confessing Church delegates were permitted to attend the Fanö Conference in Denmark, although men like Bonhoeffer managed to get there in other capacities. And despite the presence of a large Reich Church delegation, the Conference, under the guidance of Ammundsen, harshly upbraided the Nazi Church as "incompatible with the true nature of the Christian Church." [30] At the meeting, Bonhoeffer and Dr. Koch of the Confessing Church were elected to the Universal Christian Council for Life and Work, a statement of the Conference's sympathy with the Confessing Church.

From this point on, Bonhoeffer tried even harder to bring ecumenical leaders to challenge Hitler on the German Church question. He had written to Dr. Henroid, Joint General Secretary of the World Alliance and Life and Work, "I feel strongly that legally and theologically the responsibility for the future relationship between the German Church and the ecumenic movement rests with the ecumenic movement itself and its actions." [31] But Bonhoeffer was up against great odds. His sudden return to Germany to operate the seminary at Finkenwalde interrupted the important direct contact with the men he had wanted to convince. Likewise, it was evident that the backbone of the ecumenic movement was still not strong enough to carry the support Bonhoeffer asked. The impressive Oxford Conference of Life and Work in 1937 revealed the extent of internal disagreement over the simple question of denouncing the German Church, much less struggling to free the Confessing Church.

Bonhoeffer had fought vigorously. His growing theology of the Church suggests the extent to which the struggle influenced his thought. He had entered the movement at a time when it was a promising idea for a young pastor and offered an outlet for his instinctive aversion to a "national church." But the struggles, intermingled with the harsh controversy of the Confessing Church, brought Bonhoeffer, still only in his late twenties, into contact with the most perilous—if most exciting—Church efforts of the period. The ecumenical experience was not for Bonhoeffer an idea, or the recognition of an ideal. It was the encounter with an openness and a sympathy beyond the Church in Germany, which give him renewed hope for the Confessing Church and a fresh perspective for his theology. As with the Confessing Church, Bonhoeffer's experience in the ecumenical conferences forged a new resilience and mature realism where earlier there had been simply a creative but academic mind.

The matter [of Christian discipleship] is handled with such depth and precision that I am almost tempted simply to reproduce them [the opening sections] in an extended quotation. For I cannot hope to say anything better on the subject than what is said here by a man who, having written on discipleship, was ready to achieve it in his own life, and did in his own way achieve it even to the point of death.

Karl Barth, 1955

7. *Christian Discipleship*

"We Lutherans," Bonhoeffer wrote in the first chapter of his book on discipleship, "have gathered like eagles around the carcass of cheap grace, and there we have drunk of the poison which has killed the life of following Christ." [1] Such a statement typifies the strong reproach and description of moral failure which provide the basis and genius of Bonhoeffer's book.

The Cost of Discipleship is certainly Bonhoeffer's angriest book—possibly his one "angry" book. Aside from sermons (which Lutheran homiletics stress *should be* a little angry), none of Bonhoeffer's early works reveal him inflamed and vehement, as this book does. The tone throughout the book is entirely serious, rarely speculative, often rhetorically powerful—but always angry.

The conditions Bonhoeffer faced are simple enough reason why. He wrote the book between 1935 and 1937, while directing the seminary at Finkenwalde. Hitler by now had roused the German people to a nationalistic furor and an utter blindness to social responsibility. The imprisonment and terrorization of

Jews raged through the large cities. Any outspoken criticisms of the Nazi regime, including those from the Confessing Church, were quickly squelched. Germany had been, not too long ago, a "Christian" nation; now men and women continued to attend church services, but the real spirit of Christianity had dimmed almost to a darkness. At this time Bonhoeffer wrote his strongest book, a challenge to Christian discipleship, because he believed that only a real return to the Christian faith could save Germany.

The book gave Bonhoeffer his reputation as a theologian. Published in 1937 under the title *Nachfolge* (*Discipleship*), it was only years later translated into English and sold widely in Britain and America. References to political conditions in Germany and the Confessing Church were scarce. This is the reason why Bonhoeffer was able to get the book past censors.

A number of critics look upon *The Cost of Discipleship* as an unfortunate detour in the direction of Bonhoeffer's theological development. Its seeming emphasis on personal sanctification, the Christians' aloofness from the world, and a "religious sense" verging on piety have, they say, distorted the real Bonhoeffer, the champion of "religionless Christianity." They are fond of quoting his letter from Tegel prison of July 21, 1944:

> I once thought I could acquire faith by trying to live a holy life, or something like it. It was in this phase that I wrote *The Cost of Discipleship*. Today I can see the dangers of this book, though I am prepared to stand by what I wrote.[2]

By quoting Bonhoeffer, such critics provide their own rebuttals. *The Cost of Discipleship* was written during a distinct phase of Bonhoeffer's life, just as *The Communion of Saints* and the *Ethics* were. In 1936 Bonhoeffer was highly conscious of the Confessing Church's precarious situation, the need for deep spiritual motivation among the ministers he was training, and, not least of all, his own state of personal danger. Such conditions hardly discourage one from leading a holy life in the sight of God, and hoping in that. It is perfectly understandable that *The Cost of Discipleship* would reflect this urgency for a holy, personal life. The book, however, reflects more; it is a sign of Bonhoeffer's faith in the world—even at this time—that nothing in *The Cost of Discipleship* really contradicts the central passage written later in the July 21 letter: "It is only by living completely in this world that one learns to believe." [3] The book might emphasize heavily the Christian's separation from the world—but never to the point of any lack of responsibility to it.

Indeed, if *The Cost of Discipleship* marks anything in Bonhoeffer's theological growth, it would be a maturity of method and approach. *Discipleship* is written in a style which is lucid and accessible to a mind not trained to follow theological arguments, something rare in Bonhoeffer's earlier writings. For the first time, likewise, Bonhoeffer combines an exegetical approach to the Scriptures with a doctrinal discussion; the technique is most effective in uniting moral exhortation with doctrinal statement. Later, Bonhoeffer will make a variation on the method in supporting a radical ethics of responsibility on a doctrinal foundation of Church and world.

A word should be said here about Bonhoeffer's exegesis. Much of *Discipleship* is structured around Matthew 5 and 7, and reveals clearly Bonhoeffer's method in approaching the Bible. In a period when revolutionary discoveries were being made in philology, archaeology, and historical research to interpret the original biblical meanings, Bonhoeffer approached Scripture without recourse to any of the new research. It was not that he distrusted the scientific efforts: his letters make it clear that he read every important new work of biblical scholarship. He simply was interested in the Scriptures from another point of view. In a paper prepared in 1935, Bonhoeffer stated that two methods of interpretation are available: the biblical message being explained in terms of the present age, and the present age being explained in terms of the biblical message. Bonhoeffer of course condemned explaining the biblical message wholly in terms of the present age. What is needed is locating the point at which the present age and the biblical message meet. "The norm of interpretation lies in us," he stated; "the Bible is the material in which this norm finds its application." [4] This is to say that the work of interpreting Scripture means finding the concrete meaning: "What is Christ asking of us today?" What the reader of Scripture must be attentive to are the inner meaning of the passage, and the contemporary needs to which the passage speaks. But more than attentive, the Christian should concentrate on each area as it affects the other. Whatever implications on Church and state, for example, are contained in Matthew 5 to 7 find mention in Bonhoeffer's treatment only when they apply to the situation he was facing. Bonhoeffer was not concerned with a fully validated exegesis of Matthew 5 to 7; rather, he was building a homiletic from the scriptural passages—and a powerful, effective homiletic at that.

This approach is true not only of *The Cost of Discipleship,* but of the other biblical writings on this period.[5] The Confessing Church struggle was *the* decisive issue before Christians during these years, and Bonhoeffer concentrated every effort on convincing men of this. That he drew from Scripture, and drew often, does not mean that his efforts were primarily to get at the intended meaning of the Hebraic or Aramaic texts. This would have been normal exegesis. His exegesis was a kind of its own; "What did Jesus mean to say to us? What is His will for us today?"

The Cost of Discipleship may be a powerful attestation to Christian fidelity, but any real understanding of it must rely on the Confessing Church struggle. The emphases in the book are distinctly those which arose from the struggle, valid in any situation, perhaps, but outstanding for Bonhoeffer. Indeed, many statements, such as the following, are not quite clear outside the context of the Church struggle:

> Wherever a group, be it large or small, prevents us from standing alone before Christ, wherever such a group raises a claim of immediacy it must be hated for the sake of Christ.[6]

The Church struggle is reflected especially in the two major tensions which underlie the entire work. The first and weaker tension lies in the problem of the Christian in the world, a problem which Bonhoeffer had never grappled with in a moral context before. One statement, drawn from a hymn by Friedrich Christian Richter, recalls St. Paul:

> They [the disciples of Christ] wander on earth and live in heaven, and although they are weak, they protect the world; they taste of peace in the midst of turmoil; they are poor, and yet they have all they want. They stand in suffering and remain in joy, they appear dead to all outward sense and lead a life of faith within.[7]

But there are other statements, which insist on the Christian's responsibility in and to the world. "The only way to follow Jesus [is] by living in the world." [8] Bonhoeffer sees no contradiction in the Christian's two allegiances; yet his presentation of the dichotomy does make for a tension. He appeals to Luther's notion of vocation: living out the Christian life in terms of his secular calling. Yet this is not completely satisfactory. As Bonhoeffer writes, "We must face up to the truth that the call of Christ does set up a barrier between man and his natural life. But this barrier is no surly contempt for life, no legalistic piety; it is the life which is life indeed, the gospel, the person of Jesus Christ." [9] Throughout the book there emerges a subtle, deepening insistence on "in the world," which does, in many ways, complement Bonhoeffer's understanding of the Christians' "true home." Yet the tension is never lifted; nor for the true disciple should it be.

The second, more prominent tension in *Discipleship* is the inherent conflict of the hidden yet visible character of Christian life. The tension, Bonhoeffer suggests, does not originate with him; it cuts through Matthew 5 and 6. "Let your light so shine before men," said Christ. (Matt. 5:16). In the next chapter, however, "Go into thy room, and closing thy door, pray to thy father in secret" (Matt. 6. 6). At first glance, the principle is apparent enough, "Our activity must be visible, but never be done for the sake of making it visible." [10] The strain under which the Confessing Church was operating, however—Finkenwalde is a case in point—made this tension between the hidden and the visible far more complex (and far more crucial) than its gospel context suggests. Chapter titles reveal Bonhoeffer's real concern with the question: "The Hidden Righteousness," "The Hiddenness of Prayer," "The Hiddenness of the Devout Life." Throughout the entire book Bonhoeffer writes with a painful awareness of the tension and a desire to allay it.

Struggling with both tensions, Bonhoeffer set out to describe, exhort, challenge. His own theme, never absent from a page, is discipleship and its demands. "When Christ calls a man, he bids him come and die."[11] The true disciple is the man willing to pay for costly grace: the man of single-minded obedience to Christ, the individual who is not swayed by the crowd, the man of decision and sacrifice, the man of community and responsibility. The book is a powerful statement on the cost inherent in entering the way of Christ, as well as an indictment of those who claim to be disciples, but refuse the cost.

Exactly what did Bonhoeffer achieve in *Discipleship?* The question is important because *The Cost of Discipleship* is considered an important book. And while it set Bonhoeffer's popularity and provided a reading public for his later works, this book did not apparently forward the young man's provocative thinking on concrete revelation. Theologically, what is its place among Bonhoeffer's other works?

In terms of Bonhoeffer's advancing thought, *Discipleship* makes important steps in two directions. For the first time Bonhoeffer clarifies doctrinally his relationship with Luther and reveals a fresh point of view not inherent in Luther's works. And in several respects *Discipleship* gives clear glimpses of the coming range of thought in *Ethics* and the prison letters.

Since his earliest seminars with Reinhold Seeberg and Karl Holl, Bonhoeffer had kept within the scope and doctrinal lines of Luther's theology. Almost instinctively, he had accepted Luther's point of view, and rarely challenged it. However, in *Discipleship,* while he keeps tightly within Luther's framework for the most part, he does make several original departures.

In particular, Bonhoeffer's insistence on obedience as the ineluctable consequence of faith reaches beyond Luther's dictum *sola fide,* through faith alone is man saved, a fundamental precept in Lutheran theology. Bonhoeffer, it should be noted, is not redefining justification; nor is he distinctly challenging the principle *sola fide*. His emphasis, however, lies elsewhere: "The call [of Christ] goes forth, and is at once followed by the response of obedience, not a confession of faith in Jesus." [12] Obviously, the Church's condition demanded an emphasis of this kind: only action could save the day, and Bonhoeffer realized that the traditional Lutheran formulation had generally encouraged passivity. And Bonhoeffer's theology of obedience is clearly a theology of action:

> The "extraordinary"—and this is the supreme scandal—is something which the followers of Jesus *do*. It must be *done* like the better righteousness, and done so that all men can see it. It is not strict Puritanism, not some eccentric pattern of Christian living, but simply unreflecting obedience to the will of Christ.[13]

Karl Barth, who stood solidly in the tradition of Luther, saw vividly what Bonhoeffer, and others like him, were doing. Barth wrote to Bonhoeffer late in 1936:

> You will also understand that I have become more and more critical in this direction . . . and am watching more and more closely to see whether these ever repeated announcements, of better solutions, do not once again amount to giving up the sparrow in the hand in favor of the dove on the roof. And now I can already see that particularly among the present young men of the Confessing Church a further wave of this nature is in the offing in which all the earlier stuff will acquire a new topicality and it may well be that you are the very ones who are called and are capable of being leaders and spokesmen here.[14]

In many respects, Bonhoeffer was the spokesman, if not the leader, of this "upstart theology," which centered in the impact of God's Word on man's actions, rather than God's Word alone. As further indication, another development similar to the insistence on obedience in aligning Bonhoeffer's thought away from Luther's is Bonhoeffer's notion of the visible Church.

Bonhoeffer had always emphasized a visible Church; for

him, the Church was "Christ existing as community," and just as much, "Christ revealed as community." Here, however, his doctrinal basis shifts, and the more original and mediating thought of the early years gives way to a highly Pauline version. Again, the Confessing Church struggle underlines every statement. In the introduction, Bonhoeffer suggests the crucial importance that the visible Church will have for Christian disciples:

In the modern world it seems so difficult to walk in the narrow way of ecclesiastical decision and yet remain in the broad open spaces of the universal love of Christ. . . . Yet somehow or other we must combine the two, or else we shall follow the paths of men.[15]

Part IV of *Discipleship* is precisely a combination of Christ's call and the Church's support. Here Bonhoeffer insists upon a structured, ordered Church, something Luther came to see only after a generation of mediocre performance without such insistence. "An unarticulated body," Bonhoeffer states, "is doomed to perish. In this context all distinctions between form and content, reality and appearance are impossible." [16] Another fresh orientation Bonhoeffer provides for the visible Church is its significance for sanctification. Luther himself had stated, "Outside the Christian Church is no truth, no Christ, no blessedness." [17] But Luther lacked the confidence in the Church's visible appearance which Bonhoeffer has. So for Bonhoeffer to state that "sanctification is therefore possible only within the visible Church" does slightly suggest that Bonhoeffer has taken up new lines of questioning, which eventually would lead him further and further from Luther.

It should be noted, however, that wherever Bonhoeffer consciously moved from Luther's theology, he would insist that Luther would have done the same. Eberhard Bethge, who studied under Bonhoeffer at Finkenwalde during the period *Discipleship* was written, linked his teaching with Kierkegaard in saying:

For Bonhoeffer dared to claim—and he based his claim on grounds that were hard to controvert—that today Luther would say the opposite of what he actually had said in his own day.[18]

There is little explicit doctrinal break with Luther in *The Cost of Discipleship;* the book, however, does not reflect a mind which is keeping strictly to the mold of Lutheran thought. Indeed, much of *Discipleship* is exploratory and tentative, and many passages anticipate the major themes of *Ethics* and the prison letters.

That Bonhoeffer would have formulated the doctrine of "conformation" by the time he was writing *Discipleship*—man's transformation into Christ through the action of the Spirit—is not surprising; the notion is entirely Pauline. "Be not transformed according to this world; but be transformed by the renewing of your mind, that you may prove what is the good and acceptable and perfect will of God." (Rom. 12,2) However, throughout the work, Bonhoeffer continually suggests that it is precisely this action of conformation which enables man to be man, and which frees him from a state of real inhumanity, a notion fundamental to Bonhoeffer's later "secular theology."

> The call of Jesus teaches us that our relation to the world has been built on an illusion. All the time we thought we had enjoyed a direct relation with men and things.[19]

Other doctrinal developments are foreseen in *The Cost of Discipleship*: for example, the relation between Church and world, the Lordship of Christ, the Christian charge of "living for others," and the presence of God in the center, not at the periphery, of men's lives. None of these receive individual treatment, but are briefly touched upon as requisites of discipleship and passed over. There can be no doubt, however, that already Bonhoeffer has been disturbed by the questions which would guide him after 1940. Nor is there doubt that his thought develops from this period with continuity: the emphasis on discipleship and a holy life in this period gives way to a wider vision of Christian life in the world under the Lordship of Christ, a vision which does not negate discipleship, but which includes it in a larger synthesis.

The Cost of Discipleship may indeed show some subtle divergences from Luther's thought, and it may anticipate the later writings. But does it have no more significance in Bonhoeffer's work than that? The final assessment of such a book can be made only in terms of what the author attempted. He probably did not consciously attempt either a break from Luther's theology or a preview of his later thought. Bonhoeffer tried to make the reader face his own Christian life and question it, without relying on props. Systematically, throughout the book, the props are eliminated. Bonhoeffer is insistent that the question be asked honestly, and faced in all its fury and truth. Anticipating the day of judgment, which the apocalyptic climate of Nazi Germany suggested, Bonhoeffer wrote the following:

> Here is the crucial question—has Jesus known us or not? First came the division between Church and world, then the division within the Church, and then the final judgment on the last day. There is nothing left for us to cling to, not even our confession or our obedience. There is only the word, " I have known thee." [20]

There is, Bonhoeffer states decisively, no middle way for the disciple. The one way Christ has offered—his own—demands a moral precision which Bonhoeffer recognized in extremely few Christians. "To be called to a life of extraordinary quality, to live up to it, and yet to be unconscious of it is indeed a narrow way." [21]

The suggestion that Bonhoeffer was at heart an existentialist theologian is an interesting question; but in terms of *The Cost of Discipleship* it is decidedly irrelevant. Bonhoeffer set out to defend Christian responsibility in a time when his government was forcing men to forget it. His defense is, in effect, a powerful, eloquent, and continuously unsettling tribute to the real demands that Christ is making of men today.

Behold how good and how pleasant it is when brothers dwell in unity!
Psalm 132. 1

8. *The Finkenwalde Experiment*

Eberhard Bethge, Bonhoeffer's close friend and colleague, has said that to the two classical characters of the Church (Word and Sacrament), Bonhoeffer added a third—Community. The statement is no exaggeration. Bonhoeffer believed in community as urgently as he believed in the Word. However, it was not until Finkenwalde that he was able to experiment with a living Christian community and pursue its meaning for the Church.

On April 26, 1935, Bonhoeffer met his first Confessing Church seminarians, a class of twenty-five young ministers at Zingst, on the Baltic Sea. The seminary was set in rickety cottages, which Bonhoeffer finally decided to abandon. Soon the seminary moved to an old private schoolhouse in Finkenwalde, near Stettin, again on the Baltic. Here Bonhoeffer began his venture in common life, a venture hardly viewed by him as more than tested Christian living, and yet of vital significance for the years to come in the European Church.

Bonhoeffer had long been convinced that the Church can come fully to life only in the communion of men living daily for one another. The golden phrase of *The Communion of Saints,* "Christ existing as community," was the guiding idea for his two early treatises. In *Act and Being,* he had described the community as the revelation of Christ in the world today:

> God reveals himself as a person, in the Church. The Christian communion is God's final revelation: God as "Christ existing as community," ordained for the rest of time until the end of the world and the return of Christ.[1]

Through the early 1930's, Bonhoeffer spoke frequently of the Church in terms of community and its life of Christ in the world:

> The people of this community . . . do not consider themselves superior to the world, but persevere together in the midst of the world, in its depths, in its trivialities and bondages.[2]

Unfortunately, during those early years Bonhoeffer could only speak and write of community as a theoretical form. Except for his confirmation class, the work those years was too mobile, too random for any serious attempts to give life to a personal community.

In many ways, Bonhoeffer's stay in England convinced him even more of the need not only for community but for the sense of communion which life together creates. He was deeply impressed by a visit to Kelham, the noted Anglican monastery, and brought from his experience there a keen awareness of a small community's power to witness to the whole community of the ecumenical church.

But he saw another meaning for community: in the preparation of pastors and the men who would guide the Church. The English monasteries were actually being used as Anglican seminaries; and Dietrich recognized that in such an atmosphere—with its discipline and intensity—the kind of growth needed for a firmly committed pastor was possible. One of the reasons Dietrich wished to visit India so seriously later in 1934 was to observe the role of community in preparing Gandhi's followers for passive resistance.

When the news came that Bonhoeffer was asked to run a seminary for the Confessing Church, he was quick to recognize the opportunity. Of course the decision was painful: Dietrich had just begun to discover the possibilities open to the Confessing Church through the ecumenical movement, but he realized that only he could draw fully on these. He also regretted postponing his visit to Gandhi a second time. But in a letter written to the Youth Commission in January of 1935, he suggested the importance of community at that time in the Church:

> A group of young Christians are seriously considering the possibility of forming a Christian community in the form of a seminary, or any other form. . . . Only by a clear and uncompromising stand can we face Hitler. . . . We are now thinking if we could combine the idea of Christian community mentioned above with a new secretary. . . . I know of some similar ideas in England among some student groups.[3]

Dietrich hardly wanted Finkenwalde to be an isolated experiment. Even before beginning Finkenwalde, he wished to see common life developed—especially in the training of Confessing Church leaders.

For centuries, common life had been almost a dead issue in the Lutheran Church. Luther's excoriation of the monastic life and its "higher strata of sanctity" remained with the Church, and barring a few exceptions, discouraged the experiments in communal living which sprang up among Anglicans and Calvinists. The result as Bonhoeffer saw it was critical: among the ministers a mentality of individualistic piety and the absence of a sense of responsibility for others, or for the Church. The hope he placed in a strong communal life can only be inferred from his unceasing efforts in the "Finkenwalde experiment," and from the tenor of the little book he wrote after the seminary years, *Life Together*.

Bonhoeffer knew well the conditions he and the seminarians confronted. In earlier years the great challenge to a minister had been largely theological: as such, the training of a theologically adept mind was considered sufficient. Today the Confessing

Church needed men of responsibility and spiritual integrity, a type of formation which the German universities assuredly made no effort to provide. Bonhoeffer's attempt to create a Christian community of shared possessions and daily intervals of common prayer was one response to the need and, to listen to many of the seminarians who lived at Finkenwalde, the most effective one conceivable.

"Christian brotherhood," Bonhoeffer wrote in *Life Together,* "is not an ideal which we must realize; it is rather a reality created by God in Christ in which we may participate."[4] Bonhoeffer began the seminary with this recognition. Actually, Finkenwalde was a *Predigerseminar,* a special training seminary of about six months which followed upon the completion of a minister's theological studies and his year as curate. Some training in homiletics and the practical ministry was expected during these months. Beyond this, Bonhoeffer had the freedom to provide whatever forms of preparation he thought most valuable.

Life at Finkenwalde was informal. Bonhoeffer had made a schedule, but, typically, he set down no written rule. The atmosphere of Finkenwalde added to the warmth and hominess: there were no formal names, but "Brother Bonhoeffer" instead of "Herr Studiendirecktor." Each day began and ended in silence, a quality which Bonhoeffer prized for its contribution to the life of prayer. The first exercise after rising each morning was a formal prayer: alternate psalms and hymns. As Bonhoeffer wrote in *Life Together,* "For Christians the beginning of the day should not be burdened and oppressed with besetting concerns for the day's work. At the threshold of the new day stands the Lord who made it."[5]

Before breakfast the seminarians sat down for half an hour to make a meditation on a short passage of the Bible. They were to limit themselves to one passage each week, not attempting any formal exegesis (the Bibles were purposely in German), but to listen to what the text spoke, to pray over it and interpret their lives according to it. The seminarians, lacking any training in meditation, found this exercise particularly difficult. Eberhard Bethge has remarked that whenever Bonhoeffer was away, this period of meditation was quickly dropped. Upon his return, the seminarians would apologize, but admit that they didn't know what to meditate about. Bonhoeffer would say, "Chase after your thoughts, get them together, concentrate."

The spiritual atmosphere of Finkenwalde, especially the emphasis on prayer and silence, gave the seminarians a fresh experience of the Christian life, a serious absence in their heavily academic schedules. What Bonhoeffer described in *Life Together* as the goal of Christian community, that brothers "meet one another as bringers of the message of salvation," [6] gradually began happening. Bonhoeffer introduced confession, in which the members went to one another with their sins; common meditation, in which one would pray openly in the presence of his brothers; and frequent singing of the German hymns, and Negro spirituals which Bonhoeffer had brought with him from America. Always, however, the focus of such spiritual exercises was clear: to lead men nearer to Christ, and nearer to one another through Christ.

For two or three periods of the day the seminarians gathered for courses on the Bible—sometimes lectures by Bonhoeffer or his assistant, Wilhelm Rott, though, very often, discussions and seminars. Aside from the pastoral training—preparing drafts of sermons, discussing approaches to an effective ministry—Bonhoeffer attempted to teach a concept of the Church which was highly ecumenical, and which built upon the awareness of common life the seminarians were experiencing. One seminarian has reported how the seminarians were impressed by an exegesis of the opening chapters of the Book of Acts, in which Bonhoeffer drew out the early Church's exploratory efforts to take a visible, active shape in the world—an impressive comparison to the situation of the Confessing Church.

The routine might seem to have become stifling; it was not, if only for the reason that Bonhoeffer, with his natural exuberance, broke out of it so often. One morning at breakfast he would call for a day's hike; another morning, a ball game or the beach. Bonhoeffer took part in all the games; and indeed, lost few of them. He frequently embarrassed students younger than he by outrunning them in competition. He took part in frequent walks over the weekends, and always helped out washing the dishes, a rarity for a German seminary director. In the evenings the group often gathered in a large room of the house to discuss anything from Bonhoeffer's American tour to political conditions in Germany; there was even a small chamber quartet which performed frequently. All the constraints of the older life—the pressures of work, study, and family— had been lifted, and the men took part freely in the healthy communal life of Finkenwalde.

The seminarians were not without a ministry. Bonhoeffer thought that a life too distant from the problems the men would soon face could smother the courage it sought to create. The seminarians had always helped preach in local Sunday schools and churches; early in 1936, Bonhoeffer began sending them out for weekends or even entire weeks to serve in communities lacking sufficient help from the Confessing Church. The seminarians travelled in fours, and depended on the hospitality of villagers for food and board. During the days they would canvas door-to-door, visiting people and inviting them to an evening meeting in a local church or hall. During the evening meetings the four young ministers described the challenge of leading a Christian life today.

The impact of such a life of community and apostolate upon the young men who took part in it was powerful. The seminarians never forgot Finkenwalde; nor did their fellow seminarians permit them. Up to the outbreak of the War, a *Rundbrief,* or circular letter, was sent to the alumni; it gave news of events and happenings at Finkenwalde, listed the texts chosen for morning meditations, and provided drafts of sermons by Bonhoeffer and the seminarians. Likewise, graduate classes would frequently have reunions, as did the first class in April, 1936.

If Finkenwalde was successful as a place of intense spiritual formation, that success was largely due to two forces: the "Brethren House," a special community living within the seminary; and the remarkable spirit of Bonhoeffer during these years.

The *Brüderhaus,* or Brethren House, came into existence after Finkenwalde's first term. Bonhoeffer recognized his shortcomings in trying to direct a seminary alone with the intensity he desired, and early in 1936 he asked a few of the original graduates to stay and help him with the work. Their purpose was to help Bonhoeffer in the instruction and direction, as well as to provide a more energetic core of men in the religious exercises, seminars, and the seminary's other activities. Above all, these men would exemplify, as much as was humanly possible, the life of community to the younger seminarians. The idea worked. Bonhoeffer found the Brethren House to be a powerful stimulus to the life he had envisioned for Finkenwalde.

But no doubt a more powerful stimulus was Bonhoeffer himself. Eberhard Bethge has described his first encounter:

> It was on the yellow sands of the Baltic beach that I first met Dietrich Bonhoeffer in 1935; he was a tall, strongly built man of scarcely thirty years, with lively eyes, a sensitive but controlled mouth, free and relaxed in all his movements.[7]

The seminarians found him a remarkable figure: highly intellectual, yet instinctively distrustful of theory; deeply involved in the Confessing Church struggle, yet with a casual freedom which betokened an inner peace. He ran Finkenwalde without condescension, even without the ordinary symbols of authority used by heads of schools and seminaries. Seminarians would remember him best for the simple moments after lunch when a group would congregate on a small stairway outside the inspector's room. One has written of such moments:

> The picture is unforgettable: the small wooden staircase, the man sitting on it with crossed legs, reaching now and then for a cigarette, or accepting a cup of coffee poured out of the only coffee machine of the house.[8]

Dietrich personally found in Finkenwalde a haven, and the first full chance to mold the Church into what he thought it should become. Bonhoeffer took to Finkenwalde with zest and a deep belief that what he was attempting would give needed direction to the future Confessing Church. The harassing doubts of earlier years, doubts of a future torn between theology and the pastorate, died at Finkenwalde. In 1935 he wrote his eldest brother:

> When I began to study theology I imagined that it was something quite different, I daresay, a purely academic affair. But now I finally feel certain that for once I have landed on the right track—for the first time in my life. And that often makes me very happy.[9]

Something about the opportunity of Finkenwalde: its freedom, its potential for a struggling Church, but above all the opportunity it afforded to help men find Christ in both theological and active contexts convinced Bonhoeffer that this was where he belonged, this was where he could do the most good. For the first time in his life he could speak daily to men of prayer, which (often to their disgruntlement) he did; for the first time he could merge a highly active life in the Confessing Church with a responsibility which drew equally upon his theological resources and his vibrant personality. Indeed, it could be said that from his academic life at Berlin to the final months in prison, no single period of his life was so fruitful, or so attuned to Bonhoeffer's goals and outlook. Later he told his friend Eberhard Bethge that the days of Finkenwalde were the happiest and most satisfying of his life.

The work at Finkenwalde did not consume all his energy. Bonhoeffer at the same time was lecturing intermittently at the University of Berlin, and working at a furious pace with the Brethren Council of the Confessing Church. Throughout 1936, and during some of 1937, Dietrich was involved in a heated polemic centering on his firm statement, "He who deliberately separates himself from the Confessing Church separates himself from salvation." Sometimes he would race to Berlin in his Mercedes two or three times in a week, returning in the early hours of the morning. Yet within all the activity—and, in a sense, guiding it—was Finkenwalde, and the hope and warmth that Finkenwalde meant for Bonhoeffer. He was never at home in Berlin (even in his parents' house) the way he was at home among the brethren at Finkenwalde.

The change from a disturbing uncertainty to the fulfillment at Finkenwalde was a major one. But underlying it lay another, a less perceptible (though perhaps more critical) change. Dietrich described this himself in an important letter to his girl friend which he wrote in the winter of 1935-36. He had been at Finkenwalde almost a year, and was in the midst of a period during which the Bible dominated his thought. The letter, discovered by Bethge only after the volumes of Bonhoeffer's papers were published, is worth quoting at length:

> Before 1933 I hurled myself into my work in an almost un-Christian and proud manner. . . . Then something else came along, something which has permanently changed my life and its direction . . . . For the first time I discovered the Bible. . . . I had often preached, I had seen a lot of the Church, I had talked and written about it, but I had not yet become a Christian.
>
> I knew that until then I had been using the cause of Jesus Christ to my own advantage. I had never prayed, or at least very little. In spite of my isolation I was quite pleased with myself. The Bible, most particularly the Sermon on the Mount, has freed me from all this. Since then everything has changed.
>
> I now realized that the life of a servant of Jesus Christ must belong to the Church, and step by step it became clearer to me to what extent this must be so.
>
> Then came the distress of 1933. That strengthened my conviction. And then too I found others ready to concentrate their attention on this goal. All that now mattered to me was the renewal of the Church and of the pastoral profession. . . .
>
> Christian pacifism, which I had attacked passionately until shortly before, suddenly revealed itself as a matter of course. And so it went on, step by step. I could see and think of nothing else. . . . My vocation lies before me. What God will make of it, I do not know. . . .
>
> I believe that we shall only perceive the gloriousness of this vocation in the times to come and the events they will bring. If only we can hold out.[10]

The transformation, as Bonhoeffer thought it to be, gave Finkenwalde the intense moral seriousness felt by its seminarians. And it gave Dietrich a sense of confidence and clarity, that what he was doing had a true motive, and the right direction. Above all, however, Bonhoeffer now sensed in Christ and the Bible a new centrality, which for the remainder of his life would never leave him.

Finkenwalde, however idyllic, could not last long in Nazi Germany. On December 1, 1935, a decree signed by Heinrich Himmler, the notorious leader of the Secret Police, declared all examinations for the Confessing Church invalid, all training centers outlawed by the state with the subjects liable to punishment. The decree came as a blow, but Finkenwalde persisted. Bonhoeffer suspected that the Gestapo knew about the seminary, but for some political reasons permitted it to continue.

Finally, it came. In late September of 1937, Himmler launched a fierce campaign against the Confessing Church. Pastors were forbidden to travel or convene, and hundreds of them were arrested. Police came to Finkenwalde and disbanded the seminary by force. Bonhoeffer, fortunately, was away on a holiday at the time.

Bonhoeffer didn't stop. For the next two years he attempted to continue instructing two groups of ministerial candidates, with about ten living in Köslin and another eight or ten in the village of Gross-Schölnwitz near Schlawe. Bonhoeffer during those years nominally accepted a vicarage, but to keep suspicion from falling on himself, moved from place to place. The two years were for Bonhoeffer insecure and confusing; the Confessing Church had gone underground, and the mainstaff leaders like Martin Niemöller had been imprisoned. In April, 1940, the activities were halted for the second time; again, Bonhoeffer was not arrested.

Despite its sudden termination, Finkenwalde had been a powerful and an inspiring experience for those who had taken part in it. And, largely due to the little book, *Life Together,* Finkenwalde became a force in the emergence of a reborn European Church after the War.

For its size and lack of theological luster, the popularity of *Life Together* is surprising. Bonhoeffer wrote most of the book in 1938, after Finkenwalde had been shut down. When the book appeared a year later, it became quite popular in Germany and has remained a prominent work on community ever since.

The book is simple and homiletic in form, and it bears notable resemblance both to St. Benedict's *Rule* and some of Luther's pastoral writings. The chapter headings—only five—are revealing: "Community," "The Day with Others," "The Day Alone," "Ministry," and "Confession and Communion."

The theme of the book is distinctly Bonhoeffer's: "Not religion, but revelation, not religious community, but Church." With the same insistence as his sermons and personal discussions with the seminarians, *Life Together* stresses the sources of true Christian community in Christ. "Not what a man is in himself as a Christian, his spirituality and piety, constitutes the basis of our community," he wrote; "what determines our brotherhood is what that man is by reason of Christ." [11] Finkenwalde itself is a commentary on the concreteness of this community borne in Christ.

Bonhoeffer's development in *Life Together* is a rich description of both the demands and fruits of Christian community. Probably few Lutherans have gone so far as Bonhoeffer in distilling the implications of Luther's ministry of brothers.

> God has willed that we should seek and find his living Word in the witness of a brother, in the mouth of man. Therefore, the Christian needs another Christian who speaks God's Word to him.[12]

The thoughts, drawn from life, are vivid and practical, often disturbing in their harsh demands:

> It is inconceivable that the things that are of utmost importance to each individual should not be spoken by one to another. It is un-Christian consciously to deprive another of the one decisive service we can render to him. If we cannot bring ourselves to utter it, we shall have to ask ourselves whether we are not still seeing our brother garbed in his human dignity which we are afraid to touch,

and thus forgetting the most important thing, that he, too, no matter how old or highly placed . . . is still a man like us, a sinner in crying need of God's grace.[13]

Because of its homiletic and practical character—and because it emerges not from a theological framework but from the Finkenwalde experience—*Life Together* does not directly forward Bonhoeffer's theology. It simply bears out the intense question of community for Bonhoeffer in his concern for the Church. One of the greatest pities of his death before the War ended is the fact that he would not help rebuild the Church from the ashes—an activity which would, no doubt, have brought a deeper sense of community to the postwar Church.

Despite his death, Bonhoeffer's passion for community did figure in the rebirth of the German and European churches, especially in the renaissance of lay academies and semi-monastic communities. Before the War Finkenwalde had aroused some excitement; it was accused of Catholic and monastic tendencies. After the War, however, experiments similar to Finkenwalde began sprouting up throughout free Europe. The evangelical academies for laymen—there were well over forty—provided training in the Christian life in a modern society for thousands of laymen. Many of these academies attempted some degree of common life, committed to the belief that communal life is a prerequisite for the Church's full vitality and commitment to the world. Even more in step with Finkenwalde and *Life Together* were some of the neo-monastic efforts of men to live separately for a time with stable forms of worship; the two notable examples are the Iona Community off the coast of Scotland, and the Taize Community, near Cluny.

Precisely how influential *Life Together* and its recollection of Finkenwalde were for the postwar Christian "renaissance" in Europe can never be known for sure. There can, however, be no doubting the influence of the Finkenwalde experience on Bonhoeffer's own thought.

To Bonhoeffer, Finkenwalde was more than an experiment, more than the gestation period of an "idea." A personal belief, born of personal struggle, had created the community at Finkenwalde. Bonhoeffer for years hoped in the Confessing Church, hoped it would re-awaken the Christian spirit, hoped it would summon the spiritual vigor to challenge not only the German Church but the entire Nazi Regime, with all its brutal tactics and military muscle. Too many of the Confessing Church leaders disappointed him, however; the prison letters show the disheartenment caused by pastors who bickered about organization or method and gradually lost touch with the Church's original mission. A new generation of Church leaders was needed, men committed to the Church and its mission in the midst of violent struggle. Bonhoeffer saw no other genesis for such men than community.

Never in his Finkenwalde community did Bonhoeffer let the seminarians forget what they were being perpared to enter, nor did he ever permit them to look upon Finkenwalde as an "escape," a haven shielding them from the baneful contagion of Nazi Germany. "Jesus Christ lived in the midst of his enemies," Bonhoeffer wrote in *Life Together*. "So the Christian, too, belongs not in the seclusion of a cloistered life but in the thick of foes. There is his commission, his work." [14] In *The Cost of Discipleship,* written during the Finkenwalde period, Bonhoeffer had run fine swords through the monastic ideal as an "escape" from discipleship in the world; he would clearly have none of that. His community was to prepare men to step fully conscious into the seething conditions of an underground pastorate in Hitler's Germany and attempt there not only to minister to the Church, but to create wherever possible a genuine community life of resisting Christians.

If Bonhoeffer's experience with community was partially successful, that success stemmed from Bonhoeffer himself, and the integrity that he could confer upon thought and life. In his academic years Bonhoeffer had constructed an impressive theology of community. Yet he always felt that such theory was not enough; it was, indeed, essentially incomplete. Bonhoeffer craved action, decision, struggle in the world. But he feared that action would be impotent unless it drew from faith and solid theological guidance. In Finkenwalde, for the first time in Bonhoeffer's life, faith and action coalesced, and a new generation of pastors, a new vitality for the Church sprang from that union. Finkenwalde, as an experiment, had succeeded. Finkenwalde, as a step in Bonhoeffer's life, had given his thought a fresh resolution, and a firm promise for the future Church.

The ultimate question the man of responsibility asks is not, "How can I extricate myself heroically from the affair?" but, "How is the coming generation to live?"

"After Ten Years" (Meditation written in Tegel Prison)

9. *Ethics—the Attempt and the Result*

"It all depends," wrote Dietrich Bonhoeffer from his prison cell in 1943, "on whether or not the fragment of our life reveals the plan and material of the whole." [1] If the later writings of Bonhoeffer—his unfinished *Ethics,* and the assembled letters he sent from prison—resemble so many broken and scattered pieces of glass, the same brilliant light and the same expansive sky are reflected in each piece. For despite their fragmentary character, these writings have revealed Bonhoeffer as one of the most significant theologians of the twentieth century and perhaps the most prophetic for the needs of the coming Church.

The first work, the *Ethics,* did have an intended unity, though the conditions of writing it, the absence of unwritten major sections, and the destruction by the Gestapo of parts of it, have left the book decidedly incomplete. The widely-read prison letters, sent to Bonhoeffer's parents and his friend Bethge over an interval of sixteen months, were hardly meant for publication, much less intended to contain a systematic framework. Yet both works have attracted enormous attention and have been at the heart of several important movements in recent theology.

The approaching discussion of the *Ethics* and the prison writings is based upon a premise that within the fragments of these two works a perceptible pattern does emerge, and this pattern reveals the later tensions and resolutions in Bonhoeffer's thought. These fragments which Bonhoeffer has left us—often suggestion rather than statement, provocation rather than precision—rise from a mind searching desperately for Christ's place in a world torn apart by National Socialism and war. Bonhoeffer wrote these works while either deeply involved in a movement to assassinate Hitler or confined to prison afterward. Without a clear notion of the profound questions gripping Bonhoeffer in his resistance work, any understanding of the *Ethics* would be fundamentally incomplete. It is this conscientious self-questioning which directly led to the fruitful ideas of the later works. As Bonhoeffer wrote in June, 1942:

> Again and again I am driven to think about my activities which are concerned so much with the secular field. I am surprised that I live and can live without the Bible for days . . . . I feel the resistance growing in me against all religiosity, sometimes reaching the level of an instinctive horror; surely, this is not good either. Yet I am not of a religious nature at all. But all the time I am forced to think of God, of Christ, of genuineness, life, freedom, charity; that matters for me. What causes me uneasiness is just the religious clothing.[2]

The period before Bonhoeffer became deeply involved in the German resistance—roughly 1938 to 1940—marked for Dietrich a time, like the early 1930's, of painful uncertainty. The work he was doing, training pastors for the Confessing Church in Pomerania (a section of northern Germany), was important; but Dietrich constantly sensed that with greater freedom he could do much more. In February of 1938 he met for the first time with key leaders in the political resistance. He recognized that the political struggles were going to increase, rather than slow down, that Germany would never again be the same as it had before Hitler. As the year progressed, events revealed Hitler's government in all its blatant ugliness. In March came the annexation of Austria, a grim harbinger of war. Germany annexed the Sudetenland, and Hitler's gaze concentrated on Czechoslovakia. The "Crystal Night" that November, when Jewish homes, shops, and synagogues were smashed and plundered by Nazis throughout Germany, suggested the true horror of the regime. Bonhoeffer came to contemplate political resistance with growing seriousness. He likewise came to recognize that his future in Germany as a pastor was reaching an impasse.

In the spring of 1939, Dietrich realized more than earlier how seriously the Confessing Church was atrophying, partly from dissension within its own leadership, partly because it had failed to maintain the vital contact with the churches outside Germany, especially the ecumenical movement. Another problem, one deeply personal, disturbed him: men his age (he was 33 in February) were soon to be called into the military. Bonhoeffer knew that with his pacifist beliefs—and especially with the approaching war bound to be nothing more than just a criminal assault on unprepared nations—he could never go to the battlefield for Hitler. But to remain and be imprisoned, perhaps killed, for pacifism would not have helped, if only because he didn't want the government identifying his personal pacifist beliefs with the Confessing Church.

In March, Dietrich wrote to his good friend, George Bell, the Bishop of Chichester. Through Bell he arranged to see Dr. Visser 't Hooft, the leading figure in the ecumenical movement. He also arranged to talk with Leonard Hodgson, a prominent ecumenical leader. Bonhoeffer and Bethge went to England on the pretext of visiting his old congregations. Both Hodgson and Visser 't Hooft spoke with him about the problem he faced in Germany, and the crisis in the Confessing Church. But most helpful in terms of a solution was Reinhold Niebuhr, then presenting the Gifford Lectures in Scotland. With Niebuhr, Dietrich made plans for a lecture trip to America. Through Paul Lehmann at Union, mimeographed letters were sent to numerous colleges and seminaries, and arrangements for the trip were made with the Confessing Church's Council of Brethren in Germany.

With Niebuhr's formal invitation, Hitler's government granted Bonhoeffer leave "for at least the next two or three years." On June 7, 1939, Bonhoeffer set sail from Southhampton, leaving behind him a continent already tense with expectation of the coming explosion.

The retreat to America paralleled Bonhoeffer's retreat to England in 1933. He was six years older than he had been when he accepted the congregations in London. Yet the same motivation was there: to escape from a situation to which he could see no alternative action. In 1933 it had been the Nazi control of the churches; now it was the threat of conscription. And Bonhoeffer knew he could never go to war for Hitler. But the fear weighed on his conscience this time, for Bonhoeffer knew Europe was about to go up in flames. When he discovered that part of his work would involve ministry to German refugees, the thought that such work would bar his return to Germany tormented him. In a letter written to one of his American benefactors only days after his boat arrived in New York, Bonhoeffer suggested how agonized he felt in America:

> My best friend in Germany [Bethge], a young Confessional Pastor who has been working with me for many years, will be in the same conflict with regard to military service, etc., at the latest by next spring, possibly in the fall of this year. I feel it would be an utmost disloyalty to leave him alone in Germany when the conflict comes up for him. I should either have to go back to stand by him and to act with him or to get him out and to share my living with him, whatever it be, though I do not know if he would be willing to leave Germany.[3]

Bonhoeffer knew what a return to Germany would entail: a stunted ministry, a sure prison term for refusing enlistment, and possibly death. He was not completely certain or convinced of his reasons for coming to America; nor, to judge from his nervous correspondence, was he convinced of the reasons for returning. Yet only ten days after his arrival, Bonhoeffer wrote to

Reinhold Niebuhr from the country house of the President of Union Theological Seminary:

Sitting here in Dr. Coffin's garden, I have had the time to think and to pray about my situation and that of my nation and to have God's will for me clarified. I have come to the conclusion that I have made a mistake in coming to America. I must live through this difficult period of our national history with the Christian people of Germany. I shall have no right to participate in the reconstruction of Christian life in Germany after the war if I do not share the trials of this time with my people. My brothers in the Confessing Synod wanted me to go. They may have been right in urging me to do so; but I was wrong in going. Such a decision each man must make for himself. Christians in Germany will face the terrible alternative of either willing the defeat of their nation in order that Christian civilization may survive, or willing the victory of their nation and thereby destroying our civilization. I know which of these alternatives I must choose; but I cannot make that choice in security.[4]

Bonhoeffer's decision to return to Germany marked his commitment to the German future, a commitment which would lead, eventually, to the attempt on Hitler's life and to Bonhoeffer's own death. But the decision had calmed him, and early in July Bonhoeffer noted in his diary, "Since coming on the ship my inner uncertainty about the future has ceased." [5] He had a vague idea what lay ahead—an underground ministry, the elemental struggle to survive as a conscientious Christian through the upheaval of the War. But at this point he hardly anticipated the defiant resistance activity or the fate it would bring. Bonhoeffer felt only the instinctive assurance that he belonged in Germany.

He arrived in Germany in late July, 1939. In August he returned to his illegal preparation of ministers for the Confessing Church. On September 1, German troops invaded Poland, and within four weeks the Polish government surrendered. With World War I and the Versailles humiliation still blazing bitterly in the German memory, the nation grew increasingly enthusiastic about a war which the Führer assured everyone he would win. Bonhoeffer and others like him watched stricken as the German people, long tempered by nationalism, hailed a way which would clearly make of Europe another senseless graveyard.

Bonhoeffer continued with his seminary activities until the Gestapo forced him to stop the second time, in March of 1940. Then, travelling with Bethge, he became something of a visiting preacher in the northern German provinces. The restrictions were tightening, and Bonhoeffer recognized the approaching end to almost all of his pastoral activity. He had been fortunate to avoid conscription by his contacts with the influential *Abwehr,* Berlin's counter-intelligence office, which was able to keep its men clear of the army. But since 1938, he had been forbidden to reside in Berlin, and was refused permission to teach. When the Reich Chamber of Literature had issued its censorship rules for publications, Bonhoeffer had refused to sign himself as a Nazi propagandist, and was thus unable to publish. In the summer of 1940 he was prohibited from preaching altogether.

The decision to enter resistance work was a slow one, dictated as much by Bonhoeffer's growing disillusionment with personal pacifism as by the events and men with which he became involved. Hitler's aggressive arm was sweeping Europe, and ultimate victory seemed imminent. After the collapse of Poland, western Europe crumbled: Belgium, Holland, Luxembourg, France. Bonhoeffer felt distressed by the sight of the destruction his homeland had launched. At an ecumenical meeting in 1941 in Geneva, he admitted, "I pray for the defeat of my fatherland. Only through a defeat can we atone for the terrible crimes which have been committed against Europe and the world." [6] But prayer—and Bonhoeffer knew this all too well—was not enough; resistance was needed, intense, defiant, effective.

On June 14, 1940, the day France capitulated, Bonhoeffer was sitting with Bethge in a crowded cafe when the news of the French defeat was announced on the radio. At such times, the broadcast would be climaxed with the singing of the Horst Wessel song. As the customers rose and vigorously joined in the singing, Bonhoeffer rose with them, flung up his arm and sang with characteristic volume. Bethge looked up in surprise, but Dietrich leaned down and whispered, "Are you mad?" He explained afterwards. "We mustn't sacrifice ourselves in protest against such ridiculous things as this. We have to sacrifice ourselves for something far graver." [7]

The chance for "something far graver" had come in the inner resistance circle centered in the *Abwehr*. This circle was fundamentally a political conspiracy, and involved high ranking Nazi leaders such as General Ludwig Beck, Carl Goerdeler, and Colonel Hans Oster. Colonel Oster was the center of the *Abwehr* conspiracy. A respected military figure, Oster was a man of clear judgment, inspiring leadership, and above all, action. He was resourceful enough to draw Admiral Wilhelm Canaris, head of the *Abwehr* and a man trusted by the Nazis, into the resistance, permitting the *Abwehr* to become a center of the revolt.

Hans von Dohnanyi, who had married Dietrich's sister Christine, was legal advisor to the *Abwehr* and one of the leading figures in the movement. Dohnanyi had already taken part in the abortive effort of 1938, in which Hitler was to have been judged insane by a "people's court." The psychiatric reports had been prepared by a panel of psychiatrists (headed by Karl Bonhoeffer, Dietrich's father), based on information secured by Oster from an early hospital record. The failure of this early scheme had led men like Dohnanyi and Oster to their present effort in the *Abwehr:* to attempt a completely military coup, based upon the assassination of the Führer.

The resistance group centered in the *Abwehr* was certainly not the only resistance effort in Germany; but it stood, by reason of its military connections, a better chance of overcoming the grave obstacles facing resistance in Germany than any other group. And the obstacles were crippling. Unlike the resistance movements in Belgium, France, Holland, and Poland, Oster's men could not count upon the support of their countrymen. Likewise, Germany lacked any tradition of revolutionary action. The religious notion of total submission to the state was rooted in Luther, and Germany's civil history was void of any popular attempts at revolt. For most German Christians rebellion against the state, no matter how extensive the abuse of power, was unthinkable. Yet Oster's men resolved to kill Hitler, and were able to come astonishingly close in the attempt of July 20, 1944.

The *Abwehr* was enthusiastic about Dietrich's entrance; Oster's worries about securing some modification to the Allies' stated policy of unconditional surrender brought him to hope that through Bonhoeffer's contacts in Britain, he could establish communication. In the meantime, Dietrich's work as V-man (a civilian employee of the Military Intelligence) involved work in the Munich Department, with frequent travel to and from Berlin.

Once he had established himself as a member of the resistance inner circle, Bonhoeffer realized the full tension of his situation. He had stepped as deeply into the resistance movement as any other religious leader. A number of deeply committed Christians had sacrificed their lives—Pastor Paul Schneider, and the Jesuit Adolf Delp, to mention two—but in heroic personal defiance of the regime, not in the tangles of a conspiracy against it. A number of people, especially Church figures in Germany since the War, have interpreted Bonhoeffer's involvement in the resistance as a purely political decision, based on political motives. No one who knew Bonhoeffer well could agree with such a statement. Bonhoeffer was beyond and before all else a pastor, a minister of the Word of God. He saw in the erratic temper of his nation a dilemma which was, at root, moral; and he could not, for all that his theological and traditional background discouraged him, ignore his responsibility.

Dietrich's first trip for Oster's resistance group took place in Geneva, in 1941. Ostensibly a V-man with a commission from the *Abwehr,* he was able to contact Karl Barth and Dr. Willem Visser t'Hooft, at that time an important ecumenical figure. His significant meeting, however, and the one which appeared crucial for the success of the overthrow was with Dr. Bell, the Bishop of Chichester, in Sweden, in late May of 1942. Dr. Schönfeld, a German pastor (and thus a member of the German

Church) had already seen the Bishop on the same mission when Bonhoeffer and Bell met in Sigtuna, a little town quite removed from Stockholm. Because of his part in the German Church, Dr. Bell had misgivings about Schönfeld. But, as Bell himself has written:

> . . . about Bonhoeffer there could be not two opinions. I had known him intimately all the nine years since 1933. He was an uncompromising anti-Nazi, one of the mainsprings of the Church opposition, entirely trusted by the Confessional Church leaders, and deeply disliked by Bishop Heckel and all tolerators or supporters of the Nazi regime.[8]

Bonhoeffer outlined his mission; it was one quite similar to Schönfeld's. Three groups, from the state administration, trade union, and the army and state police, were preparing for an overthrow of the Nazi regime. After Hitler's speech of April 26, 1942 (his last in the Reichstag), and his claims to surmount all laws, many Germans now realized the demonic power of the Führer. The *coup,* hopefully, would eventually be welcomed by a strong minority of the German people. A program had been outlined, including a new government which would become federated with other free nations in economic and major military decisions. All Jewish persecutions would abruptly cease, and all stolen property would be returned to the Jews. The new Germany would be prepared "to take its full share in the common efforts for the rebuilding of the areas destroyed or damaged by the war." [9] The central question was: Would the Allies regard a Germany purged of Hitler any differently from a Germany controlled by him? In effect, could a truce be struck with a rebellious government, which would not demand an Allied military rule in Germany and a subsequent return of the disastrous effects Versailles had wrought?

Dr. Bell asked Bonhoeffer for the names of the chief conspirators; Bonhoeffer explained the entire pattern, under the general leadership of General Beck, who had been Chief of the General Staff before he resigned in 1938. "I could see," wrote Bell in recounting the meetings, "that as he told me these facts he was full of sorrow that things had come to such a pass in Germany, and that action like this was necessary. He said that sometimes he felt, 'Oh, we have to be punished.' " [10]

Bonhoeffer did not fear repentance, even in the form of the chaos that a continued war would bring to Germany. "We do not want to escape repentance. . . . We must take this judgment of God as Christians." [11]

On June 30 Dr. Bell saw Sir Anthony Eden, Foreign Affairs Commissioner, and pleaded for a word of assurance to the resistance core. The decision was forestalled until the Americans and Russians could be contacted. The letter which arrived three weeks later was decisive: "no action . . . could be taken."

In due course Oster and General Beck learned of the failure; it struck a hard blow to the opposition's hopes. All efforts to overthrow Hitler's regime from this point had to be based on the assumptions that the German people would greet a *coup* and that the Allies would modify their demand for unconditional surrender.

Bonhoeffer's work for the *Abwehr* circle after this point was limited. In January of 1943—Bonhoeffer at the time had just become engaged to the daughter of an aristocratic family—one of the Munich officers in the *Abwehr* was caught smuggling over the border. The Gestapo forced him to confess what he knew about Hitler's opponents in the *Abwehr,* and purely by chance clue led to clue until Bonhoeffer's name and Dohnanyi's came up. One morning early in April, 1943, while Bonhoeffer was visiting his parents in Berlin, he telephoned his sister, and when a strange voice answered he realized that the Gestapo had arrested Hans. Looking to his parents he said, "Now they will come for me." All possibly incriminating documents were hidden, and others which were safe or misleading, placed in the open. He went to his eldest sister's house next door to eat a good meal—his last for a long time. In the middle of the afternoon he was arrested. The Gestapo took him to the military section of the Tegel prison in Berlin. At the time of his arrest he was thirty-seven years old.

To turn from Bonhoeffer's resistance activities to the *Ethics* he wrote during those same years—1940 to 1943—implies the question: Did he write *Ethics* to justify his efforts as a pastor working for a political revolution? There can be no doubt that the *Ethics* was deeply affected by Bonhoeffer's involvement in the opposition, and his disappointment in Christians who gave the Nazi regime no resistance. "One is distressed," he wrote in an early chapter "by the failure of reasonable people to perceive either the depths of evil or the depths of the holy. With the best of intentions they believe that a little reason will suffice them to clamp together the parting timbers of the building." [12]

But was the *Ethics* dictated and predetermined by Bonhoeffer's political activities? Or did the work simply crystallize the reflections demanded by his secular activities?

It can hardly be inferred, as the work progresses, that its author was a militant figure in the underground movement to kill Hitler. Indeed, the *Ethics* is written in sober theological German, reminiscent of Bonhoeffer's early treatises. No statement is made to the effect of Christian pacifism; precious little is said of war, tyranny, or nationalism. A justification for political activities on the part of a Christian minister could be interpreted from the concrete implications of responsibility and the Church-world synthesis. Yet such a justification is in no wise immediately evident or convincing. In effect, the book is drawn from an effort far removed from that of rationalizing a political conspiracy—and it moves toward a goal quite separate from Bonhoeffer's decisions as a resistance figure (if only because the *Ethics* is concerned with a responsible society and not with one Christian in the midst of an anarchic world).

This does not negate the influence of Bonhoeffer's resistance work upon the *Ethics,* however. Bonhoeffer's years as an *Abwehr* agent, his contact with heroic figures like Colonel Oster and General Beck, brought him to see more sharply than before the fundamental ethical failings of Christians—and of the Church—in Germany.

Bonhoeffer remained, in all his resistance work, a theologian. And the questions he unearthed about the Church and responsibility in his personal effort to prepare a political rebellion were both disturbing and provocative. Bonhoeffer always understood himself to be an exception, one who had gone further than most Christians were expected to go. The problem was that most Christians hadn't gone very far at all. And why? Because they weren't good Christians? Or because their understanding of Christian ethics stopped at the doorstep of political involvement, of personal response to social crisis? In *The Cost of Discipleship* Bonhoeffer had written furiously of the demands Christ made of his disciples; now, he could see, these demands still left the crucial spot untended, the world of men.

The questions, from this point, arose everywhere: What is the Church's responsibility to the world? How is the Church "free" from the world, and how is it bound to the world? Should the Church combat, or side with, the humanists, the artists, the cultural leaders? Presuming that the traditional doctrine of Church and state had led in great part to the tyranny of Nazism, upon what principles could a promising Church-state relationship be conceived and developed? What are the ethical demands placed upon the individual Christian if his Church is deeply committed to freedom and the maturing of whole men in the world? Realistically, how dependent is the world upon the Church and the Church's style of life?

The questions cut through several important Lutheran doctrines; they presumed, in fact, a new underlying basis for a meaningful and resilient Christian ethics. Several times earlier, Bonhoeffer had expressed discontent with the Church's diminished role in the world as presented in traditional theological schemata. The *Ethics* gave him the first distinct chance to explore possible new relationships, and suggest a tentative doctrinal framework for the Church's full-scale involvement in the world.

Bonhoeffer had considered a lengthy and elaborate work on Christian ethics since the close of Finkenwalde in 1937. It was not until 1940 that he was able to devote to it the extensive time the work deserved. He wrote most of the work over the next three years in various places: at his parents' home in Berlin; in the Benedictine Abbey of Ettal in Upper Bavaria, where he lived for several months as a V-man working in Munich; and at the summer estate of a friend, Frau Ruth von Kleist-Retzow, in Pomerania. When he began writing, the conviction grew that *Ethics* was the beginning of his actual life work. As the war progressed, however, and once Bonhoeffer was imprisoned, he came to feel that it was enough for the book to be his major work, and his major contribution to theology. "Sometimes," he wrote from the Tegel prison in December, 1943, "I think I really have my life more or less behind me now and that all that would remain for me to do would be to finish my *Ethics*." [13]

It is apparent why Bonhoeffer would consider this his major work—or the beginning of his actual life work. No previous writings are marked with the daring, almost rash originality of the *Ethics;* none are ambitious in the mature and consciously theological way this work is. The understanding of Church and world which Bonhoeffer seeks in the work proceeds with a full awareness of Christ's presence in the Church, and of His formational action upon the members of the Church. (One of the major sections is entitled, aptly, "Ethics as Formation.") Yet Bonhoeffer, as before, could not illuminate the overpowering action of Christ upon the world without providing a profound understanding of the world's own existence. His stinging criticism in a letter from Tegel prison of Karl Barth's exclusion of all but the truth of revelation shows how vehemently Bonhoeffer rejected such answers:

> The positivist doctrine of revelation makes it too easy for itself, setting up, as in the ultimate analysis it does, a law of faith, and mutilating what is, by the Incarnation of Christ, a gift for us.[14]

The effect is a delicate tension, throughout the *Ethics,* between the supernatural and the natural, or, as he interprets the two phases, between the "ultimate" and the "penultimate." Within this tension he is able to come to grips with what is fundamentally a new understanding of the Church—no longer in terms of a static pattern, or even a theologically defined "nature," but of an existential mission.

The Church is nothing but a section of humanity in which Christ has really taken form . . . . In the first instance, therefore, she has essentially nothing whatever to do with the so-called religious functions of man, but with the whole man in his existence in the world with all its implications.[15]

Such a radical orientation toward the Church in terms of the mission to the world does not stop there; Bonhoeffer continues to erect *upon this Church-world doctrine* his notion of ethics, one highly geared to "conformation" into Christ, and highly relative in its expression in different situations in the world. As much as there is a basic ethical principle (*Ethics,* it should be recalled, never was finished), the conclusive moral demand is for conscious responsibility, not naively to one's own "Christian calling," which begs the question, but to the world, where Christ carried out *His* responsibility.

It must be admitted that the structural development of these steps is hardly clear in the present, incomplete volume of Bonhoeffer's *Ethics*. However, Eberhard Bethge, to whose laborious and careful efforts we can be thankful for the clarity of the existing volume, has said:

Bonhoeffer's book did not progress chapter by chapter in accordance with a fixed and unalterable plan. Each one grew gradually by the coalescence of numerous separate studies of the subject until it formed a whole. The titles and the arrangement of the books were subject to constant change in the course of this process.[16]

The gap between the *Ethics* Bonhoeffer intended and the fragmented work he has left behind is no doubt a great one. As Bonhoeffer wrote from prison:

I was annoyed that I had not had time to finish my *Ethics* (it was probably confiscated for the time being), and it is some comfort to know I had told you the essentials, and even if you have forgotten what I told you, it will doubtless emerge again in some shape or form.[17]

In the present *Ethics,* four stages of development are present, with each stage illuminating a new probing and a new foothold; clearly Bonhoeffer was working toward a realization he never made, except sketchily in the prison letters. Bethge's description of the *Ethics* as "an absolute fragment" is, unfortunately, all too appropriate.

Yet the *Ethics* remains with little doubt Bonhoeffer's most substantial and perhaps most theologically significant work. If no carefully etched pattern controls the book, an inner unity rises out of Bonhoeffer's gripping consciousness of a kernel idea and his awareness of its impact on all Christian life. And it is this inner unity which makes the *Ethics* well worth exploring, as well as vitally important for understanding Bonhoeffer's later thought.

Man becomes man because God became man.
Ethics

10. *Bonhoeffer's Anthropology*

Throughout the *Ethics,* one question continuously, persistently emerges, a question which dominates the entire work: "What does it mean to be a Christian?" Bonhoeffer pursues the question relentlessly. What implications can be drawn from membership in the Church? What shapes the Christian's style of life, his commitment to the world of men? As Bonhoeffer sees the question, ethics and doctrine are inextricably conjoined. And in the discussion of both ethics and doctrine, Bonhoeffer begins with one fundamental equation: to be a Christian does not mean being religious, but above all being a man.

This equation—that the Christian is primarily a man, and that his encounter with Christ *makes* him a man—opens a number of questions, as it opened for Bonhoeffer the scope of his later thought. However, the most important question concerns what Bonhoeffer meant by "man," at least when using it in the context of identifying the Christian as "being a man." For unless this concept is clear—and unfortunately, Bonhoeffer did not consciously clarify it—much of the mature thought can be misunderstood, and perhaps even missed.

For the purpose of making more explicit what Bonhoeffer left implicit in his notion of manhood, and as a guideline to the major ideas of the *Ethics* and the prison writings, a term will be used to refer to Bonhoeffer's concept of man: his "anthropology." Admittedly, he never used the word to designate a doctrine he had devised—nor, for that matter, was he probably highly conscious of having a unique concept of man. Yet his understanding of man's nature and potential is seminal to the powerful developments in the last few years. The term, anthropology, as it refers to Bonhoeffer's idea of man is only a construct—certainly not Bonhoeffer's counterpart to the scientific anthropology.

Indeed, Bonhoeffer's anthropology stands at quite a distance from the empirical studies of man which have accelerated in recent years. Although primarily neither a doctrinal theology nor an ethical statement, Bonhoeffer's anthropology is rooted in the Incarnation. Consequently, it is properly theological. In many respects, the anthropology effectively combines Christology and humanism, making true humanity contingent upon Christ:

> Jesus Christ, the incarnate God: this means that God has taken upon himself bodily all human being; it means that henceforward divine being cannot be found otherwise than in human form; it means that in Jesus Christ man is made free to be really man before God. The "Christian" element is not an end in itself, but it consists in man's being entitled and obliged to live as man before God.[1]

The anthropology can well be seen as an important source of all Bonhoeffer's mature concepts—his Church-world doctrine, his ethics, the critique of religion, the "world come of age," and his outline of a "religionless Christianity." For throughout all these later efforts, the equation of Christian and man remained central; and the attempt, for example, to probe Christian responsibility in "religionless Christianity" concludes in a statement of human responsibility.

Before one attempts an analysis of the anthropology, two important points must be considered: the background to

Bonhoeffer's anthropology, and the conscious doctrinal efforts which give the anthropology its deeply christological foundation.

It has been said that since liberal theology (when anthropology was accepted as an indispensable tool), no theologian can ignore anthropology. Karl Barth, as Bonhoeffer has suggested, tried to construct a theology lacking a fully realistic understanding of man's life, his needs, his hopes. Bonhoeffer stated emphatically that this was Barth's major weakness. Without doubt, Barth's emphasis on a transcendent, almost abstract God coupled with his vehement criticism of anthropology in theology made Bonhoeffer keenly aware of the need for a clear and positive concept of man. No less influential, probably, was Luther's frequently negative emphasis: man the sinner, man incapable of good works, man whose cancerous heart can be healed only by God's justifying mercy. Indeed, the entire Protestant tradition tended to view man dimly and accept him as a sinner rather than as a potential saint. It was as much to this whole tradition as to Barth that Bonhoeffer reacted so vigorously in his optimistic notion of man. Throughout his mature writings, Bonhoeffer makes it evident that his goal is man: redeemed, given a new humanity and potential in Christ.

> What is beyond the world is in the Gospel intended to exist for this world—I mean that not in the anthropocentric sense of liberal, pietistic, ethical theology, but in the bible sense of the creation and the incarnation, crucifixion, and resurrection of Jesus Christ.[2]

The seeds of Bonhoeffer's powerfully optimistic concept of man can be found in the historical conditions to which he reacted, and his own background and temperament. His letters of the late 'thirties and early 'forties suggest how the obliteration of human lives "for the sake of a better life" shocked him into a sudden awareness of the value of one life. Perhaps more startling was the horror of seeing "religious" men and women shrink from any responsibilities to one another and tramp blindly after their Führer in the wholesale destruction of the Jewish populace. Bonhoeffer's resistance work brought him in contact with men like Hans Oster and Ludwig Beck, in whom he glimpsed an integrity, a depth of motivation, and a capacity for self-sacrifice which he came to prize as foremost marks of the follower of Christ. In thinking out and developing his anthropology, Bonhoeffer was forecasting a Church which hopefully would arise in Europe after the War; and Bonhoeffer wanted that Church to form men the caliber of Oster and Beck.

Even more fundamental for his anthropology than historical circumstances, however, was Bonhoeffer's instinctive passion for life, his zest in living and savoring every moment. The prison letters are remarkably vivid in conveying this sense of exhilaration in life:

What delightful autumn weather we are having! If only you were at Friedrichsbrunn, and I with you, and Hans and his family too! But there must be thousands who cannot have what they want. I can't agree with Diogenes that the *summum bonum* is the absence of desire, or that the best place to live is a tub. Why should we pretend that all our geese are swans? All the same, I do believe it is not good for us to have everything we want, especially when we are young, though it would be wrong to give up wishing for anything, for then we should grow apathetic.[3]

Bonhoeffer loved music, sports, a lively walk in the mountains. The prison letters go far to show his range and sensitivity. "Time lost," he wrote early in prison, "is time when we have not lived a full human life, time unenriched by experience, creative endeavor, enjoyment and suffering." [4]

Indeed, Bonhoeffer's concept of man seems to be nearer to Shakespeare and Goethe than to his own theological forebears —both the liberal theologians of his university days, and Karl Barth. Bonhoeffer saw in man a mystery, consciously and continually exploring the range and powers of his own life. Goethe especially impressed Bonhoeffer; the great writer's passion for experience, for an ever larger life was intensely shared by Bonhoeffer.

As a result of his appreciation of man, Bonhoeffer became wary of theologians and philosophers who discussed man; he sensed the grave danger that in conceptualizing man the theologian tends to deprive man of his rich humanity. The epitome of such theologians could be found, Bonhoeffer thought, in the ethical thinkers, who set out with brash self-confidence to encompass this mystery, man, in their tidy ethical systems.

The flow of life, from the conception to the grave, is incomprehensible to the ethical; it is "pre-ethical." The "ethical" is repelled and horrified by the obscurity of motives for action, by the way in which every deed is compounded of conscious and unconscious elements, natural and supernatural elements, inclination and duty. . . .[5]

In his anthropology, then, Bonhoeffer is reacting to another tendency among theologians: the reduction of the richness and vastness of human life to a schematized series of abstractions. His insistence upon the multi-dimensional nature of the Christian life shows Bonhoeffer's repeated concern for overcoming a static idea of man. "Christianity plunges us into many dimensions of life simultaneously. We can make room in our hearts, to some extent at least, for God and the whole world." [6]

As a theologian, then, Bonhoeffer brought to his thought the scope of his own theological background, and his personal appreciation for life. He brought also the overriding conviction that at the center of this beautiful and sorrowful existence is Christ, the Lord of the world. Two quotations, both from the prison letters, suggest how intensely Bonhoeffer's love for the world led him to Christ, and vice versa. "It is only when one loves life and the world so much that without them everything would be gone, that one can believe in the resurrection and a new world." [7] Later, referring to the Song of Songs, he wrote to Bethge: "I must say, I prefer to read it as an ordinary love poem, which is probably the best christological exposition too." [8]

These influences—a theological reaction to the thinkers who had influenced him, his own background, and his deep conviction that a valid theology cannot conceptualize man—were for the most part semiconscious in Bonhoeffer. Much more conscious, and far more elaborately stated in his works, are the three doctrines which give a forceful impetus to the anthropology: the urgency of the "penultimate," the absence of two spheres, and the restoration of the natural. Doctrinally, the anthropology is based upon these assumptions; as a result, it is important to understand them before clarifying the anthropology.

Bonhoeffer's notion of the ultimate and the penultimate is one of his most original and fertile concepts. The idea as Bonhoeffer develops it attempts to resolve the tension created by the Reformers' insistence upon justification. Bonhoeffer begins by equating the "ultimate" with justification: "The origin and essence of all Christian life are comprised in the one process or event which the Reformation called justification of the sinner alone." [9] Bonhoeffer's dominating concern, however, lies with the penultimate, "What goes before the ultimate." Here he sees an entire dimension which the Reformation—and, for the most part, Protestant tradition—missed, and which needs fresh emphasis.

The relationship between the penultimate and the ultimate is the crux of Bonhoeffer's doctrine. One analogy would be "pre-evangelization" and "evangelization"—a common guideline for missionary work. The work of "pre-evangelization" involves preparing men humanly to receive the Word, whereas "evangelization" means the actual proclaiming of the Word. Bonhoeffer states that the penultimate can exist only for the sake of the ultimate, otherwise it has no Christian value and becomes simply worldly activity. The penultimate is, as a chapter heading states, "The Preparing of the Way." It is an enormous and urgent demand:

> This task is . . . a charge of immense responsibility for all who know of the coming of Christ . . . to allow the hungry man to remain hungry would be blasphemy against God and one's neighbor, for what is nearest to God is precisely the need of one's neighbor.[10]

Bonhoeffer stresses the importance of the penultimate from another viewpoint. He suggests that ministers and those charged with leading men *to* the ultimate, often cannot live realistically in the penultimate. How important, he asks, is the ultimate in the lives of Christians—and how important should it be? Should Christians always relate to their situations and to the needs of others in an ultimate way? Bonhoeffer gives the example of a pastor at a bereavement who does not read the "ultimate words of consolation from Scripture, but only attempts feeble, penultimate expressions of human solidarity and compassion." [11] The question runs deep: "We are asking whether this faith is and ought to be realizable every day, at every hour, or whether here, too, the length of the penultimate must every time be transferred anew for the sake of the ultimate." [12] The call to a renewed humanity in place of the religious or "ultimate-centered" efforts of the Church is implicit here. Indeed, the penultimate leads directly to a fresh focus on man in this world and his potentialities for becoming fully Christian. By his doctrine of the ultimate and the penultimate Bonhoeffer has made deep and lively humanity a Christian imperative. Already an anthropology of some sort is necessary.

The second major assumption is set down at length in a chapter of the *Ethics:* "Thinking in Terms of Two Spheres." Bonhoeffer's statement here parallels that of Luther four centuries earlier. In his theology Luther reacted vehemently to the dualistic conception dominating the Middle Ages, in which human life was seen at natural and supernatural levels. Fallen man had lost the supernatural, and it was the work of an intense Christian life—achieved, really, only within the monastic, or "religious" life—to regain the supernatural. The dualism created by such a conception involved a dual standard of ethics—the law for those living on the natural level (Christians in the world), and the call to evangelical perfection for the religious.

Luther's reaction was doubly violent: he rejected the cloister to return to the world, and theologically he made every effort to overturn the medieval notion of two Christian strata. Luther described a world in which man lives, marries, struggles, and in which he is saved. He saw the natural world much as the water in which fish need to live: only an environment, necessary, and yet without any inherent potential or worth consideration for itself. Luther's driving thought was justification—what becomes of man *after* he is taken from the world. Consequently,

Luther fell victim by his emphasis to the very dualism which he was attempting to overthrow.

For Bonhoeffer, however, the implications of a Christian mind purged of an unrealistic division between two spheres spring up everywhere. The personal conflicts arising from a false opposition are squelched: ". . . the Christian is no longer the man of internal conflict, but, just as the reality of Christ is one, so he . . . is an undivided whole." [13] But more: the Christian lives in one reality, not two.

> The world, the natural, the profane and reason are now taken up into God from the outset. They do not exist "in themselves" and "on their own account." They have their reality nowhere save in the reality of God, in Christ.[14]

The chapter on the "two spheres" abounds in such paradoxical yet provocative statements.

Actually, the implications of dropping the "thinking in terms of two spheres" develop as part of the texture of Bonhoeffer's mature thought. While in some respects similar to the doctrine of ultimate and penultimate, Bonhoeffer's statements on the two spheres should not be seen as a doctrine, but as the reiteration of a fundamental conviction. The certainty is rooted in Luther; and what begins with Bonhoeffer as a point of emphasis concludes in a widening, encircling perspective of Christian belief.

The third premise follows from the second: if the mentality of two spheres can be discarded, perhaps renewed understanding of the "natural" can ensue. "The concept of the natural," Bonhoeffer wrote in the *Ethics,* "has fallen into discredit in Protestant ethics." The loss has been a fatal one:

> The significance of the natural for the Gospel was obscured, and the Protestant Church was no longer able to return a clear word of direction in answer to the burning questions of natural life.[15]

For Bonhoeffer, a distinct understanding of the natural—not as an abstract doctrine, but as the ground and setting for the Gospel—is fundamental for true Christian ethics.

Bonhoeffer sees in the natural the complete range of man's powers and capabilities for good or for evil. The natural has come into being only in man's breach from God; consequently, it must be treated carefully in theology, neither totally accepted, nor entirely rejected. Bonhoeffer's early years had convinced him of the dangers in such extremes. He saw that the natural lost its hope for a genuine redemption when liberal theologians attempted to reduce revelation to terms of the natural. And in Karl Barth's theology Bonhoeffer perceived what he later called a "positivism of revelation"—that the only truth we know comes from God's Word, hardly an inviting setting for a strong theology of the natural.

What Bonhoeffer has described of the role of the natural (his comments on this topic are manifestly incomplete) suggests the powerful Christ-centered direction of his thought at this stage. "Natural life must not be understood simply as a preliminary to life with Christ. It is only from Christ himself that it receives its validation." [16]

The three assumptions provide a stable doctrinal foundation for Bonhoeffer's anthropology. By stressing the penultimate, Bonhoeffer has given worldly life a new importance for the doctrine of justification—and a new urgency. The elimination of the "two spheres" mentality makes the world itself transparent, an aid rather than an obstacle to recognizing the Lordship of Christ over the world. In his concern for the natural, Bonhoeffer has faced a serious question in Protestant theology and has penetrated more deeply the Christian implications of man's life in the world. Each of these premises forces the Christian more fully into life, and into the struggles and aspirations of the secular world. The focus sharpens; the world itself has become the ground and source of the committed Christian, no longer simply the place where he acts, not simply the accepted environment which he cannot escape; the world becomes for Bonhoeffer the combination of forces that conspire to bring the whole man to life, the forces of human progress and social failure, community and indifference. Throughout his explanations of these ideas Bonhoeffer insists vigorously that the Christian can forget only at an immense forfeit that these forces are controlled and directed by Christ. The way has indeed been cleared for a positive and powerful Christian anthropology.

The fundamental question underlying any anthropology is, of course, what is man? Bonhoeffer confronts the question, but always within the context of Christ: "Man is the man who was accepted in the Incarnation of Christ, who was loved, condemned and reconciled in Christ." [17] As Bonhoeffer wrote, "Since God became man in Christ all thought about man without Christ has been a barren abstraction." [18] Christ's coming has decisively changed man, so much so that any anthropology which does not recognize Christ risks irrelevance and pointless inquiry. What is truly worth understanding in man—his powers, his capacity for goodness, his creative drive—is really inaccessible without a proper knowledge of Christ. "Only in Christ do we know what love is." [19] Only in Christ, Bonhoeffer intimates, can the range and magnificence of man's nature be understood.

Bonhoeffer is equally explicit about the futility of natural human life without Christ. Such life is "a void, a plunge into the abyss; it is movement without end and without purpose, movement into nothing." [20] Man fallen from God and without Christ is a moral ruin; "in becoming like God man has become a god against God. . . . He lives . . . in disunion with God, with men, with things, and with himself." [21]

Doctrinally, how does Bonhoeffer justify such a stand? "Anthropology" has traditionally meant the study of man, but based upon observations of man, not upon any prior theological belief. Even though he is a theologian, Bonhoeffer seems to be inverting the process: beginning with God's revelation and moving toward man. Admittedly, he does begin like Barth with revelation, but only because revelation provides a vivid picture of the paradigmatic man, Jesus Christ. Bonhoeffer's anthropology is rooted in neither humanism nor empirical research, but in Christ: yet it leads ineluctably to a vision of man profoundly humanistic, one which surprisingly parallels the findings of contemporary psychologists and anthropologists.

A Pauline doctrine undergirds Bonhoeffer's anthropology;

he calls it "conformation." The actual relationship of Christ with man is the central question, and Bonhoeffer depicts that relationship at its most demanding, if its most exalted, point:

To be conformed with the Incarnate—that is to be a real man. It is man's right and duty that he should be man. The quest for the superman, the endeavor to outgrow the man within the man, the pursuit of the heroic, the cult of the demigod, all this is not the proper concern of man, for it is untrue.[22]

Bonhoeffer's focus is intense and direct: he is not concerned with any effects of Christ's form in man apart from that of enabling man to become himself. "Man is not transformed into a form which is alien to him, the form of God, but into his own form, the form which is essentially proper to him." [23]

Bonhoeffer's terms resemble those used by St. Paul. The process of "formation" (*Gestaltung*) enables Christ's form (*Gestalt*) to become the activating force in man. Partly because "formation" had unfavorable connotations from its use in Nazi slogans and partly because Bonhoeffer wished to emphasize the extent of the process, he coined a new word, "conformation" (*Gleichgestaltung*). Conformation does not emboss every man with the same religious or moral character—quite the opposite. Bonhoeffer insists that the man conformed to Christ is man liberated to be himself, to live in the world and experience life with all the personal vividness and spontaneity of which he is capable.

Conformation in no way resembles a program, or the efforts of what Bonhoeffer slightingly calls "practical Christianity." Nor is it achieved "by dint of efforts 'to become like Jesus,' which is the way in which we usually interpret it." [24] The form of Christ acts upon and changes man; he does not make that change himself. "It is not Christian men who shape the world with their ideas, but it is Christ who shapes men in conformity with himself." [25] The will of God, which man must follow in order to receive this conformation, is "nothing other than the becoming real of the reality of Christ with us and in our world." [26]

Conformation not only gives man his own identity and maturity; it enables him to see Christ in a new perspective. In Christ the entire scope of Bonhoeffer's anthropology is distilled and set into the world as the foundation of a renewed humanity. The man Christ is paradigmatic: he stands as the exemplary man, the focal point of human values and human integrity. As Bonhoeffer wrote provocatively in one of his final letters:

In these turbulent times we are always forgetting what it is that makes life really worth while. We think that life has a meaning for us so long as such and such a person still lives. But the truth is that if the earth was good enough for the man Jesus Christ, if a man like him really lived in it, then, and only then, has life a meaning for us. If Jesus had not lived, then our life in spite of all other people we know and honor and love, would be without meaning.[27]

Too much cannot be said of the paradigmatic Christ, in whom Bonhoeffer saw mirrored the entire human race—all men, all desires, all aspirations.

Jesus is not *a* man. He is *man*. Whatever happens to him happened to man. It happens to all men, and therefore it happens also to us. The name Jesus contains within itself the whole of humanity and the whole of God.[28]

An understanding of Christ as the exemplary man, and indeed, almost as the personification of an integrated humanity, gives Bonhoeffer's anthropology its theological basis. The Christian—the man become aware that Christ is the exemplary human being—has the consequent responsibility to follow Christ, and to be conformed to Christ. This is to become a whole person. Here lies the task of explicating and analyzing Bonhoeffer's anthropology. What precisely does he mean when he says that the Christian is not religious or ascetical, but a man?

In a generalized way, Bonhoeffer does describe his anthropology:

To be conformed with the Incarnate is to have the right to be the man one really is. Now there is no more pretense, no more hypocrisy or self-violence, no more compulsion to be something other, better and more ideal than what one is.[29]

The theme of genuineness and integrity dominates Bonhoeffer's conception of man. Along with the keen sense of life to be nourished in men and their responsible commitment to the world, the ability to live wholly forms a distinct part of the anthropology.

When he spoke of wholeness, or what he called "an integrated attitude to life," Bonhoeffer meant above all an ability to penetrate different levels of life: a man who can engage with equal composure and wholeheartedness in athletics, conversation, work, art, prayer. One of Bonhoeffer's most successful phrases, "the polyphony of life," expresses this ability well.

There is always a danger of intense love destroying what I might call the 'polyphony' of life. What I mean is that we should love God eternally with our whole hearts, yet not so as to compromise or diminish our earthly affections, but as a kind of *cantus firmus* to which the other melodies of life provide the counterpoint. Earthly affection is one of these contrapuntal themes, a theme which enjoys autonomy of its own.[30]

The "polyphony of life" is Bonhoeffer's effort to keep perspective and respect for the multiple dimensions of contemporary life. "To everything there is a season," he wrote in a letter from his cell in Tegel prison.[31] Again, in the prison letters he spoke of a "sense of quality," which should dominate human relationships, an awareness of the proper time, the proper person. This is not to suggest that Bonhoeffer was attempting to introduce into his theology an aristocratic snobbery. But he was highly sensitized to the quality of a man's life, and the ever-present danger that such quality might be submerged by an unthinking allegiance to cliches, or the numbed use of precious words and experiences. In an unfinished drama attempted in prison, the second scene includes a passage where a friend reads the following in Christopher's diary:

I tell you to guard from misuse the great words which have been given to man. They do not belong in the mouth of the masses and in the headlines of the newspapers, but in the hearts of the few who guard and protect them with their lives. It is never a good sign, when what has previously been the silent and firm possession and the self-responsible attitude of all right-minded persons in the land is shouted aloud in the streets as the very latest wisdom. . . . Let us learn to do what is right for a time without words. Around the silent sanctuary of the great values there will then be formed in our time a new nobility. Not birth and not success will establish it, but humility, faith, and sacrifice.[32]

"The Christian," Bonhoeffer wrote in his *Ethics,* "is no longer the man of eternal conflict, but just as the reality of Christ is one, so he too, since he shares in this reality of Christ, is himself an undivided whole." [33] The sense of wholeness and the consequent reverence for respective values permeates Bonhoeffer's anthropology.

The second quality of the anthropology, man's ability to live every moment intensely, is no less important. Bonhoeffer personally esteemed hearty and vigorous effort, as much in writing a theological treatise as on a tennis court. As he later wrote in his letters, Bonhoeffer believed that God should be found in men's lives, not in their anticipation of death.

I am sure we ought to love God in our *lives* and in all the blessings he sends us. We should trust him in our lives, so that when the time comes, but not before, we may go to him in love and trust and joy.[34]

Consequently, Bonhoeffer prized strength more than weakness in bringing man to God, triumph more than failure, enthusiastic and ardent living over grim meditation. He spoke once of a book on the Greek gods by W. E. Otto, which he found fascinating and stimulating:

To quote from his closing words it [the book] is about "this world of faith, which sprang from the wealth and depth of human existence, rather than from its cares and longings." I wonder if you will understand me when I say I find something attractive in this theme and in the way it is treated in this book. In fact, I find these gods—*horribile dictu*—less offensive when treated like this than certain brands of Christianity! I believe I could pretty nearly claim these gods for Christ.[35]

"A full life" was important for Bonhoeffer, not only for himself personally, not only as a basis of reaching God and having a mature relationship with God, but as an intrinsic component of the anthropology. He wrote once about living in the present moment:

But is it not characteristic of a man, in contrast to an immature person, that his center of gravity is always where he actually is, and that the longing for the fulfillment of his wishes cannot prevent him from being his whole self, wherever he happens to be?[36]

Bonhoeffer grimly realized how few men there were who could live this way. How few, he wrote, "can still indulge some strong personal feeling, and make a real effort to spend all their strength on enduring their longing, assimilating it and turning it to gain in their lives!"[37] Yet it was this caliber of man that Bonhoeffer championed, this quality of man that he sought and for which he pleaded. If a man was incapable of living each moment in its fullness, of facing the world with strength and vigor, then he lacked a vital dimension of his humanity and was not, in effect, a real man.

The third quality proceeds from the other two: the man of integrity and intense living had to be one committed to his neighbor, a man of conscience and responsibility. The theme of responsibility recurs frequently in Bonhoeffer's later writings. He saw in it the natural yet decisive corollary to genuine Christian manhood. It is the distinguishing mark of his anthropology. His ethics begins and concludes with a commitment to the responsible man:

Christ was not essentially a teacher and legislator, but a man, a real man like ourselves. And it is not therefore his will that we should in our time be the adherents, exponents and advocates of a definite doctrine, but that we should be men, real men before God.[38]

Later descriptions of Bonhoeffer's thought will show what responsibility meant for him and its extent in his theology.

Based upon a firm Christology and the doctrine of conformation, Bonhoeffer's anthropology contains three major elements: a wholeness (or "polyphony") of life; the ability to live the moment; and a keen sense of responsibility. Bonhoeffer probably did not realize the extent and depth of his anthropology in its potential for opening out radical horizons in theology. His growing criticism of religiosity was one effect of the anthropology of which he was highly conscious. For the conviction that Christ humanizes and intensifies man's life brought Bonhoeffer to challenge a good many of the presuppositions present in Church teaching and practice. However, the more positive consequences of a rich theology of human life—notably "holy worldliness," his ethics of responsible manhood, and the brilliant Church-world doctrine—were developed without the stirring sense of the revolutionary.

Yet it may be that Bonhoeffer's anthropology, understood as a christological anthropology, will remain his most distinctive contribution to theology. For here is the basis of the brutal dethronement of religion in the prison letters; here is the guiding force which impelled a new effort to define the Church, Christian ethics, and the entire scope of Christian life. And perhaps in a highly organized, highly functionalized world, where a complete human life is threatened at every attempt, Bonhoeffer's anthropology is a real boon to theologians. Admittedly, for centuries humanists, and more recently psychologists, have stressed the same creative burgeoning of human efforts and desires which underlie Bonhoeffer's anthropology. But Bonhoeffer set human life firmly into a Christian perspective, and succeeded in showing that to follow Christ leads to a more genuine humanity and a deeper involvement in the world. As he wrote in one of his final letters to Bethge:

. . . it is only by living completely in this world that one learns to believe. One must abandon every attempt to make something of oneself, whether it be a saint, a converted sinner, a churchman (the priestly type, so-called!), a righteous man or an unrighteous one, a sick man or a healthy one. This is what I mean by worldliness—taking life in one's stride, with all its duties and problems, its successes and its failures, its experiences and helplessness. It is in such a life that we throw ourselves utterly in the arms of God and participate in his sufferings in the world and watch with Christ in Gethsemane. That is faith, that is *metanoia,* and that is what makes a man and a Christian.[39]

To do and dare—not what you would, but what is right. Never to hesitate over what is within your power, but boldly to grasp what lies before you. Not in the flight of fancy, but only in the deed there is freedom. Away with timidity and reluctance! Out into the storm of event, sustained only by the commandment of God and your faith, and freedom will receive your spirit with exultation. "Stations on the Road to Freedom"

Written the day of the failure of the July 20 assassination attempt.

11. *A Church to the World*

The most important point to realize in approaching Bonhoeffer's Church-world doctrine and his subsequent ethical theory is the direction which he takes in developing both of these. Luther came to the problem of Church and world (and its ethical implications) in viewing man's need to live out the Gospel under God's justifying grace. Consequently, the problem of Christian involvement in the world was never a fiery one for Luther. But when Luther's dictums collapsed under the tread of National Socialism, the problem became a crucial one for the Confessing Church, and for Bonhoeffer.

The *Ethics* was clearly written with a vibrant sense of the need for a vital relationship between the Christian community and the world. In a sense, this tension guides and dominates the work. But the resolution, Bonhoeffer's doctrine of a Church to the world, comes less from the tension itself than from an extensive application of his anthropology. Bonhoeffer begins with a conviction that the Church belongs in the world and has obligations to the world; there is no question of a dichotomy or polarity between Church and world. He questions the mode of the Church's involvement in the world—its extent, its style, its purposes. He questions, moreover, the wisdom of the older conceptions of Church and world, especially of their tendency to distrust man's creative and invigorating powers—as artist, scientist, and shaper of the world. The direction of the *Ethics* is evident: Bonhoeffer is attempting to bring to the Church-world relationship his confidence in the man reshaped by Christ, and his immense hope for the world. The effort involves more than offsetting the dangers in traditional thought on Church and world. Bonhoeffer is attempting a new understanding of the Church, of Christian ethics, and, perhaps above all, of the individual Christian's self-understanding.

The early signs of a new Church-world theory are not hard to locate. Bonhoeffer's favorite themes were all directed toward the problem of Church and world: the urgency of a concretely proclaimed revelation, a Church in which Christ exists "as community," an instinctive distrust of theory in theology, the gripping problem of authority in the Church's proclamation, and the conviction that man must follow Christ into the midst of the world. The question of Church and world loomed increasingly larger in Bonhoeffer's writings of the late 'thirties. It is hardly surprising that, in an expansive volume on ethics, Bonhoeffer would concentrate upon a Church-world doctrine even more conscientiously than on the problem of ethics.

The historical influences upon the new doctrine are especially important for a clear understanding of the Church-world doctrine, because these influences help to assess the value of this doctrine outside the strained conditions of Nazi Germany. How valid, for example, would Bonhoeffer's description of the Church's responsibilities be elsewhere than in a state in which defiant action was perilous, but nonetheless morally necessary? Many commentators see in Bonhoeffer's thought a response to one extreme situation. Yet in his formulation of the Church-world doctrine, Bonhoeffer was primarily influenced *not* by the Nazi and Confessing Church conflict, but by his hopes for a new Church, serving a war-scarred world.

Bonhoeffer, it must be recalled, was young; he was only thirty-four when he began work on the *Ethics*. His yet hearty idealism, combined with the conviction that the War would end Hitler's tyranny, made the end of the War a focal point for his hopes of a renewed Church. As he wrote to his nephew in the sermon for his christening from the prison cell in Tegel:

> By the time you have grown up, the Church's form will have changed greatly. . . . It is not for us to prophesy the day (though the day will come) when men will once more be called so to utter the word of God that the world will be changed and renewed by it. It will be a new language, perhaps quite non-religious, but liberating and redeeming—as was Jesus' language; it will shock people and yet overcome them by its power. . . .[1]

There are other references, generally from the war years, which suggest that the force behind Bonhoeffer's most creative thinking was precisely this: the changing shape of the Church in the coming age. It would be a Church, Bonhoeffer hoped, not mainly intent upon insistently opposing the misuse of power in a Hitler or in Communism, but engaged in the world in such a way as to nurture the sense of responsibility which would obviate the rise of a Hitler. In his *Ethics* Bonhoeffer speaks of a "justification and renewal" of the West, which would follow in the wake of a restored peace and a forgiven guilt. But this justification and renewal would only come

> . . . when the Church of Jesus Christ, as the fountainhead of all forgiveness, justification, and renewal, is given room to do here work among the nations.[2]

The efforts of the Church, then, would be imperative for the future of peace, and imperative for the spiritual renewal within each nation. The question of how to engage in that effort is of central concern in the *Ethics*.

There can be no denying the dual impact, on the one hand, of Bonhoeffer's chagrin at the failure of Christians to oppose Hitler, and, on the other, of the moral commitment of the secular men he met in the resistance. Bonhoeffer's acid remarks about the Confessing Church's cringing withdrawal from its mission to the German people only suggests his passionate desire for a painful awareness of social crisis on the part of the Church. But Bonhoeffer saw further than the German situation; he had, after all, visited America and lived in England. He moreover saw the futility in approaching the Church-world question in terms of any one problem, even Church and state. As a theologian, he conscientiously sought a synthesis which, because it provided clear guidance for the Church in other countries, would provide a clear guidance for the Church in Germany.

Beyond the appallingly evident need for a renewed Church-world understanding, and Bonhoeffer's anticipation of the coming Church, one other important influence upon his Church-world thought is unmistakable: the resistance. Bonhoeffer has himself stated at several junctures how decisive his own "political activities" were for his thought.

> Again and again I am driven to think of my activities which are now concerned so much with the secular field . . . all the time I am forced to think of God, of Christ, of genuineness, life, freedom, charity—that matters for me. What causes me uneasiness is just the religious clothing. . . .[3]

The men of the resistance, the Osters and Becks, were no less influential. That these men could struggle at precarious odds for human justice and yet be apart from Christ was a paradox Bonhoeffer could not admit. Such men are, he stated in the *Ethics,* led to Christ and become Christians in their struggles and their bare faith in justice. In the section where he spoke of this, Bonhoeffer was insistent: this is not an abstract deduction, but an experience, "in which the power of Jesus Christ became manifest in fields of life where it had previously remained unknown."[4] There can be little doubt that Bonhoeffer's secular activities, and especially his experience with great men whose lives literally "belonged" to the secular sphere, powerfully influenced his assessment of the secular world.

The influences, then, are threefold: the apathy of Christians, which reflected the need for searching renewal; the hope of a new form of the Church; and the inspiration of a secular resistance. Each gave, in its own way, the search for a vital Church-world doctrine a fresh imperative. Each fastened Bonhoeffer more firmly to his search.

The search was a brief one. Bonhoeffer knew almost from the outset the terms of his Church-world doctrine. The Church, since the Patristic Age, had generally been considered in terms of its nature and its religious functions. Luther's definition of the Church is typical: "The Church is the place where the Word is preached, and the sacraments are received." The idea of the Church which Bonhoeffer proposes in the *Ethics* is therefore a startling one: "The Church is the place (or space) in the world where the reign of Jesus Christ over the whole world is evidenced and proclaimed." This does not at first sound so startling; but what Bonhoeffer in effect has done is to move away from the Church in terms of its static nature of religious function and concentrate on its relation to the world. "The Church is the place where Jesus Christ's taking form is proclaimed and accomplished." [5] It is amazing how every definition or description of the Church in the *Ethics* is worded in such a way that the Church exists only *in terms of* the world. "The Church is the place in the world. . . ." "The Church is a piece of the world. . . ." "The Church is her true self only when she exists for humanity." "The Church is the place in the world where testimony and serious thought are given to God's reconciliation of the world with himself in Christ, to his so having loved the world that he gave his Son for its sake." [6]

In *The Communion of Saints* Bonhoeffer had insisted that if the Church is to exist, it must exist in earthly form—human, tenuous, empirical. As with the later *Ethics, The Communion of Saints* attempted to redefine the Church. In the *Ethics,* however, Bonhoeffer achieves the new definition in a way that encompasses the world far more conclusively than in *The Communion of Saints.*

The question arises, however, what are these terms in which the Church is defined in relation to the world? It must be admitted that Bonhoeffer wrote no specific section on the doctrinal basis of a Church-world theology, and a carefully elaborated description of the relationship is wanting. Perhaps the best guideline in this respect is what Bonhoeffer often refers to as the "essential character" of the Church: its responsibility to the world.

> The congregation of Jesus Christ is the place at which Christ is believed and obeyed as the salvation of the whole world. This means that from the outset the congregation, according to its essential character, bears responsibility for the world which God loved in Christ. If the congregation fails to fulfill this responsibility it ceases to be the congregation of Christ.[7]

In a different context Bonhoeffer suggests the same point by stating: "The only way the Church can defend her own territory is by fighting not for it but for the salvation of the world." [8]

Responsibility for the world gives the Church-world doctrine a strong focus. Questions yet arise, but these are secondary. Bonhoeffer has redefined the Church primarily as the community of Christ responsible to mankind.

To understand the demands and extent of this responsibility requires, however, a solid footing in Bonhoeffer's theology of the Incarnation and his anthropology. Bonhoeffer set down the fundamental principle with one statement: ". . . the relation of the Church to the world is determined entirely by the relation of God to the world." [9] Like Christ, and through Christ, the Church has become fully part of the world, sharing in its anticipations, its failures, its sufferings. Bonhoeffer is most insistent on this point:

> In Christ we are offered the possibility of partaking in the reality of God and in the reality of the world, but not in one without the other. The reality of God discloses itself only by setting me entirely in the reality of the world, and when I encounter the reality of the world it is always already sustained, accepted, and reconciled in the reality of God. This is the inner meaning of the revelation of God in the man Jesus Christ.[10]

Bonhoeffer follows the basic line of thought closely; what Christ has done for the world and the manner in which Christ has taken part in the world should guide the Church in its own commitment. This means a complete orientation to Christ's Incarnation, and a worldly life steeped in the anthropology.

An incarnational emphasis dominates the *Ethics;* in discussions of the penultimate, the two spheres, and the natural, Bonhoeffer's strong incarnational thrust drives his ideas forward. The importance of Christ's humanity for the Church never leaves Bonhoeffer's sight: "We can testify to Jesus Christ and proclaim him always only as him in whom God took manhood upon Himself in the body. . . ." [11] Throughout the *Ethics* as well as the prison writings, he continues the insistence: "It is only through God's being made man that it is possible to know the real man and not to despise him." [12]

For Bonhoeffer, the implications of a Church following Christ in his Incarnation are extensive, but immediately evident. That Church partakes to the lees of the world, and of human life. Its mission, consequently, is to the whole of human life:

> The Church is the man in Christ, incarnate, sentenced and awakened to a new life. In the first instance, therefore, she has essentially nothing to do with the so-called religious functions of man, but with the whole man in his existence in the world with all its implications.[13]

For this reason, the best guideline for Bonhoeffer's notion of the Church in the world would be his anthropology. The insistence on a life expanded and not contracted by faith in Christ, the Christian meaning of a man's strength over against his weakness, the central demand of a firm moral and spiritual integrity: these themes recur and emerge as essential elements of the Christian's life. The Christian, Bonhoeffer later wrote from prison, must "plunge himself into the life of a godless world, without attempting to gloss over its ungodliness with a veneer of religion or trying to transfigure it." [14]

The Church then stands in the midst of the world as the community of men who have been restored to wholeness, and who keenly recognize their responsibility to other men. These are men who suffer with and for the world. "Jesus calls men, not to a new religion, but to life. But what does this life look like, this participation in the powerlessness of God in the world?" [15]

At this point, an important distinction is necessary. Christ has indeed communicated his life to the Church, and the Church draws its identity from an awareness that God has reconciled the world with God and enlarged the scope of man's life. However, Bonhoeffer carefully insists that the Church cannot too easily equate itself with the presence of Christ in the world—much less constrict Christ's power and love *to* the Church.

> Everything would be ruined if one were to try to reserve Christ for the Church and to allow the world only some kind of law, even if it were a Christian law. Christ died for the world, and it is only in the midst of the world that Christ is Christ.[16]

But in another way, Christ's Lordship over all creation can never be envisaged as the dominion of the Church. The Church's purpose, and the breadth of its responsibility, are determined not by the dominion of Christ, but by the inner necessity of man's response to God's Word. As Bonhoeffer had said earlier in *The Cost of Discipleship,* ". . . the Word of God must go forth from the Church into all the world, proclaiming that the earth is the Lord's." [17]

The Church then follows Christ in his Incarnation and becomes fully human in being conformed to Christ. Never, though, does it think of Christ as "its own," as belonging only to the Church and to be kept within the Church. On the contrary, each statement Bonhoeffer makes on the Church shows that exactly the opposite effect is demanded of Christ's Church:

> The Church is the place where testimony and serious thought are given to God's reconciliation of the world with himself in Christ, to his having so loved the world that he gave his son for its sake.[18]

Bonhoeffer asks, above all, that Christians think of themselves—and especially of Christ—in outgoing terms. "All men are taken up, enclosed and borne within the Body of Christ," he states in the *Ethics;* "this is just what the congregation of the faithful are to make known to the world by their words and by their lives." [19]

The question will still be asked of Bonhoeffer: in itself, what is the nature of the Church? Not what is the Church *for,* but what is the Church in itself? The very question, however, undercuts Bonhoeffer's fundamental conviction that the Church exists dynamically in going out to the world. There can be no other way of looking at the Church without turning it lifeless and impotent.

The only way in which the Church can defend her own territory is by fighting not for it but for the salvation of the world. Otherwise the Church becomes a "religious society" which fights in its own interest and thereby ceases at once to be the Church of God and of the world.[20]

Bonhoeffer's reaction against the self-enclosed and highly defensive Confessing Church becomes evident here. Less apparent is his inference that the Church achieves its identity only in sacrificing itself for the world. During his last few months in prison, when Bonhoeffer was working on the outline of a proposed book, he stated:

The Church is her true self only when she exists for humanity. As a fresh start she should give away all her endowments to the poor and needy. . . . She must take her part in the social life of the world, not lording it over men, but helping and serving them. She must tell men, whatever their calling, what it means to live for Christ, to exist for others.[21]

One of the most crucial hazards for the Christian community lies in coming to think of the Church as an end in itself. Bonhoeffer sees this danger in Catholicism, just as he saw it in the Confessing Church. Indeed, he describes the Church in too fluid and active a way to leave open much hope for a settled, definitive doctrine of the Church as a religious congregation or community. "If one wishes to speak . . . of the space or sphere of the Church," he wrote in the *Ethics,* "one must bear in mind that the confines of this space are *at every moment being overrun and broken down by the testimony of the Church to Jesus Christ."* [22] (italics added)

If the Church cannot be defined in the terms of essence and form, or even of static function, Bonhoeffer admits that its action in the world gives testimony to certain sources, and a certain style of life. "It is, of course, to be assumed," he says for example, that the Church's proclamation "can be delivered in the right way only if it springs from a hallowed life in the congregation of God." [23] He therefore does not disparage the sacraments, community life, prayer; these are with the Church as never before. They exist in the Church, however, with a new dynamic, the inspiration of the world which they have been called to serve.

A final question about the Church "itself" arises, long unsettled throughout Bonhoeffer's writings: the Church as identified with and apart from the world. *The Cost of Discipleship* had probed the tension, but without a conclusive doctrinal resolution. The tenor of the book, however, encouraged the Church to shrink from the world rather than to take part in it. For example:

> The value of the secular calling for the Christian is that it provides an opportunity of living the Christian life with the support of God's grace, and of engaging more vigorously in the assault on the world and everything it stands for.[24]

In the *Ethics* Bonhoeffer admits a separation of the Church from the world, but again only *in terms of* the positive relationship which the Church has made to the world. "The Church is divided from the world," he states, "solely by the fact that she affirms in faith the reality of God's acceptance of man, a reality which is the property of the whole world." [25] In the *Ethics* there is no tension between the Church as part of and as apart from the world—not, at least, any of the tension so powerful in *Discipleship*.

> The Church as a self-contained community is subject to a twofold divine ordinance and rule. She must be adapted to the purpose of the world, and precisely in this she must be adapted to her own purpose as the place at which Jesus Christ is present.[26]

Bonhoeffer makes a presumption here which was completely absent in *The Cost of Discipleship* and, for that matter, in the Church-world thought of Luther and Barth. Bonhoeffer sees the Church as the already Christian world conscious of itself in this community of men. The Church, then, is separate from the world only as a "summoning of the world into the fellowship of this body of Christ to which in truth it already belongs." [27] By affirming God's acceptance of the world and permitting Christ to take effect and be conformed within her, the Church may be setting herself apart from the world. But in doing so, she testifies that Christ's action is effectual for the entire world. So at no time does the doctrine of "separation from the world" move from the one direction which Bonhoeffer follows: bringing *all* men to a completeness of life in Christ.

There is, then, the seeming ambivalence: adapt to the world, take part in it and help nourish its secular hopes; likewise, be conformed to Christ in a way that all men can see what has happened to the world in the coming of the man Jesus. The principle is firm. Never should the Church's "separation" from the world lead anywhere than to a greater summoning of the world into the Church. Seen this way, the responsibility is an awesome one, but Bonhoeffer expects a great deal of men who claim to be following Christ.

> The Church, then, bears the form which is in truth the proper form of all humanity. The image in which she is formed is the image of man. What takes place in her takes place as an example and substitute for all men. But it is impossible to state clearly enough that the Church, too, is not an independent form by herself, side by side with the form of Christ, and that she, too, can therefore never lay claim to an independent character, title, authority or dignity on her own account and apart from him. The Church is nothing but a section of humanity in which Christ has really taken form.[28]

Up to this point the focus has been the Church, whether seen from its source in the Incarnation, or its terminus in the world. A major question, however, which must be put to Bonhoeffer's new Church-world doctrine and which will shift the focus, regards the Church's action: in what does the Church's responsibility consist in and to the people of the world? The question has perenially been an urgent one, and in Bonhoeffer's schema it takes on a renewed urgency. In an essay in the *Ethics* entitled, "On the Possibility of the Word of the Church to the World," Bonhoeffer probed the questions perceptively:

What lies behind that longing, which is awakening everywhere among the Christians of the world, for the Church's word of solution to the world? . . . The social, economic, political and other problems of the world have become too much for us; all the available offers of ideological and practical solutions are inadequate. In this way the world of technical progress has reached its limits. The car is caught in the mud; the wheels are rotating at the highest possible speed, but they still cannot draw the car clear. In their extent and in their character the problems are so universally human that some quite fundamental remedy has become necessary.[29]

Bonhoeffer seriously questions the extent to which the Church *should* answer, or be expected to answer, the problems facing the world in any age. "*Are there,*" he asks, "Christian solutions at all for worldly problems?" [30] He notes that Jesus hardly seemed preoccupied with the world's problems; His Word ignores all the world's problems and looks down upon them from another height; "it is not a solution, but a redemption." [31]

The responsibility of the Church, consequently, is not to present the world with answers to its problems—at least not in such a simplistic version as Bonhoeffer has disclaimed. How then should the Church be responsible to the world? To what extent, and at what peril to itself?

Bonhoeffer's descriptions of the Church's "proclamation to the world," its "witness before men," and its mandate to action in the secular sphere abound in the *Ethics*. However, he does not clarify the nature and extent of this responsibility; it must simply be inferred.

Bonhoeffer carefully notes one condition fundamental to the Church's responsibility. "There are a number of completely different ways," he states, in which the congregation may fulfill its responsibility towards the world. It will fulfill it differently when it is in the situation of a mission and when it is in a situation in which the Church is recognized by the state, and differently again in times of persecution.[32]

Again, no totally correct standards can be set upon the Church's commitment; the situation determines this commitment to a great extent. It should be noted, however, that Bonhoeffer is here speaking of the *Church's* responsibility. That of the individual Christian will be taken up in a later chapter.

Three levels of the Church's responsibility emerge in Bonhoeffer's discussion in the *Ethics:* the Church as witness, the Church as men crystallizing the world's guilt and hope for a new future, and the Church as an active force in the secular world.

The first fundamental level of witness demands that Christians reflect the man Christ in whom they have been conformed:

. . . the first demand which is made of those who belong to God's Church is not that they should be something in themselves, not that they should, for example, set up some religious organization or that they should lead lives of piety, but that they shall be witnesses to Jesus Christ before the world.[33]

During the mid-'thirties Bonhoeffer had been absorbed with the problem of a concrete revelation. Is it possible to proclaim the Gospel concretely (with a deep insight into the present situation and its demands) and with authority? Late in the *Ethics* Bonhoeffer states that "the Church as a community is not to be separated from the office of proclamation." [34] Its very bearing and its day-to-day witness are its most intense, and most honest, and certainly most concrete, proclamation of Christ's love for the world. And by its integrity, this proclamation of the Church's witness mirrors the authority which so concerned Bonhoeffer.

The Christian congregation stands at the point at which the whole world ought to be standing; to this extent it serves as deputy for the world and exists for the sake of the world. On the other hand, the world achieves its own fulfillment at the point at which the congregation stands.[35]

The second level of responsibility is less clearly delineated; yet Bonhoeffer sees it as essential for the spiritual renewal of the Western nations:

The Church today is that community of men which is gripped by the power of the grace of Christ so that, recognizing as guilt towards Jesus Christ both its own personal sin and the apostasy of the western world from Jesus Christ, it confesses this guilt and accepts the burden of it. It is in her that Jesus realizes His form in the midst of the world. That is why the Church alone can be the place of personal and collective rebirth and renewal.[36]

This second level, the responsibility to confess the guilt of the world, must be seen in the perspective of the War and Bonhoeffer's abiding consciousness of Germany's guilt. In an illuminating chapter entitled "The Confession of Guilt," Bonhoeffer speaks of guilt as the defection from Christ.

True acknowledgement of guilt does not arise from the experience of disruption and decay, but for us, who have encountered the form of Christ, solely from this form. . . . The place where this recognition of guilt becomes real is the Church.[37]

The Church kneels before God and takes upon itself the guilt of the nations. However, with this confession of the world's guilt—rather than its denial, so loudly proclaimed everywhere else—"there arises the possibility of forgiveness." [38] The community of the Church does not seek out the guilty party, or make fierce demands for expiation upon those at fault. They are "men who take all, really all, guilt upon themselves, not in some heroic resolve of sacrifice, but simply because they are overwhelmed by their own . . . guilt towards Christ." [39]

Bonhoeffer continues the chapter by describing, almost cataloging what the Church does confess. The statements are burning self-indictments:

The Church confesses that she has witnessed the lawless application of brutal force, the physical and spiritual suffering of countless innocent people, oppression, hatred, and murder, and that she has not raised her voice on behalf of the victims and has not found ways to hasten to their aid. She is guilty of the deaths of the weakest and most defenseless brothers of Jesus Christ . . . .

The Church confesses that she has desired security, peace and quiet, possessions and honor, to which she had no right, and that in this way she has not bridled the desires of men but has stimulated them still further.[40]

Bonhoeffer insists that the confession of guilt does not belong to the Church only at this time and this place. Nor is this confession in any sense optional.

For indeed the free confession of guilt is not something which can be done or left undone at will. It is the emergence of the form of Jesus Christ in the Church.[41]

Without the confession of guilt—and recognized in the proportions Bonhoeffer has suggested—the congregations cease to be the Church of Christ.

The third level of responsibility reaches beyond witness and the recognition of guilt; here Bonhoeffer confronts the Church's moral obligation actively to shape the world. As he pressed the question in one context, "Has the Church merely to gather up those whom the wheel has crushed or has she to prevent the wheel from crushing them?" [42] Bonhoeffer sees the question as an acutely thorny one. He has clearly had enough of the "programmes" and "crusades" usually meant by the Church's "action in the world." In a brief, regrettably unfinished chapter appended to the *Ethics,* "On the Possibility of the Word of the Church to the World," Bonhoeffer faces the question directly. The essay recalls the earlier search for "a concrete word to proclaim to the world," and anticipates the world "come of age" which can grapple quite well with its own problems. The Church, Bonhoeffer stated earlier, "bears responsibility for the world which God loved in Christ." [43] He had suggested at other points what this responsibility implied: a concern "not with conserving the past only, but searching for order, and working with the forces of order." [44] And elsewhere, in speaking of the penultimate, he discussed the obliteration of conditions which block the Gospel, conditions such as poverty and seething hate.

In these references such a far-reaching measure of responsibility had only been mentioned, however.

In the brief essay dealing with the question of the Church acting in the world, Bonhoeffer seems to take a negative stand. He rules out the notion of a "Christian answer" to most secular problems; indeed, he questions whether Christians should always attempt an answer:

> Who actually tells us that all worldly problems are to be and can be solved? Perhaps the unsolved state of these problems is of more importance to God than their solution, for it may serve to call attention to the fall of man and to the divine redemption.[45]

He then states declaratively: "The essence of the Gospel does not lie in the solution of human problems, and . . . the solution of human problems cannot be the essential task of the Church." [46] The Church, however, should take action in another sense, not attempting directly to "solve" problems, but relate to them and challenge them. By the authority of God's Word, she must "necessarily declare those economic attitudes or forms to be wrong which obviously obstruct belief in Jesus Christ." [47] On another level,

> . . . not by the authority of God but merely on the authority of the responsible advice of Christian specialists and experts she will be able to make her contribution towards the establishment of a new order.[48]

Bonhoeffer keeps a sharp distinction between the first function, which he calls *diakonia,* issuing from the Word of God, and the second, which is the human effort of man to reconstruct the world on a basis of harmony and peace.

If Bonhoeffer seems reluctant to deal forthrightly with this third level of the Church's responsibility, it is largely for the reason that he sees action in the world mainly in terms of the individual Christian, and not of the community. Decisive action in society generally comes from men serving important social roles—politicians, educators, military authorities—and not from the Church as a whole. These men should share vividly in the Church's life, and should draw from the Church their keenness of conscience, their vision and courage. But their action takes place in the world, and in the roles designated for them by the world, not by the Church.

In effect, responsibility on all the three levels can well be considered the living pulse of the Church, and the essence of the Church-world relationship. This step in Bonhoeffer's thought is a most decisive one. Only a few years before he had written of a Church hidden in the world, protecting itself from the dangers of the world. By contrast, the new description is daring: a Church whose presence, sense of guilt, and action in the world reflect a profound concern for the world and, in turn, summon the world to a recognition of Christ's love for all men.

More daring perhaps are the consequences of the Church-world doctrine, consequences explored completely only in the prison letters. As with his anthropology, Bonhoeffer's doctrine of the Church's responsibility opens up a new understanding of the Christian's identity and his relationship with God and men. Unfortunately, Bonhoeffer had only begun to explore that new understanding when he was killed by the Gestapo. Yet the impulse that led to the understanding is clear.

Latent in Bonhoeffer's Church-world doctrine is an implicit critique of Luther and of the Lutheran tradition of the Church's precarious attitude to secular life. In overthrowing the medieval dichotomy of the supernatural over the natural, Luther had pleaded heartily for man's presence in the world. But it was always a presence that betokened risk, temptation, the danger of losing God's grace. The world thus became a giant testing ground, man's decisive response to the ultimate. Marriage, occupation, government, society: these had their roots in God, were his "decrees of creation." However, they were present to test the Christian's faith. And the Christian recognized in them more often their looming dangers than their promise of a richer life. Perseverance in the world, despite its trials and failures, describes most clearly for Luther the Christian's vocation; and the Christian's submission to the demands of the world is actually his obedience to God.

Luther's conception never really did overcome the medieval

other-worldliness that he was challenging. The effect is inescapable: a shakily founded insistence upon holiness present in the world's own struggles and aspirations. Admittedly, Luther did open the way to secularism, which came in the historical forms of the enlightenment, liberalism, and "godless" humanism. But he plainly did not foresee a world which could bear its own weight and believe correctly in its own progress, and his theology of the world reflects this.

Bonhoeffer had retained Luther's idea of the Church-world relationship up until the writing of *The Cost of Discipleship.* Indeed, this book may well be one of the strongest utterances of Luther's doctrine in the last century.

> In the world the Christians are a colony of the true home, they are strangers and aliens in a foreign land, enjoying the hospitality of that land, obeying its laws and honoring its government. They receive with gratitude the requirements of their bodily life, and in all things prove themselves honest, just, chaste. . . . They live their own life under alien rulers and alien laws. Above all, they pray for all in authority, and that is their greatest service.[49]

There can be little doubt about the extent of the breakaway in the *Ethics,* and especially in the prison letters. Bonhoeffer keeps Luther's conception of a "worldly life" and the mandates of family, government, occupation, and Church. However, infused with his anthropology, these conceptions take on a vivid and radical new direction, as portents of hope for a larger worldly life, rather than tests for an afterlife. Likewise, in Bonhoeffer the Christian life involves a depth of commitment *to* the world which is all but totally absent in Luther, an absence largely responsible for the apathy of Lutherans in the face of Hitler's tyranny.

Bonhoeffer's implicit criticism extends of course to the Church itself. The Protestants, he states on the last completed page of the *Ethics* proper, have failed "to perceive the inner connection between this mission [in the world] and the Church's internal functions." [50] The charge is central to the pattern of the *Ethics,* and probably one of the reasons Bonhoeffer attempted the work. In the prison letters Bonhoeffer criticized major theological figures of the century for their failure to come to grips with the Church-world problem because of their inability to accept completely the world. His comments about Paul Tillich are typical:

> Tillich set out to interpret the evolution of the world itself—against its will—in a religious sense, to give it its whole shape through religion. That was very courageous of him, but the world unseated him and went on by itself. . . .[51]

In his Church-world doctrine, Bonhoeffer likewise found a basis for the criticism of an inward-centered Christian life, later to become his full-scale attack on "religion." His vehement description of "good people" who became helpless and unconcerned in the face of social crisis anticipates the stabbing criticism of religion which would come later. The word "religion" is used only occasionally in the *Ethics,* but throughout there are suggestions of the grave dangers involved in losing sight of the Church's one guiding feature: its responsibility to the world.

More positively, the Church-world doctrine of the *Ethics* suggests a new style of Christian holiness, and a new autonomy for the secular world. The references to the Christian's life "of genuine worldliness" are brief, but give an idea of the scope of what is to come.

> A life in genuine worldliness is possible only through the proclamation of Christ crucified; true worldly living is not possible or real in contradiction to the proclamation or side by side with it, that is to say, in any kind of autonomy of the secular sphere; it is possible only "in, with and under" the proclamation of Christ.[52]

For Bonhoeffer "true worldly living" accepts the potentialities and aspirations of the world and works within these, without attempting to foist onto them a "clericalist" or "churchly" garb. If the Church exists "not . . . to deprive the world of a piece of its territory, but precisely in order to prove to the world that it is still the world . . . which is loved by God," [53] then the world's activities in which the Christian is involved should be recognized as having, in Christ, a freedom of their own. Bonhoeffer speaks often of the Church's mandate to "allow the world to be what it really is before God," clearly designating a new freedom, rather than any Church control.

The roots of a firmly Christ-centered theology of secularity are present here. And though not until the prison letters will Bonhoeffer commend the "world come of age" for shaking off the fetters of religion, already in the *Ethics* he speaks sympathetically of the process of secularization going on within Western culture. There is, he thinks, a healthy secularity, which belongs in the world; however, there is likewise a disastrous secularity, which grows like a cancer at the heart of the Church and readily dislocates Christ. Luther reacted to this later secularity violently. Bonhoeffer perceptively remarks:

> Luther was protesting against a Christianity which was striving for independence and detaching itself from the reality of Christ. He protested with the help of the secular and in the name of a better Christianity. So, too, today, when Christianity is employed as a polemical weapon against the secular, *this must be done in the name of a better secularity and above all it must not lead back to a static predominance of the spiritual sphere as an end in itself.*[54] (italics added)

In the light of the Church-world thought of the *Ethics,* it becomes clear that the Church took on for Bonhoeffer not simply a fresh doctrinal formulation, but an entirely new meaning. The traditional notions of the Church, as a fortress of the faithful protesting against the world's onslaughts, as a gathering of Christians to pray and share in a "religious" experience, or even as the place where the Word is preached and sacraments offered to men—all these interpretations lacked the one life-giving power: bearing Christ's commitment to the world. Bonhoeffer turned the idea of the Church inside out. In doing so, he restored to it much of the vitality and social concern absent from ecclesiology for centuries.

Any judgment on the significance of the Church-world doctrine upon Bonhoeffer's maturing thought would have to await the prison letters, where this doctrine is carried to its conclusion in a "religionless" version of Christianity. But the real judgment, the impact of the doctrine on the Church, can only be seen in final measure in the Church's opening out to the needs of the poor, the depressed, the value-stricken middle classes. Here, after all, is what Bonhoeffer was looking for in his theology. "The Church is her true self only when she exists for humanity." [55] Bonhoeffer's doctrine will only be its true self when the Church begins to witness before men the love of God for the world, and in that witness, serve.

Departure from the Ethical

Bonhoeffer's ethics, as much as it can be called an ethics, is grounded in his concept of a Church to the world. With his ethics Bonhoeffer reaches the avowed purpose of his book and handles many of the questions which had come to absorb him since the dissolution of Finkenwalde. Here, likewise, he takes full advantage of his anthropology, using it as a seedbed for his ethical doctrine.

The most emphatic point Bonhoeffer makes about Christian ethics is that in the older conception of ethics a Christian ethical theory is impossible.

> The knowledge of good and evil seems to be the aim of all ethical reflection. The first task of Christian ethics is to invalidate this knowledge. . . . Christian ethics stands so completely alone that it becomes questionable whether there is any purpose in speaking of Christian ethics at all.[56]

Actually, it is not so much the presence of a Christian ethics that Bonhoeffer is challenging, as the nature of that ethics. His point centers in the conflict of good and evil. The fall of Adam brought to the human race a constant struggle between good and evil, a struggle which made the knowledge of good and evil the fundamental basis of ethical choice. Human life came to be seen only in the white and black of the right or wrong ethical choice. There was room for nothing else. Fallen man's overriding concern was ethical, the proper choice between good and evil. Hence, there came about, Bonhoeffer suggests, the predominant role of Law in the Old Testament, the highly keen sense of ethical choice, and the eventual rise of the Pharisee as the characteristic religious leader.

"The Pharisee," Bonhoeffer says,

> is the man to whom only the knowledge of good and evil has come to be of importance in his entire life; in other words, he is simply the man of disunion. . . . For the Pharisee every moment of life becomes a situation of conflict in which he has to choose between good and evil. As a result, he cannot confront another man in any other way than by examining him with regard to his decisions in the conflicts of life.[57]

In short, the Pharisee is an ethical monster, created by and recreating the exaggeration of good and evil as the essence of life.

In reconciling the world with God, Christ abruptly destroyed the knowledge of good and evil as the basis of ethical choice. Man was freed, and that freedom meant that no longer was he obstructed everywhere by the need for ethical choice. Bonhoeffer sees in the clash between the Pharisees and Christ precisely the crisis which Jesus has brought to ethic-centered man. The confrontations in the gospels, especially in Matthew 22, show what is happening. As Bonhoeffer comments,

> The crucial point about all these arguments is that Jesus does not allow himself to be drawn into a single one of these conflicts and decisions. With each of his answers he simply leaves the case of conflict beneath him. . . . Jesus' answers do not appear to be answers at all, but rather attacks of his own against the Pharisees, which is what they, in fact, are.[58]

The clash is decisive. It reveals that Christ, the man of union, lives in a sphere of moral freedom completely foreign to those men of total disunion. More to the point, Christ reveals the new mode of ethical life which He has brought to those willing to share in His life. The confinement of ethical categories, the inability to perceive the fluid, simple content of human life: all this is overcome by the man who shares in Christ's life and moral freedom.

The tragedy—and Bonhoeffer here addresses his remarks to theoretical ethicists—is that many people, including supposed Christians, have not realized this new freedom. "The academic question of a system of ethics," he admits, speaking specifically of the modern generation, "seems to be of all questions the most superfluous." [59] And he says elsewhere of the ethical effort that narrows life into the terms of good and evil: "It turns the moralist into a dangerous tormentor, tyrant and clown, a figure of tragicomedy." [60] Throughout the development of a Christian ethics purged of the old ethical categories, he consistently denounces any attempt to segment and organize ethical imperatives.

What then *is* the ethical for Bonhoeffer? Fundamentally, the ethical remains the problem of deciding a moral choice without a clear recognition of the good. But in truth the truly ethical moments occur infrequently. Bonhoeffer questions how often the moral course is not self-evident—surely not every moment, perhaps only rarely. This disparity of the need for ethical choice within the whole context of life brings Bonhoeffer to conclude that life is larger, and really more important, than ethics. He is most emphatic on the point.

> But precisely this proper delimiting of the place and of the time is of crucial importance if one is to prevent a pathological overburdening of life by the ethical, if one is to prevent that abnormal fanaticization and total moralization of life which has as its consequence that those processes of concrete life which are not properly subject to general principles are exposed to constant criticism, fault-finding, admonition, correction and general interference.[61]

Effectively, then, a man's ethical concerns should be subordinated to the larger, more imminent concerns of life—work, family, leisure. Bonhoeffer is highly critical of the crisis theologians in this point who assume that man must continually be doing something decisive.

The positive notion of a Christian ethics is rooted deeply in Bonhoeffer's thought, and it is important to see the question in the perspective of his growing ideas on the Christian's life in the world. While in Spain at the age of 22, Bonhoeffer had written an address entitled, "What Is a Christian Ethic?" The ring is familiar.

Ethics is a matter of earth and of blood, but also of him who made both; the trouble arises from this duality. There can be ethics only in the framework of history, in the concrete situation, at the moment of the divine call, the moment of being addressed, of the claim made by the concrete need and the situation for decision, of the claim which I have to answer and for which I have to make myself responsible. Thus there cannot be ethics in a vacuum, as a principle; there cannot be good and evil as general ideas, but only as qualities of will making a decision.[62]

Many departures from this viewpoint would be made in the later, far more conclusive *Ethics;* but Bonhoeffer keeps the same emphasis, if undergirding it with a firmer Christology.

Throughout his mature writings, Bonhoeffer calls attention to the impasse of the Confessing Church, demanding the search for fresh ethical inquiry.

The great masquerade of evil has wrought havoc with all our ethical preconceptions. This appearance of evil in the guise of light, beneficence and historical necessity is utterly bewildering to anyone nurtured in our traditional ethical systems.[63]

Elsewhere he points out a discovery which made older ethical systems seem obsolete: "The greatest of all the dangers which threatened the Church with inner disintegration and disruption lay in the neutrality of large numbers of Christians." [64] The result is a concentration, in his fresh approach to ethics, upon the elements of his anthropology, his Church-world doctrine, upon integrity, action in the world, and a perceptive and responsible life.

The central question which Bonhoeffer sets before himself in dealing with ethics is: What is the decisive ethical standard? Twice, once in the *Ethics* and again in the prison letters, he specifically discusses the question of an ethical standard and puts to the problem the traditional and modern answers: conscience, duty, free responsibility, private virtuousness. "It is the best of men," he sadly admits of all these standards, "who go under in this way, with all that they can do or be." [65] He sees following such ethical foundations as a futile, even ludicrous effort; he compares such men to Don Quixote, so serious and yet so laughable. On the contrary, the contemporary Christian must be a man who sees reality as it is and who acts responsibly, basing his action upon a clear vision of this reality.

The fundamental notion which Bonhoeffer challenges throughout his ethical thought, yet which lies at the root of any ethical formulation, is the concept of the good. He begins one discussion discarding from the outset as irrelevant the two questions, "How can I be good?" and "How can I do good?" The whole ethical notion of good has always been dangerous, Bonhoeffer says, because it encourages a self-centered style of moral life. "A desire to be good for its own sake, as an end in itself, so to speak, or as a vocation in life, falls victim to the irony of unreality." [66] Man turns to the sphere of the "ought," what Bonhoeffer concedes to be a dubious sphere, at the least. Man wonders about how "good" he is and tends to make an increase in this personal goodness *the* standard of his moral decisions. The "good" becomes the all-embracing and decisive idea in life, so much that life again is drained of all but the categories of good and evil, and their subsequent search for the "right answers." Clearly, Bonhoeffer is reacting again to the extreme of religiosity in which the Church assures security, but at the cost of "personal righteousness." Again, the Pharisee becomes the model of moral man—and not the simple person of Christ.

The point which Bonhoeffer makes urgently and which lies at the foundation of his own ethical thought is that a "theory of good" is fundamentally a dangerous aberration of true Christian ethics.

> Christ did not love a theory of good, but he loved the real man. He was not, like a philosopher, interested in the "universally valid," but rather in that which is of help to the real and concrete human being.[67]

For Bonhoeffer, the good is bound up with Christ and the concrete human moment. As an answer to his own question about the decisive ethical standard he states firmly: the will of God. However, he means by "the will of God" something highly existential:

The will of God is always concrete, or else it is not the will of *God*. In other words, the will of God is not a principle from which one has to draw inferences and which has to be applied to "reality." A "will of God" which can be recognized without immediately leading to action is a general principle, but it is not the will of God.[68]

Good cannot be confined to principles; it cannot be held out as an ethical category. Good is reality, the human and divine, "reality seen and recognized in God." Indeed, only the man of deep faith can ever act ethically.

. . . Reality cannot be helped by even the purest of principles . . . but only by the living God. Principles are only tools in God's hands, soon to be thrown away as unserviceable. To look in freedom at God and at reality, which rests solely upon him, this is to combine simplicity with wisdom.[69]

Bonhoeffer outlines a few of the consequences of such an approach. The concrete nature of the good means that the ethical is destroyed by being detached from its concrete relations.

The question of the good is posed and is decided in the midst of each definite, yet unconcluded, unique, and transient situation of our lives, in the midst of our living relationships with men, things, institutions and powers, in other words, in the midst of our historical existence. The question of good cannot now be separated from the question of life, the question of history.[70]

By taking the point further, "the good demands the whole, not only the whole of a man's outlook but his whole work, the whole man, together with the fellow-men who are given to him." [71] The presumption of a human integrity is especially important here; without this integrity, the good can never be recognized.

The question of good embraces man with his motives and purposes, with his fellow-men and with the entire creation around him; it embraces reality as a whole, and it is held in being by God.[72]

The major implications for a style of renewed moral life as Bonhoeffer sees it are fourfold: an undergirding integrity of the person, a mind sensitized to meeting moral problems concretely, a clear summons to action in the world, and a breadth of experience in life. Each implication will be looked at briefly.

Bonhoeffer's ethics has often been described as relativist or "situational." Admittedly it is, although from different reasons than those which lie behind the situation ethics of other recent theologians. Bonhoeffer's concrete ethics originates in the Incarnation and his anthropology. The presumption of a person's wholeness is important here, for unless the man has truly been "united with himself," Bonhoeffer would admit that a completely concrete ethics is beyond the range of his moral powers. The Pharisee, who typifies disunited man, is certainly incapable of living out a concrete ethics; the demands of appreciating a situation, reflecting upon it, and perceiving the inner moral imperative, are too much for the Pharisee.

Bonhoeffer stresses secondly the concrete and immediate nature of the truly ethical experience. His starting point is the Incarnation linked with his doctrine of conformation. "What can and must be said is not what is good once and for all, but the way in which Christ takes form among us here and now." [73] In an essay written in the Tegel prison and appended to the *Ethics,* "What Is Meant by 'Telling the Truth'?" Bonhoeffer proposes the concrete ethic applied to human veracity. During the time he was writing this essay, Bonhoeffer was often drawn from his cell for several hours at a time and grilled thoroughly about his suspected involvement in the resistance. Dietrich was able to "lie" fluently and consistently enough to quiet suspicions. But the dilemma gave him a chance to think out the *context* of telling the truth—and the context of any moral act.

"Telling the truth," he wrote, "means something different according to the particular situation in which one stands." [74] A captured soldier, for example, should be extremely cautious in what he says. So should parents be discreet in what they tell their children. Bonhoeffer carries the point further. "An individual utterance," he states, "is always part of a total reality which seeks expression in this utterance. If my utterance is to be truthful it must in each case be different according to whom I am addressing." [75] In effect, then, "telling the truth . . . is not solely a matter of moral character; it is also a matter of correct appreciation of real situations and of serious reflection upon them." [76] Telling the truth must be learned; it is something with no guiding laws to hold up dictatorially over all situations.

Bonhoeffer emphasized likewise the summons to action inherent in Christian ethics. "The good of which Jesus speaks consists entirely in action," [77] Bonhoeffer states. The whole man cannot hear and fail to carry out that belief in action. The Protestant tradition, with its explicit distinction between the person and his work, has implicitly encouraged an ethics which pays lip service to action. Bonhoeffer especially lashes out with stinging force at those people—theologians, pastors, laymen—who theorize about ethics but miss their chance to alter the course of history by becoming involved in the world in those times when society is being reshaped. There are times when the ethical theme no longer needs stating, times when action alone is needed. Bonhoeffer's disappointment in the Confessing Church is again evident.

The fourth implication of Bonhoeffer's study of the "good" is the fullness of life which should precede and guide ethical choices. The whole man in Christ is the man of the anthropology: man capable of meeting life on its own terms, stepping forward with courage and the faith that in this moment he will be conformed to Christ. Consequently, Bonhoeffer sees ethics not as leading away from an enriched human life, but as leading *to* an even more intense and committed life:

> Ethics and ethicists do not intervene continuously in life. They draw attention to the disturbance and interruption of life by the "shall" and the "should" which impinge on all life from its periphery. . . .

[They] do not wish to represent goodness . . . as an end in itself . . . they wish to help people to learn to share in life, to share in life within the limits of the obligations of "shall" and "should," and not to hold themselves aloof from the processes of life as spectators, critics and judges. . . .[78]

The four implications—human wholeness, a mature ability to perceive the inner moral demands of the concrete situation, the summons to action, and a sense of life—suggest how strongly Bonhoeffer's ethics is directed to the Christian's life in the world. Indeed, the truly ethical man is man who looks to Christ and acts responsibly in history. Bonhoeffer concludes one chapter, "The Concept of Reality," defining the purpose of true ethical inquiry:

Its purpose is, therefore, participation in the reality of God and of the world in Jesus Christ today, and this participation must be such that I never experience the reality of God without the reality of the world or the reality of the world without the reality of God.[79]

Elsewhere, he condemns any ethical effort which does not take part in the world's struggles and ardor, its passions and crises:

The cultivation of a Christian inner life, untouched by the world, will generally present a somewhat tragicomical appearance to the worldly observer. For the sharp-sighted world recognizes itself most distinctly at the very point where the Christian inner life deceives itself in the belief that the world is most remote.[80]

Bonhoeffer's ethics, although never labelled as such by him, is obviously a "worldly ethics," and does serve as the basis for his later concept of "worldly holiness." One of the key criticisms running throughout his discussion of ethics has been of man's instinctive desire to set up a moral law over man's personal inner life and to follow the light of that law. Bonhoeffer prizes life in the world too highly, however. He has rejected a moral life controlled from without by any foreordained law. Wholeness, freedom, the presence of Christ: these are the ethical demands which Bonhoeffer recognizes and which he hails.

With a Church-world doctrine in which responsibility is

posited as the Church's link with the world, Bonhoeffer has set the foundation for an ethics demanding total adherence to Christ in the concrete situations of worldly life. The conclusions, however, are yet tentative; Bonhoeffer would continue the same line of thinking in his prison cell, and would eventually explore the enormous implications of a Church responsible to the world. It is tragic that he died after the preliminary effort of tearing away the primary obstacle to this exploration: the Church's "religious premise." The positive description of "religionless Christianity"—containing the *complete* Church-world doctrine, not simply its beginnings—is more mystery than description, for Bonhoeffer has left behind him only fragments.

There is all the difference in the world between a month in prison and a whole year. A year brings not only interesting and intense impressions, but opens up a wholly new and far-reaching sphere of life.

Letter of April 26, 1944, to his parents

12. *The Prison Writings*

There can be little question that of all Bonhoeffer's writings, the most provocative and the most influential have been the letters which he wrote and smuggled out during his two years in prison. The letters and fragmentary essays of this period reveal a maturity and a lucidity of thought willing to grapple with searing, frightening questions in a totally honest way. No theologian of our century has so seriously questioned the premises of our "Christian beliefs" as Bonhoeffer has. No theologian has thrust the Church into the world and so honestly explored the implications as Bonhoeffer has. Above all, no one, with the possible exception of Teilhard de Chardin, has brought to the world a vision of Christ large enough, embracive enough, to make full-hearted life in the secular efforts of our time a Christian imperative.

Why should the prison years be so decisive, so illuminating? The story of Bonhoeffer's stay, especially as revealed through his letters, is humanly inspiring, if seemingly senseless and at times grim. His description of the first days suggests the new conditions he had to live with:

The formalities of admission were correctly completed. For the first night I was locked into an admission cell. The blankets on the bed exuded such a bestial smell that in spite of the cold it was impossible to use them. The next morning a piece of bread was thrown into my cell; I had to pick it up from the floor. A quarter of the coffee consisted of grounds. The sound of the warders' vile abuse of the prisoners penetrated into my cell for the first time; since then I have heard it every day from morning to night. On parade all the new arrivals were addressed by one of the warders as "scoundrels," etc. We were all asked the reason for our detention. I said that I did not know why I was detained. The warder laughed scornfully and said, "You'll find out soon enough." It was six months before a warrant for my arrest arrived. . . . I was taken to the most isolated single cell on the top floor; a notice prohibiting all access without special permission was put outside. I was told that all my correspondence would be stopped until further notice and that, unlike all the other prisoners, I would not be allowed half an hour a day in the open air, though, according to the prison rules, I was certainly entitled to it. I received neither newspapers nor cigarettes. After forty-eight hours my Bible was returned to me; it had been searched for razor blades, a file, etc. During the next twelve days the cell door was only opened for food and in order to put out the bucket. Nobody said a word to me. I was told nothing about the reason for my detention or its duration. From various remarks I gathered—and this I confirmed later—that I was lodged in the section for the most serious cases, where the condemned and shackled prisoners lay.[1]

Tegel was a military jail; and when it was discovered that General von Hase, Berlin's commandant, was the cousin of Dietrich's mother, conditions swiftly changed. Dietrich kept the fiercely hot cell on the top floor, although he could have asked to change with a prisoner downstairs. He was permitted to receive gifts, and each week his mother or father, his sister Ursula, or his fiancée, Maria von Wedemeyer, could leave clean clothes, food, or books for him. After six months and after making a successful impression upon two of his guards, Bonhoeffer began smuggling uncensored letters to Eberhard Bethge, at that time a Wehrmacht soldier.

Bonhoeffer knew that the S. S. had nothing convincing about his activities in the resistance movement, that he was being kept only for avoiding conscription. He wrote in an early letter to Bethge, "The charge on which I would be condemned is so unobjectionable that I should actually be proud of it." [2] Meanwhile, he was pulled from his cell for endless and meaningless preliminary hearings. Much of his free time was spent in committing to scraps of paper the lies about his work in the *Abwehr* which would sound consistent and convincing. The effort to lie coolly and perseveringly was an intense and dangerous one, but Bonhoeffer succeeded.

The letters which Bonhoeffer wrote during those years were fortunately preserved by Bethge and by Dietrich's mother. Bethge's letters had been packed inside tin cans and buried in his garden. Unfortunately, a large number of letters could not be preserved. The greatest loss was probably the sheaf of letters from September, 1944 (the book, *Letters and Papers from Prison,* closes with a letter from August), which Bethge destroyed shortly before his own arrest in October.

Bonhoeffer likewise wrote a number of essays, on "The Sense of Time," "On the Possibility of the Word of the Church to the World," "The First Table of the Ten Commandments," and "What Is Meant by 'Telling the Truth'?" Beyond the essays, he attempted other literary forms; still extant are a number of revealing poems, an incomplete drama, and an unfinished novel.

The prison letters reveal Dietrich Bonhoeffer as no other writings have: as a personal, warm, and holy man; a man concerned at one moment with a monumental reinterpretation of Christianity, and at another asking his parents for "some tooth paste and a few coffee beans." Few theologians have been exposed in the highly personal light of Dietrich Bonhoeffer's letters. Extremely few would have fared so well.

The letters reveal prison life as Bonhoeffer felt it. He describes with a fresh delight the small joys of January sunshine, fragments of chorales carried to his cell on a Sunday breeze, even the reliable peals of the six o'clock prison bells. Although he had numerous books and read and wrote constantly, the heavy concentration on intellectual matters disturbed him.

And yet, you know, I should like to feel the full force of the sun again, burning the skin and making the whole frame glow, and reminding me that I have still got a body. If only I could get tired of the sun, instead of books and thoughts! I should love to have my animal existence awakened, not the kind that degrades a man, but the sort that delivers him from the stuffiness and spuriousness of a purely intellectual existence and makes him purer and happier.[3]

New themes emerge in these letters, and Bonhoeffer pursues —sometimes brilliantly, sometimes ponderously, sometimes pedantically—such thoughts as the home, solitude, foolishness, middle-class life, recollection. He comments frequently about his fellow prisoners, possibly about an enriching discussion he may have had with one, though more often about their inability to adjust humanly to prison life. Some of his comments become stinging, almost brutal:

Everybody here seems to gossip indiscriminately about his private affairs, no matter whether others show any interest or not, merely for the sake of hearing themselves speak. . . . It often fills me with shame here to see how readily men demean themselves just for a bit of gossip, how they prate incessantly about their own private affairs to people who don't deserve it, and who hardly even listen. And the strangest thing about it is that they have no regard whatever for truth; all they want to do is to talk about themselves, whether what they say is true or not.[4]

His own response to the prison is anything but a deteriorating despair. "Joy," he writes typically, "is something we can do with very badly here; it's such a serious place, no one ever laughs. It seems to get even the warden down." [5] He admits the agony of the empty, daily routine, coupled with a dreadful homesickness. Yet he forces from himself a more demanding routine. The danger of losing order by sleeping in after six in the morning, for example, is a thought that frightens him. "A good piece of self-discipline is to do a daily dozen every morning and have a cold wash down, which is a real support to one's morale," [6] he says with almost monastic confidence.

Yet Bonhoeffer learned from the prison. "Prison life," he admits at one point, brings home to a man how nature carries on its quiet, care-free life quite unconcerned, and makes one feel almost sentimental towards animal and plant life—except for flies; I can't work up any sentiment towards them! [7]

The growth of a deeper wisdom is evident:

Above all, we should avoid getting absorbed in the present moment, and foster that peace of mind which springs from noble thoughts, measuring all other things by them. . . . It is weakness rather than wickedness that degrades a man, and it needs profound sympathy to put up with that.[8]

Probably one of the most beautiful features of the prison letters are Dietrich's recurring comments on friendship. In an elaborate, theologically-tainted discussion of friendship, he places it within the sphere of freedom; yet his personal comments to Bethge are far warmer, and more revealing. Following a visit in November with his parents, his fiancée, and Bethge, Bonhoeffer wrote:

When I got back to my cell afterwards I paced up and down for a whole hour, while my dinner lay waiting for me on the table until it got quite cold, and in the end it made me laugh when I caught myself saying from time to time, "How wonderful it was!" I never like calling anything "indescribable," for it is a word you hardly ever need use if you take the trouble to express yourself clearly, but at the moment that's just what this morning seems to be.[9]

He asks Bethge, later, should he be released from prison, whether it would be possible to join his regiment. Bonhoeffer's thoughts on other people slowly take on body:

In the last month or two I have learned for the first time in my life how much comfort and help I get from others. . . . When we want to calculate just how much we have learned ourselves and how much we owe to others, it is not only un-Christian, but useless. What we are in ourselves, and what we owe to others makes us a complete whole.[10]

And in one period of fear about the dangerous future:

And if it should be decided that we never meet again, let us remember one another to the end with thoughts of gratitude and forgiveness—and may God grant that we may stand together before his throne one day, praying for one another and joining together in praise and thanksgiving.[11]

Prison life did not go on for Bonhoeffer without events—dramatic, international, or at home. Berlin bombings and the terror among the prisoners during the bombings kept even the well-guarded inmates at the edge of the War. In May, 1943, only two months after his imprisonment, Eberhard Bethge married Dietrich's niece, Renate. The child born a year later was christened Dietrich, and Bonhoeffer wrote a baptism sermon for him, which included some of his most forward thinking on the future Church. In a letter to Bethge written while contemplating pictures of young Dietrich, Bonhoeffer wrote:

I think he's lovely, and if he takes after me in looks, I only hope he will be as free from toothache and headache as I am, and be blessed with my leg muscles and sensitive gums—though that can sometimes be a disadvantage. For other things he can do better elsewhere. . . . He has also inherited the best thing about me, my name. . . . Believe me, I shall always be a good godfather to him and do all I can to help him. In fact, I don't believe he could have a better one![12]

Beyond his growing ability to live sensitively and sympathetically, Bonhoeffer's developing thought and the influences which silently shaped it over the prison months demand attention. It was not until late April, 1944, that he described the ideas which would guide the theologians of a decade. In the meantime he came to read and question with a freedom which had been denied him since the academic years at Berlin. His reading, described in the books he asked for throughout the letters home, testifies to a wide range of interests. He read far more than the copious theological tomes of the university days. Some books which he admits impressed him were von Weizsacker's *The World View of Physics,* W. E. Otto's *The Homeric Gods,* Harnack's *History of the Prussian Academy,* and the extensive works of two important literary figures, Goethe and Stifter. He admits, however, "My real ambition was to become thoroughly familiar with the nineteenth century in Germany." [13] His reading was almost entirely confined to 19th century German thought and literature, and he remarked once of the period:

Hardly anyone has the slightest idea what was achieved during the last century by our own grandfathers. How much of what they knew has already been forgotten! I believe people will one day be utterly amazed at the fertility of that age, now so much despised and so little known.[14]

He likewise read the Bible with a renewed concentration, especially the Old Testament. His insights into the theology behind the Old Testament beliefs gradually built toward the severe questions and radical suggestions of the later months.

The other influences are apparent. A major one, which kept the sense of a new beginning alive, was Bonhoeffer's continuing hope that his prison term would be short-lived, and that once the resistance effort had destroyed Hitler (which he expected would happen any day), he would soon take part in the reconstruction of Germany. Another influence came in the condition of his fellow prisoners. Their frequent inability to cope with the strains of prison life brought home to him the drastic need for men of strength, a need stressed in the *Ethics* and now confirmed all the more forcefully in the letters.

To look upon Bonhoeffer's thoughts on "religionless Christianity" and the "non-religious interpretation of biblical concepts" as emerging solely from his reading and thought of the prison months, however, is to miss a central element in the pattern of his mature theology. Bonhoeffer's growing self-consciousness, his heightened self-reflection, combined with a distaste for unhealthy introspection, his constant efforts to unearth the moral failures of his generation—these factors brought out in him a continuous, probing search for a moral identity and a freedom which together mark the man conformed to Christ. His poem, "Who Am I?" written in response to his popular image among the prisoners as a saint and comforter suggests the tone and thoroughness of the search:

Who am I? They often tell me
I stepped from my cell's confinement
Calmly, cheerfully, firmly,
Like a squire from his country-house. . . .

Who am I? They also tell me
I bore the days of misfortune
Equably, smilingly, proudly,
Like one accustomed to win.

Am I then really all that which other men tell of?
Or am I only what I myself know of myself?
Restless and longing and sick, like a bird in a cage,
Struggling for breath, as though hands were compressing my throat,
Yearning for colors, for flowers, for the voices of birds,
Thirsting for words of kindness, for neighborliness,
Tossing in expectation of great events,
Powerlessly trembling for friends at infinite distance,
Weary and empty at praying, at thinking, at making,
Faint, and ready to say farewell to it all?[15]

Bonhoeffer asked the question elsewhere, in a letter to Bethge; it is the same question, with the same frightened overtones:

Am I the man who keeps scourging himself and outwardly pretends to others (and to himself as well) that he is a contented, cheerful, easy-going fellow, and expects everyone to admire him for it?[16]

Bonhoeffer recognized, however, the importance of such searching: "There is something more at stake than self-knowledge." [17] Indeed, the honesty with which Bonhoeffer faced himself throughout the letters is impressive. "You are the only person," he wrote in his first letter to Bethge, "who knows how often I have nearly given away to *acedia, tristitia,* with all its damaging effects on the soul." [18] He kept trying to perceive the wider context of his search, and admitted, in speaking of the period after the War, that "the task laid on our generation will not be once more 'to desire great things,' but to save ourselves alive from the debris, as a brand plucked from the burning." [19]

The search for a moral identity provides, certainly, one of the guiding lines to the rebellion against religion and the effort to articulate a "religionless Christianity." The search appears in one form or another throughout the prison letters. Looking back, can infer that it led successfully to a serene death on that grim April morning at Flossenbürg.

It is surprising that despite the hardship of prison life, especially separation from his family at such a time of crisis, Bonhoeffer rarely complained about being at Tegel. On the contrary, he deeply believed that something worthwhile would emerge:

> The turbulent events in the world outside during the last few days make me feel how much I should like to be somewhere where I could be useful. But for the time being my job is to stay in prison, and what I can do here makes its contribution to the unseen world, though that hardly comes under the category of active service.[20]

Throughout these months the growing suspicion of religion and the notion of a Christianity centered in the anthropology of man conformed to Christ can be seen slowly emerging. The themes basic to the anthropology—the penultimate, a healthy polyphony of life, meeting the moment in its fullness—resound over and over again, giving the letters that spontaneous and provocative charm which is distinctively theirs. Already in November, 1943, Bonhoeffer mentioned his growing intolerance for the religious:

> Don't worry, I won't come out of here a *homo religiosus!* On the contrary my suspicion and horror of religiosity are greater than ever. I often think of how the Israelites never uttered the name of God. I can understand that much better than I used to.[21]

When finally Bonhoeffer did develop his ideas at length, events brought his writings to a close before he could. The Normandy landing, June 6, 1944, was a clear sign to Bonhoeffer—and, he knew, to the other resistance figures—that the end of the War was approaching. One of the stated goals of Oster's resistance group had been to cut short the War by seizing power before a total Allied Victory. The invasion of France demanded the immediate destruction of the Führer, if Germany was to survive.

After the imprisonment of Hans von Dohnanyi and Dietrich

Bonhoeffer, the resistance center at the *Abwehr* had taken on a different color. Oster had been banned from his office. A new figure had taken over much of Beck's and Oster's former leadership, Claus Schenk, Count von Stauffenberg. A young man of rare nerve and inspiring fortitude, Stauffenberg decided single-handedly to murder Hitler. As full colonel and appointed Chief of Staff to General Fromm, Stauffenberg had the most precious advantage of anyone in the *Abwehr* circle—access to Hitler's staff conferences.

The date was July 20, 1944. Stauffenberg carried his briefcase, equipped with bomb and timing mechanism, into the wolf's lair, Hitler's conference station in East Prussia. On the pretext of making a telephone call, Stauffenberg left the room; he heard the explosion a few moments later. The Count rushed back to Berlin to alert his men to take control of central communications, and eventually to take over the army. But the hope was futile. Hitler lived, and he moved quickly and effectively to destroy the movement.

The purge that directly followed the attempted assassination was bloody and reckless. By midnight Colonel Stauffenberg and a number of others involved in the plot were shot at the resistance headquarters. Clues appeared, and although it took months to follow them up, the Gestapo eventually reached the older roots of the July 20 attempt. In early October, 1944, Bonhoeffer was abruptly transferred from Tegel to the Gestapo's maximum security prison on Berlin's Prinz-Albrechtstrasse. The original order was to execute everyone implicated immediately, but Hitler intervened and asked that a number of the conspirators be kept alive and tortured to secure the names of further conspirators. Bonhoeffer was kept alive.

In February, 1945, as the Russian armies closed in upon Berlin from the East, Bonhoeffer and other important prisoners were transported to Buchenwald. The American forces now crowded in from the southwest. Beginning April 3, Bonhoeffer and fifteen other Buchenwald prisoners were driven in a small truck between camps and prisons which were too overcrowded to take more. On April 7, a bus appeared. The driver found a bridge, and after crossing the Danube, the prisoners spent the night in a Bavarian schoolhouse. The next day was Sunday, April 8. As Payne Best, a British Secret Service Agent present with Bonhoeffer, later wrote:

Pastor Bonhoeffer held a little service and spoke to us in a manner which reached the hearts of all, finding just the right words to express the spirit of our imprisonment and the thoughts and resolutions which it had brought. He had hardly finished his last prayer when two evil-looking men in civilian clothes came in and said: "Prisoner Bonhoeffer. Get ready to come with us." Those words, "come with us"—for all prisoners they had come to mean one thing only—the scaffold. We bade him goodbye—he drew me aside—"This is the end," he said; "for me, the beginning of life." And then he gave me a message to give, if I could, to the Bishop of Chichester.[22]

Again Bonhoeffer was traveling on the road, although this time knowing where he would be going. The car pressed through the thin-partitioned sector which still belonged to Germany. Only a few days later, the entire region would fall into Allied control. When Bonhoeffer reached the concentration camp and crematorium at Flossenbürg, he was put through a mock high treason trial. Then, as the dawn broke, he filed into the sandy courtyard alongside Canaris, Oster, and other leading resistance figures. There he was hanged. The body, like those of his companions, was dumped into the giant crematorium. "There is no grave," writes Bethge. "The ashes were scattered in the wind. There was no religious comfort and ceremony around him. The camp, stoves, uniforms in a dreary quarry, that was the last. No shroud, no hymn, no church." [23]

Bethge and Bonhoeffer's own family did not discover his fate with certainty until months later, when they heard the memorial service given for him in Trinity Church, Kingsway, which was broadcast over B.B.C. The Bishop of Chichester spoke there. And men who had known Bonhoeffer began to assess the disaster that had befallen the Church in Germany.

The letters from prison which survived, and which testify to a startling growth in Bonhoeffer's thought, range from pleasant notes to his parents within weeks after he was taken to Tegel, to the important final letters to Bethge which have been preserved up to August 23, 1944. These later letters, boldly pursuing the theme of a Christian life stripped of its religious premise, have aroused every reaction conceivable: vehemence, shock, intolerance, confusion, agreement, enthusiasm. Karl Barth has said of Bonhoeffer's non-religious interpretation of biblical concepts that he can reach a certain understanding of it, which is no real understanding.[24] Bethge has reported a remark made sincerely at a pastor's conference: "We can only hope that at the very last Bonhoeffer recovered his faith again." [25]

Dietrich Bonhoeffer himself realized that his thinking would provoke some severe reactions. Early in his correspondence with Bethge, he commented on the penultimate:

> You cannot and must not speak the last word before you have spoken the next to last. We live on the next to last word, and believe in the last, don't we? Lutherans (so-called) and pietists would be shocked at such an idea, but it is true all the same.[26]

He slightly suggested such a reaction once or twice later; but it seems clear that Bonhoeffer was not concerned about the impression his thoughts would make. He wanted to get at the truth—by himself, and to a large extent for himself. "You would be surprised and perhaps disturbed," he wrote to Bethge, "if you knew how my ideas on theology are taking shape." [27]

Bonhoeffer, however, refused to believe that any changes of a crucial nature were at work reshaping his life or his thought. As he wrote to Bethge in the letter before the storm of questions which brought on his fresh thought:

> You say my time here will be very important for my work, and that you're looking forward to what I shall have to tell you later, and to read what I have produced so far. Well, you mustn't expect too much; I have certainly learned a great deal, but I don't think I have changed very much. There are some who change a lot, but some hardly change at all. I don't believe I have ever changed very much, except at two periods in my life, the first conscious impact of Papa's personality, and the second when I was abroad.[28]

Perhaps one of the reasons Bonhoeffer "undervaluated" the significance of his ideas about religion and a secular interpretation of biblical concepts is the direction by which he arrived at these ideas. Bonhoeffer *began* with a firm belief in the Incarnation and the Cross, and, consequently, in the potential of a renewed humanity. This belief led him to a criticism of religion, to an attempt to describe "religionless Christianity," and finally, to wholehearted recognition of the world come of age. The process is profoundly theological. Bonhoeffer does not begin, as he criticized Troeltsch and other liberal theologians for doing, with the "world come of age" and moving *toward* a self-styled "religionless Christianity." With a fear as grave as his fear of apathy and indolence, Bonhoeffer dreaded the easy reduction process which makes the Church an accessory to the world, and Christ a versatile conceptual tool.

With such a strong christological foundation, Bonhoeffer never thought his ideas were exceptionally "radical" or "dangerous." Yet from a theological point of view it was precisely his brilliant and insistent vision of the centrality and nearness of Christ which made his thought a dangerous threat to many views and dogmas of the past. For however much Bonhoeffer's thought is fragmentary and imprecise, it must be reckoned with; Bonhoeffer was a deeply serious theologian who tackled the most vital question of his age without for a moment losing sight of Christ.

The question which opens the floodgates of Bonhoeffer's new ideas appears in a letter dated April 30, 1944. The first questions are, it should be noted, specifically about Christ, not the world come of age. "The thing that keeps coming back to me is, what *is* Christianity, and indeed what *is* Christ, for us today?" [29] The question drops like an explosion. Thoughts about present practices and future needs appear rapidly, crowding one another out:

> The time when men could be told everything by means of words, whether theological or simply pious, is over, and so is the time of inwardness and conscience, which is to say the time of religion as

such. We are proceeding towards a time of no religion at all: men as they are now simply cannot be religious any more.[30]

Bonhoeffer's insistence on the presence and action of Christ had always characterized his thought. Yet not until the *Ethics* had he explored Christ's impact upon the world with enough depth and urgency to realize that a radical focus on Christ meant a radical focus on the world. As the distinguished German theologian, Gerhard Ebeling, stated in his perceptive essay on the prison letters, the doctrine of reconciliation—that man lives in a world where God and the cosmos are reunited—can be most demanding:

Really to grasp that reconciliation, to understand it thoroughly, to live it, to reckon with it in all its furthest implications, to make it expressible, communicable, to be able to express it liberatingly and redeemingly—that is a task which demands our being incessantly exercised by the question, what Christ really *is* for us today.[31]

Bonhoeffer's question, then, is a most potent one. It recalls the question at the source of much of Bonhoeffer's biblical exegesis throughout the 'thirties: "What did Jesus Christ mean to say to us today?" Now the question takes on a deeper, more unsettling form: What is Jesus Christ for the man who can no longer take religion seriously, the man who has fully felt the impact of the Darwinian and Freudian revolutions? What is Christ if the religious premise has to be cut away, like the dead half of a living body, from the Church? The question is above all a question about Christ, not man; and if Bonhoeffer summons his rich anthropology and a historical interpretation of "man come of age," it is only to see Christ more sharply.

The development of Bonhoeffer's Christology shows a growing equation of the power of Jesus Christ with the whole of reality. In *The Communion of Saints* and *Act and Being,* Bonhoeffer had approached Christ from the Church; Christ was seen, primarily, in His body, His presence in the Church. In the summer of 1933 he prepared a Christology class for his students at the University of Berlin. Here he clarified the importance and centrality of Christ, rather from a personal than a social or "worldly" sphere: "Christ is our center even when he stands on the periphery of our consciousness; he is our center even when Christian piety is forced to the periphery of our being." [32] The insight grew. In *The Cost of Discipleship* and *Life Together,* published five years after the Christology lectures, the personal commitment to Christ within a community was Bonhoeffer's restless concern. Not until *Ethics,* however, did the full scope of an original understanding of Christ emerge. Throughout the *Ethics,* no chapter from Scripture is quoted nearly as often as Colossians I, in which St. Paul describes the cosmic Christ:

> He is the image of the invisible God, the first-born of all creation; for in him all things were created, in heaven and on earth, visible and invisible, whether thrones or dominions, or principalities or authorities—all things were created through him and for him. He is before all things, and in him all things hold together (Col. 1. 15-17).

Two christological doctrines are developed in the *Ethics:* the Incarnation, which serves as a basis for the anthropology and the Church-world relationship; and Christ's Lordship, the temporal consequence of the Incarnation. The notion of Lordship is hardly a new one to Bonhoeffer. In the early 'thirties he continuously stressed the reality of the world under Christ's Lordship. In "Thy Kingdom Come," a conference given in November of 1932, Bonhoeffer had contrasted the Church under Christ (which recognizes it *is* under Christ) with the state (which may or may not recognize it). The idea of Lordship took on a clearer focus in the *Ethics;* here Bonhoeffer saw it as the "setting free" of all worldly institutions to pursue their unique goals and aspirations:

> The commandment of Jesus Christ does indeed rule over Church, family, culture and government; but it does so while at the same time setting each of these mandates free for the fulfillment of its own allotted functions.[33]

Bonhoeffer carried his point further; he saw Christ's Lordship not only as a liberation, but as the only possible liberation.

The dominion of Christ and the Decalogue do not mean that the secular institutions are made subservient to a human ideal of "natural law," not yet to the Church (this being a contradiction of the medieval Thomist doctrine), but they mean their emancipation for true worldliness, for the state to *be* a state, etc.[34]

Bonhoeffer's effort here is plain: he is constructing a theology of secular life upon the doctrine of Christ's Lordship. Even within the *Ethics* his assertions in this direction are strong and decisive. Under Christ the world comes into its own, and its new freedom and new autonomy are taken up in a higher unity which Bonhoeffer terms "Christonomy."

The effort of much of the decisive thought in the later prison letters is to explore this Lordship, which Bonhoeffer sees as fundamental to Christianity stripped of its religious premise. "Christ is . . . not an object of religion, but something quite different, indeed and in truth the Lord of the World." [35] Christ's Lordship, and its immediate consequence in terms of the Christian's responsibilities in the world, take on sharper and sharper form during the last months.

All this time, it should not be thought that Bonhoeffer conceived Christ's Lordship or His centrality as apparent to the world at large; quite the opposite. Bonhoeffer at no moment fails to remember that personal faith in Christ is the crux, in many ways, of His presence and action in the world. Like Luther he insists upon a deeply personal faith, rather than a bland consent to the precepts of the Church. In the sketchy outline to his book (which never survived), he stated:

What do we really believe? I mean, believe in such a way as to stake our whole lives upon it? The problem of the Apostles' Creed? "What must I believe?" is the wrong question. . . . Barth and the Confessing Church have encouraged us to entrench ourselves behind the "faith of the Church," and evade the honest question, what is our real and personal belief? Hence lack of fresh air, even in the Confessing Church. . . . We cannot, like the Catholics, identify ourselves *tout court* with the Church.[36]

His brief but acid comment about the Confessing Church,

which he could have applied to other churches as well, was made in the same outline: "Generally in the Confessing Church: standing up for the Church's 'cause', but little personal faith in Christ. 'Jesus' is disappearing from sight." [37]

As a consequence of his Christology, Bonhoeffer launched out on his castigation of an outworn religious premise and began searching for a new secular language. There can be no question that Bonhoeffer's vision of Christ and Christ's action upon man gives his awakening thought its major thrust. "How can men endure earthly tensions," he wrote, "if they know nothing of the tension between earth and heaven?" [38] Indeed, it soon becomes obvious that in Bonhoeffer's criticism of religion only a firm adherence to Christ as the source of attack could inspire a meaningful and faithful effort to handle the non-religious terms for biblical concepts.

The attack, following the onslaught of questions which Bonhoeffer threw open in the April 30 letter, came fiercely and brutally. At this first mention of "religion," Bonhoeffer recognized it not as one specific danger among others, but as the premise upon which traditional Christianity has hinged:

> Our whole nineteen-hundred-year-old Christian preaching and theology rests upon the "religious premise" of man. What we call Christianity has always been a pattern—perhaps a true pattern—of religion. But if one day it becomes apparent that this *a priori* "premise" simply does not exist, but was an historical and temporary form of human self-expression . . . it means that the linchpin is removed from the whole structure of our Christianity to date.[39]

What, exactly, does Bonhoeffer mean by "religion"? The question is central to an understanding of his mature thought, and only a careful study of his use of the word can unearth its full meaning. He suggests several times that religion means "to speak on the one hand metaphysically, and on the other individualistically. Neither of these is relevant to the Bible message of today." [40] There is, however, something incomplete about the categories of metaphysical and individualistic awareness, especially when compared with Bonhoeffer's sweeping judgments about the function of religion for nineteen centuries of Christianity. The whole truth comes much nearer in a discussion of recent history.

> Man has learned to cope with all questions of importance without recourse to God as a working hypothesis. In questions concerning science, art, and even ethics, this has become an understood thing which one scarcely dares to tilt at any more. But for the last hundred years or so it has been increasingly true of religious questions also: it is becoming evident that everything gets along without "God," and just as well as before.[41]

Bonhoeffer's most immediate and most urgent sense of the need to do away with the "religious premise" rises from such historical speculations. "Religion" as such is equated with man's effort to call upon God to "fill in for" some aspect of the world and life which man hasn't taken under control. As Gerhard Ebeling says, religion means "supplementing reality by God." [42]

Religion never meant for Bonhoeffer any exterior phenomenon or doctrinal truth. He considered it a mode of thought, albeit an often diseased mode of thought, more of a tone and approach than a conclusive dogmatic stand. This understanding made an explicit definition of religion all the more difficult —perhaps, in the final effort, impossible.

Bonhoeffer does give his critique of religion a doctrinal handle, however, by equating its importance for Christianity with St. Paul's problem of circumcision. The equation is a bold one; Bonhoeffer has stepped beyond making a simple analogy, and is suggesting that in the "new age," religion has the same irrelevance for Christians as the Law had for early Christians:

> The Pauline question whether circumcision is a condition of Justification is today, I consider, the question whether religion is a condition of salvation. Freedom from circumcision is at the same time freedom from religion.[43]

Bonhoeffer's equation makes a complete understanding of religion all the more important. With St. Paul, the extent and demands of the Law were sharply outlined; the same is hardly true of religion. *What* should be eliminated from the Church's practices? To what extent does religion infiltrate a Christian's beliefs, and his actions? How, as Bonhoeffer asks, do we speak of God without religion, i.e., without "the temporally influenced presuppositions of metaphysics, inwardness, and so on"? [44] The questions go on. How speak in a secular fashion of God? And what of the Church? As Bonhoeffer asks,

> In what way are we in a religionless and secular sense Christians, in what way are we the *Ekklesia,* "those who are called forth," not conceiving of ourselves religiously as specially favored, but as wholly belonging to the world? Then Christ is no longer an object of religion, but something quite different, indeed and in truth the Lord of the world. Yet what does that signify? [45]

The search for a new self-understanding runs throughout the questions and probing suggestions of the last prison letters; apparently Bonhoeffer feels that only through a fresh insight into the Christian's personal life severed from its religious roots can any change, any *metanoia,* come about.

Bonhoeffer himself hardly perceived the extremes to which his questions would drive him. He probably saw, if somewhat vaguely, that to overthrow the area of "religious understanding" meant to topple the usual manifestations of God to men—in other words, to leave Christians without the older ways of "sensing God." The result was almost inevitable, a recognition of "Christian atheism," a realization that to discover God in nature, in the "unknown" that science stands on the brink of knowing, or in man's deepest failings is not really to discover God at all. Such efforts to perceive God in the "unknown" result in a false and unnecessary religious delusion. A "Christian atheism" would challenge such efforts. Whether Bonhoeffer actually anticipated such a movement there is no way of knowing; the prison letters suggest that he would have welcomed it, provided, of course, it kept the proper christological perspective.

The roots of Bonhoeffer's devastating critique of religion reach back, as do the roots of all his later ideas, to the formative years both before and during the 'thirties. In his two theses the revelation-centered emphasis which he had drawn from Karl Barth kept him highly wary of man's efforts to construct the Church. In 1932 he excoriated Christians for falling into a "pious, Christian secularism," which amounts to the "Christian renunciation of God as the Lord of the earth." [46] In the same context he wrote:

We are otherworldly—ever since we hit upon the devious trick of being religious, yes even "Christian," at the expense of the earth. Otherworldliness affords a splendid place in which to live. Whenever life begins to become oppressive and troublesome a person just leaps into the air with a bold kick and soars relieved and unencumbered into so-called eternal fields. . . . An otherworldly Church can be certain that it will in no time win over all the weaklings, all who are only too glad to be deceived and deluded, all utopianists, all disloyal sons of the earth.[47]

The Cost of Discipleship and *Life Together* challenge a number of the religious premises that Bonhoeffer later describes, but not in an unequivocal way. Only in the *Ethics* does the critique of a religious, closed-off mentality on the part of Christians become a distinct judgment. From four points of view—Christ's Lordship, the anthropology (Bonhoeffer's vision of whole and responsible man), the Church to world doctrine, and the concrete ethics—he launches his criticism. It took only the months of reflective quiet which Bonhoeffer found in his prison cell to bring the criticism to the height it reached in the final months.

A sensitive question but nonetheless an important one in the critique of religion is Bonhoeffer's relationship to other theologians who had attempted a similar critique—notably Ludwig Feuerbach and Karl Barth.

Ludwig Feuerbach (1804-1872) lived and wrote in the turbulent years which felt the full impact of Georg Wilhelm Hegel, the great idealist philosopher. Feuerbach was primarily a theologian, although one who avoided the question of God, and attempted to clarify, instead, the nature of religion. A flagrant materialist, Feuerbach made a profound impact upon Karl

Marx, as can be seen in the latter's excoriation of religion as the "opium of the people."

Feuerbach's efforts, consistent throughout his works, to tear away the false God and uncover the real substance of religion, blazed the pathway for Marx, Nietzsche, Freud, and the 20th century temperament, which could see in religion little more than a cultural anachronism. In the process of his work, however, Feuerbach had clearly leveled theology to anthropology; there is no serious appeal to revelation in Feuerbach, only to man's experience. Karl Barth reacted violently to such a reduction of theology—violently enough, in fact, to swing full circuit and issue another critique of religion, with religion meaning a quite different thing.

Religion rises from man, says Barth, and it consists in man's efforts to create or project a God in man's own terms. Barth generally speaks of religion in contrast with revelation: "If man believed, he would listen, but in religion he talks. . . . If he believed, he would let God himself intercede for God, but in religion he ventures to grasp at God." [48] He repeats a favorite statement several times, "Religion is unbelief," which attacks the religious man who makes his own efforts the measure of his sanctification. It should be mentioned, however, that Barth's attitude toward religion is not totally negative; he admits that faith can, and is, nurtured in religion—but his main point is that religion should exist for faith, not the other way around.

In his own critique of religion, Bonhoeffer acknowledges Barth as the origin of the religious critique. "Barth was the first theologian to begin the criticism of religion—and that remains his really great merit. . . ." [49] But Bonhoeffer sees immediately the limitations of Barth's approach:

> But he set in its place religion the positivist doctrine of revelation which says in effect, "Take it or leave it": Virgin Birth, Trinity or anything else, everything which is an equally significant and necessary part of the whole, which latter has to be swallowed as a whole or not at all. This is not in accordance with the Bible.[50]

Bonhoeffer did not take after Barth in the revelation-dominated notion of religion. Indeed, despite his early links to Barth, it is clear that in his critique Bonhoeffer lies nearer to Feuerbach than to Barth—although Bonhoeffer's Christology sharply distinguishes him from Feuerbach. It is obvious that Barth and Bonhoeffer began their critiques from widely different vantage points. Barth wanted to emphasize the total gratuitousness and unmerited nature of revelation by contrasting it with religion. Bonhoeffer's critique sprang from a long period of reflection on the Lordship of Christ, compelled by painful observations of the world around him.

Throughout Bonhoeffer's numerous remarks on religion in the later prison letters, five characteristics emerge with strong consistency: God as a metaphysical support, the tendency to think in terms of two spheres, the use of God as a stopgap for the holes in our knowledge, man's weakness as his focus in relation to God, and the neurotic inwardness which makes the god of Christian life personal salvation. All of these characteristics can be summed up under the main notion of religion—the compulsive need to make room somewhere for God, "supplementing reality by God." [51] Throughout his comments on the historical growth of a "world come of age," Bonhoeffer refers back to this need, felt so deeply by the weak and the supporters of the Christian religion: ". . . it always seems to me that in talking thus we are only seeking frantically to make room for God." Or again: "At this point nervous souls start asking what room there is left for God now. . . ." [52]

The first characteristic, a metaphysical awareness of God, sees God as the completion of the world, a supernatural "second story" to the universe. "The 'beyond' of God," Bonhoeffer states emphatically, "is not the beyond of our cognitive faculties. The transcendence of epistemological theory has nothing to do with the transcendence of God." [53] A clearer statement can be found in the outline to his unwritten book:

> What do we mean by "God"? Not in the first place an abstract belief in his omnipotence, etc. That is not a genuine experience of God, but a partial extension of the world. . . . Our relation to God

is not a religious relationship to a supreme Being, absolute in power and goodness, which is a spurious conception of transcendence. . . .[54]

Bonhoeffer sees in the metaphysical summons of God a constant reversion to the limits of man's experience, and, as a result, to the boundaries of his real life. "The transcendental is not infinite and unattainable tasks, but the neighbor who is within reach in any given situation." [55] The criticism extends, actually, to any notion of God which attempts to know him in terms of what man does not know. As Bonhoeffer had suggested in *Act and Being,* "A God who 'is' isn't." A God known only as the completion of a supposedly incomplete world is hardly the Christian God, but merely the God of religion.

Resulting from the notion of God as a "superstructure" is the mentality described in *Ethics* as "thinking in terms of two spheres." The description provided in the *Ethics* is clear:

Reality as a whole now falls into two parts, and the concern of ethics is with the proper relation of these two parts to each other. In the scholastic scheme of things the realm of the natural is made subordinate to the realm of grace; in the pseudo-Lutheran scheme the autonomy of the orders of this world is proclaimed in opposition to the law of Christ. . . . In all these schemes the cause of Christ becomes a partial and provincial matter within the limits of reality. . . . So long as Christ and the world are conceived as two opposing and mutually repellent spheres, man will be left in the following dilemma; he abandons reality as a whole, and places himself in one or other of the two spheres. He seeks Christ without the world, or he seeks the world without Christ.[56]

The two spheres are a most convenient escape from the demands of the world in all its fury and pain. But the concept cuts even deeper than in discouraging hearty life in the world: it suffocates belief in the *real* Christ, the Christ of flesh and emotion, who belonged to the world as no man ever has. Here Bonhoeffer agrees somewhat with Barth that religion not only hinders the Word of God but subtly constricts man's full response to revelation.

The third characteristic, God as a "stopgap," strikes at religious leaders, preachers especially, who in their embarrassment that God is disappearing from the world, constantly search out the limits of men's capacities and achievements as the place where "God is":

Religious people speak of God when human perception is (often just from mental laziness) at an end, or human resources fail: it is in fact always the *deus ex machina* who is marched on to the stage either for the so-called solving of insoluble problems or as a support in human failure—always, that is to say, in exploitation of human weakness or on the borders of human existence. Of necessity, that can only go on until men can, by their own strength, push those borders a little further, so that God becomes superfluous as *deus ex machina*.[57]

This is one of Bonhoeffer's most persistent and severe criticisms of religious people; not only are they themselves incapable of accepting the new universe which man knows and gradually is coming to control, but they must attempt to convince others that God is "still to be found" at the other edge of science or experience. In explaining this notion, Bonhoeffer's thoughts about the world take on clearer shape. For example, in discussing friendship and the separation of friends, Bonhoeffer remarks: "It is nonsense to say that God fills the gap; he does not fill it at all, but rather what he does is precisely to keep it empty." [58]

The fourth characteristic is aligned with the third: for religious people, "God becomes the answer to life's problems, the solution of its distresses and conflicts." [59] Running through Bonhoeffer's anthropology is a lively confidence in man's strength, and repudiation of man's weakness. To judge from the length of the discussions about religious man's penchant for weakness, Bonhoeffer finds this "excuse" for God the most repelling.

We should find God in what we do know, not in what we don't. . . . This is true not only for the relation between Christianity and science, but also for wider human problems such as guilt, suffering and death. It is possible nowadays to find answers to these problems which leave God right out of the picture. It just isn't true to say that Christianity alone has the answers. In fact the Christian answers are no more conclusive or compelling than any of the others. . . . We must not wait until we are at the end of our tether: he must be found at the center of life, and not only in death; in health and vigor, and not only in suffering; in activity, and not only in sin. . . . Christ is the center of life, and in no sense did he come to answer our unsolved problems.[60]

The appeal which religion makes to man is an appeal to his weakness; Bonhoeffer sees in this idea a profound danger—that man at his most vulnerable and shameful point should find there his deepest relationship with God. Relationships of that sort could only breed a queer neurosis.

When God was driven out of the world, and from the public side of human life, an attempt was made to retain him at least in the sphere of the 'personal,' the 'inner life,' the private life. And since every man still has a private sphere, it was thought that he was most vulnerable at this point.[61]

In this particular context, Bonhoeffer goes on to chastise, if somewhat narrowly, the psychotherapists and novelists who are never satisfied until they have spied out man in his most personal, and very often unbecoming moments. Then he attacks the priests.

This irresponsibility and absence of bonds has its counterpart among the clergy in what I should call the "priestly" snugging around in the sins of men in order to catch them out. It is as though a beautiful house could only be known after a cobweb had been found in the furthermost corner of the cellar. From a theological point of view the error is twofold. First, it is thought that a man can be addressed as a sinner only after his weaknesses and meannesses have been spied out. Second, it is thought that man's essential nature consists of his inmost and most intimate background, and that is defined as his "interior life"; and it is in these secret human places that God is now to have his domain![62]

The final characteristic which Bonhoeffer describes is the inwardness in which a man sees little more than his own salvation, and the escape to a world beyond the earth. Bonhoeffer remarks about this inwardness frequently; he sees the two components of religion as an obsession with a metaphysical God, and an unhealthy inwardness.

The pietistic tradition in Protestant thought, and especially consequent devotional practices, provided Bonhoeffer with much to criticize. The central role afforded conscience, the often overwhelming concern for personal salvation, the steady tendency to reduce life to a moral battlefield: Bonhoeffer saw how these tendencies shrank the Christian life to a self-preoccupation, draining it of any concern for action, social responsibility, or true communion with God.

Bonhoeffer speaks often of life under Christ as being far more than something "of the heart." Describing God's Kingdom, for example, he says, "For it is a Kingdom stronger than war and danger . . . not a Kingdom of the heart, but one as wide as the earth, not transitory, but eternal. . . ." [63] He also speaks disparagingly of conscience, as he already had in the *Ethics:* "The man with a conscience fights a lonely battle against the overwhelming forces of inescapable situations which demand decisions. But he is torn apart by the extent of the conflicts. . . ." [64] Bonhoeffer's vehement attack on the moralization of life, a consequence of the "interior-centered" man, is also to be found in *Ethics.*

He is careful, however, to point out the important distinction between the interior-centered and the biblical man:

On the second point it must be said that the Bible does not recognize our distinction of outer and inner. And why should it? It is always concerned with *anthropos teleios,* the *whole* man, even where, as in the Sermon on the Mount, the Decalogue is pressed home to refer to inward disposition. It is quite unbiblical to suppose that a "good intention" is enough. What matters is the whole good. The discovery of inwardness, so-called, derives from the Renaissance, Petrarch perhaps. The "heart" in the biblical sense is not the inward life, but the whole man in relation to God. The view that man lives just as much from outwards to inwards as from inwards to outwards is poles apart from the view that his essential nature is to be understood from his intimate background.[65]

Combined, the five elements create a vivid, if mosaic, impression of the "religious premise" which Bonhoeffer is decrying. The impression Bonhoeffer leaves is one not at a great distance from Feuerbach, or Marx who followed him. Like Feuerbach, Bonhoeffer glorified in man's powers and dreaded the often disruptive and retarding effect of religion upon these powers. Like Feuerbach and Marx, Bonhoeffer wanted to speak to man in his strength, in his wholehearted life and aspirations. Perhaps for this reason, Bonhoeffer has been quite popular among theologians in Communist Germany. However, more important that the similarities is the one striking difference: Bonhoeffer's critique grew from, and was directed toward, an extraordinary faith in Christ, Lord of the world. Without this faith such a critique would be impossible and meaningless.

Out of Bonhoeffer's critique there emerges a new effort to define and explore the coming tenor of Christianity. Since the Gestapo's discovery of his resistance work cut short his letters, the lines seem hazy and difficult to follow. But however difficult, his thought is most urgent at this period. For the death blow to the religious premise has raised the enormous question: What now?—a question which no one could answer better than Dietrich Bonhoeffer.

How this religionless Christianity looks, what form it takes, is something that I am thinking about a great deal.

Letter of 30 April, 1944

13. *The Shape of Religionless Christianity*

Deeply enmeshed in Bonhoeffer's comments about the "religious premise" are remarks, fragmentary and suggestive, about Christianity as it should be for the coming age. In one of his last letters to Bethge, Bonhoeffer described a book which he was preparing to write, *The Essence of Christianity,* on the world's coming of age, the dissolution of religion, and the "real meaning" of the Christian faith. Obviously such a book would have been invaluable in clarifying Bonhoeffer's thought in the critical area of "religionless Christianity" and a "non-religious interpretation of biblical concepts." Unfortunately he was never allowed to finish the book. What he had finished was seized by the Gestapo and destroyed when he was taken from Tegel. His own earlier words best describe the significance of such a blow, and the condition to which Bonhoeffer's most mature and important thought has been reduced.

We have grown up in a society which believed that every man

had the right to plan his own life. There was, we were taught, a purpose in life, and it was every man's duty to accept that purpose resolutely, and pursue it to the best of his powers. Since then, however, we have learned that it is impossible to plan even for one day ahead, that all our work may be destroyed overnight, and that our life, compared with our parents', has become formless and fragmentary. [1]

For Bonhoeffer, the religious premise was replaced with a new premise: that man has "come of age." The concept is one that can easily be, and has often been, seriously misunderstood. Bonhoeffer is not speaking of the Western world as reaching any decisive stage of progress which sets it morally or spiritually beyond earlier centuries. In all his historical reflections he makes no commitment to a "progressing humanity." He merely states what to him is an apparent observable cultural fact:

Man has learned to cope with all questions of importance without recourse to God as a working hypothesis. In questions concerning science, arts, and even ethics, this has become an understood thing which one scarcely dares to tilt at any more.[2]

Bonhoeffer speaks of the "world come of age" only in the context of a world which no longer needs—and is *aware* it no longer needs—the religious premise which has long characterized Christian preaching, devotion, and self-understanding. The man come of age is one whose work, family, education, and awareness of the world have made daily recourse to God unnecessary. He attempts no conscious movement of atheism and would not admit he was an atheist; very possibly he attends church on Sunday mornings. Yet he does not think that he needs God; and the preaching he hears, the books he may read, the sin he is told surrounds him—these do not summon the whole man, in complete involvement, as do his family, his work, his friendships. In short, he is a man able to live a human, relatively complete life in the midst of a secular culture and with an immense confidence in that culture—without God.

For Bonhoeffer, the "world come of age" is more than a premise to a new form of Christianity; it is the perspective from which that new form might be envisioned and awakened. Indeed, evidences are clear that Bonhoeffer welcomed the secular forces in the world, and saw in them a growing liberation from man's enslavement to religious forms—a liberation to be fuller men in Christ. To cope with reality without God is to exert a full humanity, a humanity in the past too often cramped and restricted by religion.

Bonhoeffer's notion of the "world come of age" hinges on the historical thrust of the last four centuries as Bonhoeffer interprets them. In his *Ethics,* Bonhoeffer spent a chapter describing the historical heritage of the Christian West. His historical analysis in that chapter has come under heavy criticism, but several points suggest the importance of the thinking that went into the chapter. In speaking of the 18th century Enlightenment, for example, he wrote:

> Yet it was not so much in the question of belief and life that emancipated reason displayed its immense power, but rather in the discovery of that mysterious correspondence between the laws of thought and the laws of nature. . . . The technical science of the modern western world has emancipated itself from any kind of subservience. It is in essence not service but mastery, mastery over nature. It was an entirely new spirit that evoked it, and it will continue only so long as this spirit continues. This is the spirit of the forcible subjugation of nature beneath the rule of the thinking and experimenting man. Technology became an end in itself. It has a soul of its own.[3]

Emphasizing the importance of the technology which has reshaped men's lives so thoroughly, he continues: "The age of technology is a genuine heritage of our western history. We must come to grips with it. We cannot return to the pre-technical era."[4] Clearly, Bonhoeffer has already recognized the dimensions of change, and the need for a change in the Church of similar revolutionary proportions.

The historical analysis which Bonhoeffer provides in the prison letters is, like that of the *Ethics,* more of a thumbnail version of historical events than a careful study of precise historical causes. He finds in the Renaissance what he calls the "*one* great development which leads to the idea of the autonomy of the world."[5] This development occurs side by side in theology, ethics, politics, philosophy—every area of thought. As Bonhoeffer says:

In theology it is first discernible in Lord Herbert of Cherbury with his assertion that reason is the sufficient instrument of religious knowledge. In ethics it first appears in Montaigne and Bodin with their substitution of moral principles for the ten commandments. In politics, Machiavelli, who emancipates politics from the tutelage of morality, and founds the doctrine of "reason of state."[6]

He continues with philosophy, in which he shows how Descartes saw the world as a mechanism, operating without the intervention of God. More recent philosophers have followed the pattern; "all along the line there is a growing tendency to assert the autonomy of man and the world."[7] The same development, if more apparent, has been going on in natural science; the overthrow of the classical cosmos meant an infinite universe, one which was conceivably self-sustaining. "It is true that modern physics is not so sure as it was about the infinity of the universe," Bonhoeffer remarks, "but it has not returned to the earlier conceptions of its finitude."[8]

Bonhoeffer definitely accepts, indeed welcomes, this historical thrust. He poses one question, however, "How can we reclaim for Christ a world which has come of age?"[9] It is this question which guides him, and which keeps his criticisms of the religious efforts to "redeem" a godless world as solid as they are.

As violent and penetrating as his criticism against religion itself is Bonhoeffer's criticism against the "Christian apologetic" which attempts to destroy the world's faith in itself and restore a medieval faith in God.

The attack by Christian apologetic upon the adulthood of the world I consider to be in the first place pointless, in the second ignoble, and in the third un-Christian. Pointless, because it looks to me like an attempt to put a grown-up man back into adolescence, i.e., to make him dependent on things on which he is not in fact dependent any more, thrusting him back into the midst of problems which are in fact not problems for him any more. Ignoble, because this amounts to an effort to exploit the weakness of man for purposes alien to him and not freely subscribed to by him. Un-Christian, because for Christ himself is being substituted one particular stage in the religiousness of man, i.e., a human law.[10]

The effort, as Bonhoeffer sees and stabbingly describes it, amounts to a blindness of the present world and a groping search for the world that was the Middle Ages. Bonhoeffer sharply denounces the search as ultimately dishonest.

At this point, nervous souls start asking what room there is left for God now. And being ignorant of the answer they write off the whole development which has brought them to this pass. As I said in an earlier letter, various emergency exits have been devised to deal with this situation. To them must be added the *saltum mortale* back to the Middle Ages, the fundamental principle of which however is heteronomy in the form of clericalism. But that is a counsel of despair, which can be purchased only at the cost of intellectual sincerity. It reminds one of the song:

It's a long way back to the land of Childhood.
But if I only knew the way! [11]

Bonhoeffer's remarks probably would not be so strong, but for the effects of such nostalgia, which he sees as profoundly harmful to Christ. For the defenders of religion—whom Bonhoeffer calls Christian apologetic, as if they were some corporate entity—too readily identify the historical movement, which is increasingly godless, as being anti-Christian. For Bonhoeffer it certainly is not.

Catholic and Protestant historians are agreed that it is in this development that the great defection from God, from Christ, is to be discerned, and the more they bring in and make use of God and Christ in opposition to this trend, the more the trend considers itself to be anti-Christian. The world which has attained to a realization of itself and of the laws which govern its existence is so sure of itself that we become frightened. . . . Efforts are made to prove to a world thus come of age that it cannot live without the tutelage of "God." [12]

The result, then, is twofold: the modern world is identified as anti-Christian, immediately becoming unattractive and ultimately dangerous for the "true Christian." Likewise, the Christian attempts to convince this world that it cannot really, after all, live without God; it lives presently only under an illusion.

Bonhoeffer's lengthy descriptions of the tactics taken by the Christian apologetic to convince the world that it needs God prove to be some of the most biting passages throughout the prison letters. He attacks two levels: those preachers and others who attempt to prove somehow that people need a God; and the theologians who make the same attempt, although on a theoretical level.

In the first category, Bonhoeffer is deliberately vague. He sees many of the attempts to bring Christ into the world as no more than attempts to force upon people a consciousness of their need for religion, a need which in fact they no longer have.

As the border is edged back on sickness, guilt, mystery, even death, the so-called "ultimate questions" which only "God" can answer lose their force.[13]

Bonhoeffer speaks slightingly of the

. . . secularized offshoots of Christian theology, the existentialist philosophers and the psychotherapists, who demonstrate to secure, contented, happy mankind that it is really unhappy and desperate, and merely unwilling to realize that it is in severe straits it knows nothing at all about, from which only they can rescue it.[14]

The criticism reaches further than this, however. "You see," Bonhoeffer later wrote to Bethge, "this is the attitude I am contending against. When Jesus blessed sinners, they were real sinners, but Jesus did not make every man a sinner first. He called them out of their sin, not into their sin." [15] He directs his remarks also to the efforts mentioned earlier, of hitting man at his most vulnerable spot and attempting to direct him to God this way. Bonhoeffer speaks quite disdainfully of these people: "In a flower garden they grub around for the dung on which the flowers grow." [16] Yet he recognizes the extent of this "revolution from below, a revolt of inferiority," and this recognition drives him to state all the more energetically that man should confront God at man's strongest and most dynamic point. "I should like to speak of God not on the borders of life but at its center, not in weakness but in strength, not, therefore, in man's suffering and death but in his life and prosperity." [17]

Bonhoeffer's criticism of the theologians for their attempt to ignore the modern world is far more direct. A strong attack is made upon Karl Barth. When Bonhoeffer first asks the question, "Then what is a religionless Christianity?" Barth's name appears:

> Barth, who is the only one to have started on this line of thought, has still not proceeded to its logical conclusion, but has arrived at a positivism of revelation which has nevertheless remained essentially a restoration. For the religionless working man, or indeed, man generally, nothing that makes any real difference is gained by that.[18]

"Positivism of revelation" expresses forcefully, if not too lucidly, Bonhoeffer's chief disappointment in the man most influential in shaping his own thought. The old tension is still present: the urgent insistence on the Gospel's relevance to the world in the liberal theologians, against Barth's drastic return to revelation. Bonhoeffer never forgot the value which Barth's emphasis had instilled: the ability to see Christ as the directing, central factor in all theological discussions. But a return to revelation (what Bonhoeffer calls "essentially a restoration") does little good to the people for whom the Christian message, even if restored, has lost all meaning. Barth's work, Bonhoeffer is suggesting, has served its purpose well; but now theology is summoned to a new purpose.

Two other theologians who come under fire are Paul Tillich and Rudolf Bultmann. Bonhoeffer's remarks about Tillich are direct and effective:

> Tillich set out to interpret the evolution of the world itself—against its will—in a religious sense, to give it its whole shape through religion. That was very courageous of him, but the world unseated him and went on by itself: he too sought to understand the

world better than it understood itself, but it felt entirely *mis*understood, and rejected the imputation.[19]

These remarks are especially instructive. Bonhoeffer sees no future in theology which refuses to listen, and most attentively, to the world, and to accept the world's own self-understanding as a starting point for theological search.

Bonhoeffer's criticism of Bultmann is not so clear or consistent as his criticisms of Barth and Tillich, possibly because Bonhoeffer lacked the knowledge of Bultmann he had of Barth and Tillich. His first mention of Bultmann is in connection with the effort to clear religion from the Christian life:

I expect you remember Bultmann's paper on the demythologization of the New Testament? My view of it today would be not that he went too far, as most people seem to think, but that he did not go far enough. It is not only the mythological conceptions, such as the miracles, the ascension and the like (which are not in principle separable from the conceptions of God, faith and so on) that are problematic, but the "religious" conceptions themselves. You cannot, as Bultmann imagines, separate God and miracles, but you do have to be able to interpret and proclaim *both* of them in a "non-religious" sense. Bultmann's approach is really at bottom the liberal one (i.e., abridging the Gospel), whereas I seek to think theologically.[20]

Bonhoeffer remarks elsewhere about Bultmann that in reacting too heavily to Barth, he had gone off into "the typical liberal reduction process (the 'mythological' elements of Christianity are dropped, and Christianity is reduced to its 'essence')."[21] Bonhoeffer concludes with some remarks which better clarify his own effort than Bultmann's:

I am of the view that the full content, including the mythological concepts, must be maintained. The New Testament is not a mythological garbing of the universal truth; this mythology (resurrection and so on) is the thing itself—but the concepts must be interpreted in such a way as not to make religion a pre-condition of faith. . . .[22]

Bonhoeffer apparently mistrusted the theological effort to

come to grips with the faith without beginning with a Christ-dominated expurgation of the religious elements so deeply imbedded in the theological patterns of thought. "The world's coming of age," he states, "is no longer an occasion for polemics and apologetics, but it is really better understood than it understands itself, namely on the basis of the Gospel, and in the light of Christ." [23]

The "world come of age" was for Bonhoeffer a conclusion and a premise. From his observations of the death of religion as an established fact and as a liberating force for the world historically, he could accept a world built upon and daily guided by secular hopes. But more importantly, Bonhoeffer accepted the religionless condition of twentieth-century man as the foundation of a new form of Christianity, described significantly by him as "religionless Christianity." This new form did not simply mean new institutional patterns, but a drastic change in the Church's inner self-awareness. For Bonhoeffer it meant first and foremost the guidelines of understanding this new Church—what he called the "non-religious interpretation of biblical concepts."

The term "non-religious interpretation of biblical concepts" is an intriguing one. Bonhoeffer's insistence in the 'thirties that the preached word should grow from knowledge of the circumstances and be intensely concrete, no matter at what cost, anticipated a totally secular language for the fundamental Christian truths. And the Church-world doctrine, in which the Church acts in the world and in terms of the world's needs and structures, implicitly demanded the break from a narrow ecclesiastical vocabulary. "In ethics, as in dogmatics," Bonhoeffer wrote in the *Ethics,* "we cannot simply reproduce the terminology of the Bible. The altered problems . . . demand an altered terminology." [24] Now the critique of religion adds a fresh and urgent demand. "The time when men could be told everything by means of words, whether theological or simply pious, is over." [25] There can be no effort made to clarify a Church free of its religious premise without a fundamental overhauling of the language by which that very freedom can be explored. A

Church existing in and for the world can only understand itself in the language which is the impelling force of the *world's* present vitality—the language, for example, of science, of business, of politics, of social consciousness. Indeed, the employment of secular language—and Bonhoeffer does not mean simply spoken language—is *the* crucial step in the process of eliminating religion, for immediately the Church will find itself speaking not to the "religious" Christians, but to the man of Bonhoeffer's anthropology.

There is little question that Bonhoeffer's hope in a renewal of Christianity freed of its religious premise lies in proclamation, and not a radical shift in forms. Indeed, Bonhoeffer was highly critical of making the change in the Church's form—the parish structure, the shape of worship, and the community of Christians—the basic source of renewal. "By the time you have grown up," he wrote in the baptismal sermon to Bethge's son, "the Church's form will have changed greatly. We are not yet out of the melting-pot, and any attempt to help the Church prematurely to a new expansion of its organization will merely delay its conversion and purification." [26]

Bonhoeffer, however, never divided renewal through proclamation from renewal through a change in formal structures; he saw the two elements combined. For example, following a discussion of "speaking of God," he wrote, "The outward aspect of this religionless Christianity, the form it takes, is something to which I am giving much thought. . . ." [27] Or again: "How do we speak . . . in secular fashion of God? In what way are we in a religionless and secular sense Christians, in what way are we the *Ekklesia,* 'those who are called forth'?" [28] Bonhoeffer decidedly intended no critical division between proclamation and form, even though he felt that proclamation was the only way to arrive effectively at a renewal of the forms.

Bonhoeffer believed firmly in the proclamation of a renewed language drawn from the secular world. Immediately following his statement that hastening matters will only delay the Church's conversion, he wrote:

It is not for us to prophesy the day, but the day will come when men will be called again to utter the Word of God with such power as will change and renew the world. It will be a new language, which will horrify men, and yet overwhelm them by its power.[29]

Bonhoeffer speaks here of a power "which will change and renew the world." It should be noted how this power, by its effect upon the world, achieves far more that what is expressed as the intentions of those whose "attempt to hasten matters will only delay the Church's conversion and purgation." [30] The slight upon would-be Church reformers was intended. A conscious effort to "renew the Church," especially through a change in forms, is doomed from the start. Only the proclamation of God's Word through the power of secular language and a new meaningfulness can charge the world with a fresh spiritual vigor. The world, after all, is the real field of effort for the Christian in a religionless Church.

Bonhoeffer did not entirely understand what this new language would consist of, and as soon as he began working with it, the overwhelming size of the task became evident. He wrote to Bethge early in July, "It's high time I said something concrete on the worldly interpretation of the Bible, but it's too hot!" [31] A week later he wrote: "I find it very slow going trying to work out a non-religious interpretation of biblical terminology, and it's a far bigger job than I can manage at the moment." [32]

Yet certain suggestions about the nature of this non-religious interpretation appear throughout the later letters. Bonhoeffer left, however, no more than suggestions. In mentioning the need to speak this language, for example, he uses a number of terms which broadly outline the notion he is working toward: "claiming the person for God"; "speaking pertinently"; in one case the statement, "There seems to me no way of getting hold of such a person and bringing him to his senses." [33]

A number of other suggestions emerge: comments made at random throughout the letters which, combined, offer at least segments of a pattern for this new "non-religious" interpretation. Bonhoeffer speaks of the quality which the Church's preaching should instill: "There are degrees of perception and degrees of significance," he says, "i.e., a secret discipline must be re-established whereby the *mysteries* of the Christian faith are preserved from profanation." [34] Elsewhere he discusses the importance of preparing men for a life of "Christian polyphony": "We have to drag men out of one-track thinking, as a sort of 'preparation' or 'enablement' for faith, although it is only faith itself that can make possible a multi-dimensional life." [35] Finally, in his baptismal sermon he makes an especially tantalizing suggestion:

> So our traditional language must lose its force and fall silent, and our Christianity today will be confined to two things: praying, and doing the right among men. Christian thinking, speaking and organizing must be reborn out of that action . . . . Until then the Christian cause will be a silent and hidden one; but there will be those who pray and do right and await God's time.[36]

These three suggestions are helpful—the nurturing of mystery, the preparation for a multi-dimensional life, and rooting the coming Church in prayer and action. However, one of these hints touches at the essence of the "non-religious interpretation" itself. The nearest guide to that essence lies in the searing question Bonhoeffer asks in the outline to his book: "What do we really believe? I mean, in such a way as to stake our whole lives upon it? The problem of the Apostles' Creed? 'What must I believe?' is the wrong question." [37] Bonhoeffer's direct, honest confrontation of the question forces a naked answer—and this answer may be the key to his "non-religious interpretation." To "really believe" in the Church, the word of God, justification, a man must have brought these mysteries into his life and integrated them in the pattern of his values, commitments, and hopes. At the point of integration, "justification" is no longer a biblical word but a profound personal meaning, a meaning palpable and concrete for that individual. This concrete interpretation and this ability to insinuate a depth of meaning enable the biblical concepts to come alive in a religious interpretation. How to spark that life? Bonhoeffer left no answer, only a handful of random thoughts.

Gerhard Ebeling has seen one clear indication of measuring the validity of true non-religious interpretation, however. He suggests shifting the criterion of the Church's preaching from the response of the believer to the response of the worldly-believer. The thought is striking, if perhaps self-evident for a Church to the world. It is also far-reaching. As Ebeling has written:

> This reversal of the relation of Word and faith, which comes not of letting the non-believer be the criterion of whether our proclamation is understandable, results not only in silencing the genuine faith which must repudiate any religious talk that no longer speaks to real man because it does not speak of him. Thus the peculiarly sympathetic nearness of the believer to the non-religious man, as Bonhoeffer testifies to it in his own case, becomes a genuine symptom of the present state of Christianity.[38]

The very effort to speak forcefully to nonbelievers will itself impel an honest search for the "secular expression" of biblical concepts. This search has always characterized the most earnest missionary efforts; and if Bonhoeffer was right in admitting that the world has found its own identity and speaks its own language, then perhaps the Church's future enterprise could best be perceived in terms of the culturally sensitive missionary.

It is unfortunate that Bonhoeffer was denied the opportunity to say more than he did about the "non-religious interpretation of biblical concepts." The idea is seminal to the critique of religion and especially to his description of the new "religionless Christianity."

Apart from the urgency to use secular language and secular modes of thought in proclaiming the Gospel, how clearly does Bonhoeffer present his notion of "religionless Christianity"? The question is a difficult one, for from the start "religionless Christianity" has a fundamentally negative basis. It is Christianity *without* religion, and Bonhoeffer's very term—religionless—provides few indications of exactly what will take the place of religion. Actually, the term "religionless Christianity" is so vast that it discourages any attempt at a conclusive definition. Yet the suggestions scattered through the final letters reveal three themes which were very close to Bonhoeffer and which provide a glimpse of what he hoped to see in the future Christianity. These themes are "holy worldliness," an extension and completion of Bonhoeffer's anthropology; a Christian atheism, which enables the believer to live "without God in the presence of God"; and a sense of responsibility and social commitment which must characterize Christians in the coming era.

The first of these themes, "holy worldliness," resounds throughout all the letters, just as it had throughout much of the *Ethics.* The theme is a challenging expression of Bonhoeffer's anthropology, a summons to live out the arduous and exhilarating life of a man who has drawn his life from Christ. "It is only by living completely in this world that one learns to believe." [39] Bonhoeffer's concept of "holy worldliness" is vividly exemplified in Kierkegaard's well-known Knight of Faith from *Fear and Trembling*:

> He is always making the movement of infinity, but he makes the movement with so much precision and assurance that he possesses himself of the finite without anyone, even for a moment, suspecting anything else. . . . Most men's lives are lost among the joys and sorrows of the world; they "sit out" and take no part in the dance . . . they are strangers in the world. . . . To be able to fall in such a way as to appear at once standing and walking, to be able to transform the leap into life into a normal gait, to be able to express perfectly the sublime in terms of the pedestrian—only the knight can do this—and this is the single miracle.[40]

Kierkegaard's description was not used by Bonhoeffer, but it does capture in summary form much of what Bonhoeffer suggested in various contexts. The ability to move freely, amiably, intensely in the present can only come of a commitment to the future and to the eternal. "Move into the storm of event," wrote Bonhoeffer, "sustained only by the commandment of God and your faith, and freedom will receive your spirit with exultation." [41]

To Bonhoeffer, "holy worldliness" is the only genuine form of holiness possible for the contemporary Christian—anything else is sham or illusion. By the term (which he uses only a few times), he means a complete dedication to life, a commitment in one stroke to a man's own potential and the needs of the world. He speaks of the virtue of *hilaritas,* which he grants to such men as Rubens, Karl Barth, Kierkegaard, and Nietzsche. *Hilaritas* is:

Confidence in their work, a certain boldness and defiance of the world and of popular opinion, a steadfast certainty that what they are doing will benefit the world, even though it does not approve, a magnificent self-assurance.[42]

The affirmation of life central to worldly holiness reaches far. In the fragment of a letter written in 1943 there are the words:

Even if you must scorn life in order to master it, at least do not forget to love it once you have done so. Beware of speaking too lightly of happiness and of flirting with misery: that is the negation of living, an abuse of man as he was created and as he lives his life, a poor sinner yearning for happiness as a slight sign of friendliness from God. It is not so easy to be unhappy, and he who is so does not scorn or abuse the man who is happy. There is no good reason to be willing to bear misery unless it is to make other people happy. Unhappiness comes of itself, or rather from God, and we have no need to run after it. To become unhappy is fate. But to want to be unhappy is blasphemy, and a grave spiritual illness.[43]

One of Bonhoeffer's favorite authors was Goethe, whose works convey a magnificent quest for life, the full range of *hilaritas.* Among the few remains found with Bonhoeffer's clothes at Flossenbürg the morning of April 10 were a Bible and a volume of Goethe. The impression left by Goethe, as well as the numerous other writers of the 19th century whom Bonhoeffer had read in prison, was a fresh and deeper understanding of human life and its meaning for the Christian believer. The insistence upon "a full life," the stabbing criticisms of fellow prisoners who "miss the fullness of life and the wholeness of an independent existence," [44] the constant return to the theme of involvement in the world: these give some indication of Bonhoeffer's direction. Throughout the letters Bonhoeffer equates this new holiness not with any "virtue," but with a mind and soul open widely enough to embrace the world. W. E. Otto's book on the Greek gods captured and thrust forward Bonhoeffer's hope for a new and religionless Christian life. An excerpt from Otto's conclusion might suggest why:

> Thus the belief of the most perceptive of all peoples has remained unheeded and unpraised—this wonderful and admirable belief which arose out of the riches and depths of life, not out of its anxieties and yearnings—this meteor of a religion which could not only see the brilliance of life with an eye more luminous than the rest of mankind but is also unique in that its lucid gaze confronted the insoluble conflict of life with candor and out of its most terrifying darkness conceived the majestic achievement of tragedy.[45]

Within his notion of holy worldliness, Bonhoeffer suggests three qualities which describe the Christian's relationship to God: knowing God in the blessings He sends us; relating to God in strength, and not in weakness; and sharing with God in His suffering in the world. Each quality is sketched only briefly, but each one seems to have attracted Bonhoeffer as an important characteristic of the Christian living a holy life before God in the world.

"The intermediate theological category between God and human fortune is, it seems to me, that of blessing." [46] He considers the point a vital one; God's blessings, he says, whether health, fortune, or vigor, form a central concern in the Old and New Testament. There has been an unhealthy insistence on the asceticism of the cross, which has overshadowed the primary relation of God's blessing. Bonhoeffer detects the insistence in the lonely and tortured Kierkegaard.

> And this is just what gives rise to an unhealthy asceticism, and deprives suffering of contingency upon a divine ordinance. . . . The only difference between the two Testaments at this point is that in the Old the blessing also includes the cross, and in the New the cross also includes the blessing.[47]

Bonhoeffer's thought on blessing is decisive. "We ought to find God and love him in the blessings he sends us." [48] He doesn't neglect suffering, the cross, the sense of this world's doom; "to everything," he writes, "there is a season." In the meantime, however,

> . . . we should love God in our lives, so that when the time comes, but not before, we may go to him in love and trust and joy. But, speaking frankly, to long for the transcendent when you are in your wife's arms is, to put it mildly, a lack of taste, and it is certainly not what God expects of us. . . . If he pleases to grant us some overwhelming earthly bliss, we ought not to try and be more religious than God himself.[49]

The remarks on blessings, made at several junctures in the letters, implicitly criticize religion and the religious man's inability to cope fully with human life. The man of holy worldliness accepts the rhythm of life, of blessing and pain, and uses this rhythm as part of the *cantus firmus,* his polyphony of life in which God is praised simply by the man's fullness of freedom and joy.

However much God wishes men to love Him from the center of their lives, in their joys and blessings, it is also true that He wishes man to remain faithful in suffering. Bonhoeffer's comments on suffering are prolific and provocative. Without forgetting the rhythm in which suffering is only one strain, he gives considerable attention to the role of pain in the Christian's worldly life:

> . . . not only action, but also suffering is a way to freedom. The deliverance consists in placing our cause unreservedly in the hands of God. Whether our deeds are wrought in faith or not depends on our realization that suffering is the extension of action and the perfection of freedom.[50]

Recurring often with the mention of suffering is a phrase, "participating in the suffering of God in the world."[51] In a poem, "Christians and Unbelievers," Bonhoeffer suggests what he might mean:

> Man goes to God when he is sore bestead,
> Finds him poor and scorned, without shelter or bread,
> Whelmed under weight of the wicked, the weak, the dead:
> Christians stand by God in his hour of grieving.[52]

Deeply rooted in Bonhoeffer's Christology had always been a profound appreciation of the suffering Christ—the crucified, ignoble one, immersed in the world at its most grueling point. In the final letters Bonhoeffer identifies the Christian's suffering with his most intense participation of God's life.

"Christians range themselves with God in his suffering; that is what distinguishes them from the heathen." As Jesus asked in Gethsemane, "Could ye not watch with me one hour?" This is the exact opposite of what the religious man expects from God. Man is challenged to participate in the sufferings of God at the hands of a godless world. . . . He must live a "worldly" life and so participate in the suffering of God.[53]

The radical identification of suffering the intense life of this world with participation in Christ marks a major tenet of the notion of "holy worldliness." Unhappily, like many of Bonhoeffer's other original concepts, there is no extensive development, only traces running throughout the letters.

The third quality, and the one most characteristic of Bonhoeffer, is a summons to strength:

I should like to speak of God not on the borders of life but at its center, not in weakness but in strength, not, therefore, in man's suffering and death but in his life and prosperity.[54]

God's blessing may well be the origin of this strength, but it is man's responsibility to nurture and develop it. "I have noticed," he wrote to Bethge, "how much depends on stretching ourselves to the limit." [55] At another juncture he remarks that, according to St. Paul, God not only wishes us to be holy; He wishes us to be strong.

Bonhoeffer's athletic and competitive temperament had always helped him appreciate the importance of a firm will and concentrated human effort. As his letters indicate, he had difficulty sympathizing with men who collapsed or gave in at the first demands. Speaking of a whining Nazi cellmate, Bonhoeffer seems almost rigidly stoical:

I told him in no uncertain terms what I thought of people who can be very hard on others and make grand speeches about living dangerously, etc., etc., and then crumble up themselves under the slightest test of endurance. It was downright disgraceful, I said, and I had no sympathy whatever with such behavior.[56]

Bonhoeffer's insistence on strength may lack some of the theological firmness undergirding much of his other mature thought; yet the insistence plays an important role in his version of "holy worldliness." Moreover, it sets the tone to the type of life Bonhoeffer expects.

These three qualities—blessing, suffering, strength—give some indication of a description of the holiness toward which Bonhoeffer is moving in his last letters. The reliance upon, and the movement toward a profound anthropology rooted in Christ is evident. For Bonhoeffer, as much as ever,

. . . to be a Christian does not mean to be religious in a particular way, to cultivate some particular form of asceticism . . . but to be a man. It is not some religious act which makes a Christian what he is, but participation in the suffering of God in the life of the world.[57]

"Holy worldliness" may describe the qualities of man's relationship with God, but it does not get at the biting question of what is, without religion, the nature of man's relationship with God. To strip away the religious premise is to tear from man his overwhelming sense of conscience, his inwardness, a sense of some metaphysical being holding the universe together. It is, in effect, to undermine the traditional needs which gave birth to prayer and liturgy. And, as Bonhoeffer himself asks:

What is the significance of a Church (Church, parish, preaching, Christian life) in a religionless world? How do we speak of God without religion, i.e., without the temporally-influenced presuppositions of metaphysics, inwardness, and so on? How do we speak (but perhaps we are no longer capable of speaking in such things as we used to) in secular fashion of God? [58]

The questions are frightening in their vastness and revolutionary character. Yet, given Bonhoeffer's consignment of the religious premise to the past, or at best to a fragment of contemporary society, such questions are unavoidable. What solid footing—if a "Christian atheism" can be considered solid—he has left us needs a great deal of cautious but honest exploration, for it is central to the pattern of "religionless Christianity."

The death blow to religion came in a world where man realized he no longer needed a *deus ex machina* to fill in for his unsolved problems. Bonhoeffer keeps a clear distance theologically between this *deus ex machina* of laziness and human weakness and the God of Scripture. But he recognizes that many Christians do not. The surging effort of his description of God and man's relation to God in an era without religion is to condemn decisively the *deus ex machina,* the god men "use," and establish clearly the sense of the true God which should predominate.

Bonhoeffer is attempting, then, a type of atheism, at least as far as a false image of God is concerned. This will explain his paradoxical language, and his fury in chastising the use of a *deus ex machina.*

Bonhoeffer believes that for most men a sense of God has dwindled to some childhood reminiscence. Speaking of his effort to expound the first three commandments, he wrote: "Idols are objects of worship, and idolatry implies that people still worship something. The truth is, we've given up worshipping everything, even idols. We're absolute nihilists." [59] Bonhoeffer sees no danger in this situation; if anything, he foresees promises:

> When we speak of God in a non-religious way, we must not gloss over the ungodliness of the world, but expose it in a new light. Now that it has come of age, the world is more godless, and perhaps it is for that reason nearer to God than ever before.[60]

For to Bonhoeffer, the greatest insurance of a deeply worldly and committed life is a right outlook on God and a clear withdrawal from the religious outlook of the past. That is why he can say, with paradoxical clarity:

> The only way (to the truth) is that of Matthew 18. 3, i.e., through repentance, through *ultimate* honesty. And the only way to be honest is to recognize that we have to live in the world *etsi deus*

non daretur (to which God is not given). And this is just what we do see—before God! So our coming of age forces us to a true recognition of our situation vis-á-vis God. God is teaching us that we must live as men who can get along very well without him. The God who is with us is the God who forsakes us (Mark 15. 34). The God who makes us live in this world without using him as a working hypothesis is the God before whom we are ever standing. Before God and with him we live without God.[61]

The heightening paradoxical tenor of the passage suggests that as Christians move further and further from the religious premise, they will be moving further and further from their old notions of God—a naturally frightening, yet nonetheless essential, prospect.

With the *deus ex machina* overturned, what, positively, should *be* the Christian's awareness of God? Bonhoeffer suggests two ideas, but their context and his expression of them suggests that these, like many of the other notions of religionless Christianity, are largely exploratory.

He speaks, as earlier, of God's sufferings in the world, as the point at which the Christian meets God:

God allows himself to be edged out of the world and on to the cross. God is weak and powerless in the world, and that is exactly the way, the only way, in which he can be with us and help us. Matthew 8. 17 makes it crystal clear that it is not by his omnipotence that Christ helps us, but by his weakness and suffering.[62]

The idea, firmly lodged for many years in Bonhoeffer's Christology, is that by *His weakness* in the world, God is able to conquer the world. As Bonhoeffer states, the idea is radical, but thoroughly biblical.

This is the decisive difference between Christianity and all religions. Man's religiosity makes him look in his distress to the power of God in the world; he uses God as a *deus ex machina*. The Bible however directs him to the powerlessness and suffering of God; only a suffering God can help. To this extent we may say that the process we have described by which the world came of age was an abandonment of a false conception of God, and a clearing of the decks for the God of the Bible, who conquers power and space in the world by his weakness. This must be the starting point for our "worldly" interpretation.[63]

The alternative, then, to a God of supernatural power supporting the universe from without is a God entering the world as man, with all the emotion and distress of man, and suffering powerlessly in that world. Once again Bonhoeffer turns to the Incarnation and to his anthropology: Christ supports whole men, men committed to the world by the inexorable pain and sadness of His own life in the world.

The second point which Bonhoeffer suggests for "finding God" in a post-religious age follows closely upon the first. For Bonhoeffer the "experience of transcendence" takes on a reshaped meaning. In his first of the important final letters Bonhoeffer touched on the question: "God is the 'beyond' in the midst of our life. The Church stands not where human powers give out, on the borders, but in the center of the village." [64] Later, in a section entitled "Miscellaneous Thoughts," there is the single statement: "The transcendent is not infinitely remote, but close at hand." [65] The statement recalls *The Communion of Saints*. Not, however, until the outline to his book does he explore the idea with any thoroughness.

What do we mean by "God"? Not in the first place an abstract belief in his omnipotence, etc. That is not a genuine experience of God, but a partial extension of the world. Encounter with Jesus Christ, implying a complete orientation of human being in the experience of Jesus *as one whose only concern is for others. This concern of Jesus for others* is *the experience of transcendence.*[66]

The question of a "transcendent God" or an "imminent God" has always been one of the keenest disputes in Protestant theology. Generally "transcendence" implied an experience of the "beyond," man's sudden confrontation with the overwhelming immensity of a Being greater than any experience. Bonhoeffer's statement here overturns the traditional meaning of transcendence by forcing that experience into a totally human context: not the " 'beyond' of our perceptual faculties" now, but the beyond of a human self-sacrifice for others which defies an understanding. Here, as nowhere else in Bonhoeffer's later thought, the anthropological element almost exclusively dominates his thinking. Faith comes about purely *in terms of* the human; it is one man's incredible concern for others which spurs on faith. Although Bonhoeffer might be seen here as swerving away from some very fundamental Christian doctrines, he actually is leading back toward them.

> This freedom from self, maintained to the point of death, the sole ground of his omnipotence, omniscience and ubiquity. Faith is participation in this Being of Jesus (incarnation, cross and resurrection). Our relation to God not a religious relationship to a supreme Being, absolute in power and goodness, which is a spurious conception of transcendence, but a new life for others, through participation in the Being of God.[67]

The thought here is charged with Bonhoeffer's renewed way of looking at God. He is demolishing the "religious relationship to a supreme Being" by challenging the transcendence in which that Being is understood. What he suggests, "a new life for others, through participation in the Being of God," is not at all new; what is new is Bonhoeffer's way of arriving there. What Bonhoeffer demands, in effect, is a new premise for Christian preaching and teaching: a sense of humanity insuring the ability to recognize in this one man Jesus a transcendent gift, and therefore God.

> The transcendence consists not in tasks beyond our scope and power, but in the nearest thing to hand. God in human form, not, as in other religions, in animal form—the monstrous, chaotic remote and terrifying—nor yet in abstract form—the absolute, metaphysical, infinite, etc.—nor yet in the Greek divine-human of autonomous man, but man existing for others, and hence the Crucified. A life based on the transcendent.[68]

This new premise, which in some ways takes the place of the religious premise, can be identified largely with Bonhoeffer's anthropology, i.e., with his concept and appreciation of man. What is above all important here is that men be able to look to Christ and see *there* His transcendence, to locate in Him the hope not simply for a saviour in the traditional sense, but for a paradigm of humanity and of life. As Bonhoeffer wrote in one of the last preserved letters to Bethge:

> The key to everything is the "in him." All that we rightly expect from God and pray for is to be found in Jesus Christ. The God of Jesus Christ has nothing to do with all that we, in our human way, think he can and ought to do. We must persevere in quiet meditation on the life, sayings, deeds, suffering and death of Jesus in order to learn what God promises and what he fulfills.[69]

For Bonhoeffer "holy worldliness" and the renewed relationship to God in an altered form of transcendence bring the Christian before Jesus Christ in a startling, much more human way. The wellsprings of "religionless Christianity" can be seen here: a richness and rhythm of life; the ability to find God in the blessings He sends us; the spirit of *hilaritas,* freedom, and strength; union with God in His suffering in the world; living before God but without recourse to the *deus ex machina,* and thereby completely living by the human resources of mind and will; finding in this "man for others" the fullness of God. But what of its outcome? What do we know of the Christian man nurtured in such a spirit? Throughout the letters, to an astonishing degree, Bonhoeffer stresses one concept central to the nonreligious man of God: responsible action.

Bonhoeffer's "theology of responsibility"—for his thought amounts, in the end, to that—is a rich and surprisingly well-developed area of his later theology. The theme of responsibility dominates many sections of the *Ethics,* and there are few important letters from prison in which Bonhoeffer does not plead for this basic trait. If any virtue or capability typifies the whole of his anthropology, it is responsibility. Indeed, at several junctures Bonhoeffer equates the whole or conformed man with the responsible man.

It is difficult to render what Bonhoeffer meant by "responsibility" in theological language, or any language at all. Language has a way of obscuring the decisive issue, of softening the impact. As Bonhoeffer wrote in the baptismal sermon, "We have learned a bit too late in the day that action springs not from thought, but from a readiness for responsibility."[70] What he said following this statement shows the extent of his hope in another generation:

For you thought and action will have a new relationship. Your thinking will be confined to your responsibilities in action. With us thought was often the luxury of the looker-on; with you it will be entirely subordinated in action. "Not everyone that saith unto me, Lord, Lord, shall enter into the kingdom of heaven; but he that does the will of my Father who is in heaven." (Matthew 7:21).[71]

The relation of thought and action: as a theologian and highly active member of the resistance—this question had a burning urgency for Bonhoeffer. The growth of that urgency can be seen in the development of the *Ethics,* where responsible action takes on an increasing role at every stage. By the fourth, final stage he included such chapters as "The Structure of Responsible Life," "Deputyship," "Correspondence with Reality," "The Place of Responsibility," and "Vocation." Early in the prison letters is a meditation, "After Ten Years," in which Bonhoeffer asks the decisive question: Who stands his ground? Who, Bonhoeffer asks, can be sure he is doing the right thing in this great "masquerade of evil"? Not, he says, the shortsighted rationalist; not the moral fanatic; not the man of conscience; not the duty-bound or the man of moral freedom; not even the man of private virtue. Only the man

who is ready to sacrifice all these things when he is called to obedient and responsible action in faith and exclusive allegiance to God. The responsible man seeks to make his whole life a response to the question and call of God.[72]

Admittedly, Bonhoeffer's treatment of responsiblity in the *Ethics* is more academic, and more remote, than the numerous scattered comments in the prison letters. Indeed, his earlier concern is with the structure and pattern of responsibility—not a sharp plea for responsible action in the midst of crisis. Yet the major theological pattern is set down within the *Ethics:* an idea of responsibility as vocation, and as limited by the institutions within which it operates. The effort throughout the prison letters is to proclaim the immediate imperative of free responsibility, and to clarify the demands of that responsibility.

There is no actual definition of responsibility in the later writings, partly because for Bonhoeffer the concept was too large and too fluid to contain within an explicit definition. The innumerable different directions from which he approaches responsibility suggest how alive the concept was for him. For example:

> We must sally forth to defy fate—I think the neuter gender of *Schicksal* (fate) is significant—with just as much resolution as we submit to it when the time comes. One can only speak of providence on the other side of this dialectical process.[73]

Or elsewhere he says, "I believe that God both can and will bring good out of evil. For that purpose he needs men who make the best use of everything. . ." [74] or again, "it is easier by far to act on abstract principle than from concrete responsibility." [75] The statements are frequent and perceptive, and suggest the importance Bonhoeffer sensed in responsible action springing constantly from the Christian life.

Pastor Zimmermann, a friend of Bonhoeffer during the critical pre-War years and into the War, has recounted a meeting about two months before Bonhoeffer's arrest. Lieutenant Werner von Haeften, a staff officer present, put the critical question to Bonhoeffer: "I shall be with Hitler tomorrow: shall I shoot him?" Bonhoeffer's careful answer suggests the extent to which he expected responsibility to carry. The question, Bonhoeffer replied, was not simply one of killing Hitler, but of achieving a political overthrow. If an effective government did not move in quickly, the consequences could be devastating. He added that Haeften's decision was his own, and could be made by no one else; the dreadful act of murder must come, above all, from a profound conviction that it was morally right and necessary. Here, the summons to full responsibility brings on a weighty yet tenuous burden. But this is as Bonhoeffer always said it should be:

We must take our full share of responsibility for the molding of history, whether it be as victors or vanquished. It is only the refusing to allow any event to deprive us of our responsibility for history, because we know that is a responsibility laid upon us by God, that we shall achieve a relation to the events of history far more fruitful than criticism or opportunism. To talk about going down fighting like heroes in face of certain defeat is not really heroic at all, but a failure to face up to the future. The ultimate question the man of responsibility asks is not, How can I extricate myself heroically from the affair? but, How is the coming generation to live? [76]

Like "holy worldliness," like the rekindled faith in God growing from a world built upon a premise of atheism, responsibility characterizes the Christian Church which has carefully torn out its religious roots. Yet in responsibility the field of vision for a renewed Church is somehow sharper—perhaps because we have not only Bonhoeffer's words to turn to as an explanation, but the vivid witness of his life.

The question, "How is the coming generation to live?" drove Bonhoeffer and steered his thought through the War years. The critique of religion, and the desperate, excited search for a new pattern of Christianity sprang from this question. "Religionless Christianity" was not for Bonhoeffer simply a field of theological exploration; in it he laid his expansive, personal faith in man; in it, indeed, he laid his hope for a future Church which could rise like the phoenix from its own ashes. Religionless Christianity was the culmination of Bonhoeffer's lifelong efforts. What remains of Bonhoeffer's mature thought may be fragmentary and at best suggestive. Yet it is a daring, audacious, and compelling challenge for the Church to face and enter the world more inextricably than she ever has before, a challenge which Bonhoeffer believed the Church must accept, or perish.

Who would deny that the German, again and again, has done his utmost in bravery, and has risked his life while obeying orders, following his calling, or doing his work. But, in doing so, he has not understood the world; he had not anticipated that his willingness to subordinate his ego, and to risk his life for his calling can be abused for evil. . . . Thus, the German never grasped a decisive and fundamental idea: the necessity to act freely and responsibly even if it impaired his work and his calling.

"After Ten Years" (Meditation written in Tegel Prison)

14. *From Pacifism to Resistance*

During the incredible years of the Nazi regime in Germany, small groups of men assembled throughout the country discussing strategies and possible conspiracies to bring Hitler's government to a quick end. The "movement," unified only by this common purpose, was admittedly small. And in terms of the effects its members desired, the resistance was a failure. It achieved no major works of sabotage, few major disclosures of military information to the Allies. And it failed completely in its major goal: the assassination of Adolf Hitler.

Yet the men remembered and honored in Germany a generation later are not the military heroes, not the leading government figures, but the heroic, dedicated few who risked treason to prevent their homeland from destroying itself.

The men who carried the resistance efforts into an active, tactical sphere were for the most part military men or had once been military men: General Beck, Colonel Oster, Lieutenant von Stauffenberg. A few pastors and Church leaders became involved in the tactical efforts, however; their presence and bearing intensified the needed moral incentive. Among these pastors, one who saw the issues perceptively and acted unhesitatingly became more completely identified with the resistance than the others. "Bonhoeffer," an eminent resistance authority has written, "stands out as a foremost representative of those who did not hesitate to carry the moral dilemma through to a radical solution—one which was not laid upon the conscience of resisters in any other country." [1]

That Bonhoeffer, having entered the resistance, became one of its leading figures, is not surprising; he was capable of brilliant leadership, trust, and rare courage. That he entered the resistance at all *is* most surprising. The Bonhoeffer of the early and middle 'thirties was a man committed to resistance, but totally nonviolent resistance, a man who prized peace and struggled persistently for it. The thought of taking part in a plot to assassinate the Führer would have been totally alien to him. Yet after 1940, Bonhoeffer became increasingly involved in the resistance work centered in the *Abwehr,* and never, once he entered the movement, did he doubt the value or morality of his choice.

Bonhoeffer's movement from a state of pacifism and nonviolent resistance to an outright effort to participate in a necessarily violent overthrow of his government marks a personal reversal of major dimensions. Had Bonhoeffer's pacifism been simply a transient, temporary position determined by the vicissitudes of the state, such a movement would be more easily credible. But Bonhoeffer's pacifism was a profound belief, an important aspect of his psychological and moral life. He abhorred violence and admired Gandhi precisely for his ability to achieve important political goals through the moral use of nonviolent techniques. During the 'thirties Bonhoeffer came to loathe Hitler, to see in him and his disfigured government a capacity for evil which could destroy Germany. But the thought of murdering Hitler to check his atrocities cut across the grain of Bonhoeffer's beliefs. As much as he sensed a responsibility to the German people, he instinctively withdrew from whatever means would involve violence or a form of destruction.

Then, after 1938, he changed. The precise turning point is

difficult to isolate. In February of that year he met with resistance leaders Sack, Oster, Canaris, and Beck, and from that time on was kept in touch with the movement through his brother-in-law, Hans von Dohnanyi. Not until his return from America, however, a year and a half later, did he become actively involved in the effort. By 1940 he was a confirmed participant, and within months a leading figure in the *Abwehr* conspiracy.

Why? What in Bonhoeffer—or the circumstances that surrounded him—changed over those critical years of 1938-39? The answer is crucial to a full understanding of the man's stature as a Christian, as well as of his later theology.

The movement from pacifism to active conspiracy must be seen in the context of pacifism's meaning for Bonhoeffer. "Pacifism" is a word too often used, which carries a wide range of meanings: from militant rebellion against a war, to a pseudo-religious reluctance to participate in one. As the Nazi crisis in Germany became exacerbated, the meaning of pacifism for Bonhoeffer sharpened. He was constantly discussing it, rethinking it, applying it to the Church. Friends who knew him in England as a pastor or later at Finkenwalde testify that peace and pacifism were conversation topics which he discussed frequently and passionately. During years of such nationalistic fervor, Bonhoeffer's fascination with pacifism was a rare and dangerous preoccupation for a German.

Over the 1930's, five major influences upon Bonhoeffer's pacifism can be identified, and in terms of these influences the quality of his pacifist beliefs can be understood. The first of these influences must have been more latent than the others, yet it probably provided Dietrich with his first encounter with pacifism. Dietrich's friendship with the French pacifist Jean Lasserre at Union Seminary lasted less than a year, and it was a curious relationship. Lasserre, a serious, retiring young man, hardly impressed Dietrich at first. Only when the two men met on a serious, open basis did Bonhoeffer discover in the Frenchman a profound sympathy—something which he could hardly share with anyone else at Union. The scrap of conversation recorded in

Bonhoeffer's prison letters suggests how the two students talked with one another. "We were discussing what our real purpose was in life. He said he would like to become a saint." Bonhoeffer admits: "At the time I was very much impressed, though I disagreed with him, and said I should prefer to have faith, or words to that effect." [2]

Lasserre was a pacifist with beliefs more deeply rooted in the Sermon on the Mount than in the experience of the Great War. Bonhoeffer came to sense in him a startling commitment to Christ's demand for peace—a commitment which led Bonhoeffer to an awareness that international peace, and not Church unity, was the crucial issue of the ecumenical movement.

Lasserre was for Bonhoeffer a start. He probably did not recognize, when he left New York in the summer of 1932, how important Lasserre would be. Bonhoeffer never became the kind of pacifist that Lasserre was: a man whose range of beliefs and activities centered around his quest for peace. But Bonhoeffer deeply respected, and certainly learned from Lasserre; later, when Dietrich was arranging ecumenical conferences, he struggled urgently to arrange for Lasserre to speak, that his voice would be heard by Church figures throughout Europe.

The second influence, one whose potential was never fully realized, was the witness of Mahatma Gandhi, the saintly liberator of India's millions. As early as his first trip to America, Dietrich looked upon Gandhi with fascination and admiration. Gandhi's method of rebelling and then retaliating to force in a totally nonviolent way suggested to Bonhoeffer the presence of a man who could combine political and religious goals without the corrupting use of destructive methods. Gandhi's pacifism, like Lasserre's, grew from a profound respect for the message of the New Testament. But Bonhoeffer saw in Gandhi, even more sharply than in Lasserre, the contemporary significance of pacifism on a social scale. Dietrich's desire to visit India in 1932 was prompted largely by curiosity and an immense respect for Gandhi as a Christian. His later ambition to see Gandhi in 1935, however, followed Hitler's abuse of power in Germany; and Dietrich hoped with a new urgency to find in Gandhi's method of *satyagraha* a tactic which the Confessing Church could use to challenge the Third Reich. His disappointment in being unable to visit Gandhi then was keen. The failure of the proposed trip forced him to search for alternative methods, and a meaningful interpretation of resistance for the Confessing Church.

Bonhoeffer's belief in nonviolence came largely from Gandhi; and the conception of pacifism which Bonhoeffer adhered to grew very much from Gandhi's belief in the power and necessity of political resistance. Dietrich never believed that a nonresistant, retiring adherence to "pacifism" was any answer; he generally regarded that as an escape. Above all he valued participation, action, the shaping of whatever social condition was desired. But that shaping had to be done in what was primarily a peaceful way, and a way which could not lead to war. Here Gandhi stood as an indication of Christ's will for the present. And here Gandhi made a powerful impact on Bonhoeffer's notion of pacifism.

The third influence, more fundamental than Lasserre or Gandhi, though discovered largely through Lasserre and Gandhi, was Christ—and Christ's admonitions on peace. Bonhoeffer found Christ's statement in the Sermon on the Mount the most relevant statement of the gospels for the present. (*The Cost of Discipleship* is in many ways a lengthy homiletic on this passage.) Bonhoeffer wished above all to follow Christ; and the contexts in which he speaks of peace are invariably as the peace prescribed by Christ and ensured not by men or weapons, but by God.

> Peace on earth is not a problem, but a commandment given at Christ's coming. . . . Peace means to give oneself altogether to the law of God, wanting no security, but in faith and obedience laying the destiny of the nations in the hand of Almighty God, not trying to direct it for selfish purposes.[3]

In a sense, the word "pacifist" does not apply to Bonhoeffer through the mid-'thirties. He believed in peace because he believed in Christ, and for him peace was simply a command of Christ which applied to the present with an exceptional force. Bonhoeffer saw peace as a very limited goal, primarily as a step to a greater purpose: the unity of men in Christ's Church. He never struggled for peace in the way that his friend Lasserre did; for Dietrich, Christ's mandate meant the effort to communicate to Christians the imperative of international peace for the sake of the Church—not the imperative of peace at any cost, for the sake of peace.

The fourth influence could be identified as Bonhoeffer's involvement in the ecumenical movement during the critical years of 1932 to 1938. As late as 1935, the War could probably have been averted by the intervention of France or any of the Allies in Germany to check the rampant build-up of arms. Although Bonhoeffer's colleagues in the ecumenical movement were internationally-minded Christian ministers—generally young—and certainly men with limited political connections, Dietrich attempted continually to make them aware of the critical need for international peace. Indeed, Bonhoeffer saw the ecumenical movement primarily as a peace-creating venture, not mainly an effort to unite the churches. Consequently, the stream of involvements with the various ecumenical organizations took on for Bonhoeffer the character of a search—for the meaning of peace, and the role of "the one great Ecumenical Council of the Holy Church of Christ" [4] in achieving that peace.

This search led Bonhoeffer to his deeper concern with peace, and, indirectly, to his personal pacifism. Through his contacts in the ecumenical movement he came to recognize the utter folly of nationalism, the desperate urgency with which peacemaking was needed, the painfulness involved in the seemingly futile struggle for peace. It was hard for a man accustomed to working with Englishmen, Frenchmen, and Norwegians to accept the need for Germany to go to war. It was harder for a man who had struggled for years in awakening men to the need for peace to see any sense or value to such a war—much less feel personal commitment to it. In this sense, then, Bonhoeffer's pacifism was simply a natural consequence of his work in the ecumenical movement.

The fifth influence, and certainly the most directly felt, was Dietrich's knowledge as early as 1938 that he was to be called to the military. For Dietrich it was not simply a matter of fighting or refusing to fight. The war which stood ominously on the horizon was an act he recognized as simply evil; the war Hitler intended was totally aggressive, totally unnecessary. As a Christian who had for years meditated on the Sermon on the Mount, Dietrich found it unthinkable to serve. He admitted that other Christians, so highly sensitized to their obligations to the state, conceivably could serve. He even accepted, if dejectedly, the fact that the Confessing Church would not make a commitment on the issue. But, as he wrote the Bishop of Chichester, it was personally impossible for him to serve:

> . . . Perhaps the worst thing of all is the military oath which I should have to swear. So I am rather puzzled in this situation, and perhaps even more because I feel, it is really only on Christian grounds that I find it difficult to do military service under the present conditions, and yet there are only very few friends who would approve of my attitude. In spite of much reading and thinking concerning this matter I have not yet made up my mind what I would do under different circumstances. But actually as things are I should have to do violence to my Christian conviction, if I would take up arms "here and now." [5]

Here an important distinction—between pacifism out of political motives and pacifism out of Christian motives—is suggested. Only later would it become evident that for Bonhoeffer the distinction could never really exist: as a purpose for pacifism, or for active resistance to Hitler's regime.

These five influences—Lasserre, Gandhi, Christ's Sermon on the Mount, the ecumenical movement, and the imminence of conscription—stand out as decisively affecting Bonhoeffer's unique style of pacifism. It was very much a pacifism with Christian roots and Christian goals, a pacifism which Bonhoeffer held to be deeply personal, and not obligating others.

But with Bonhoeffer pacifism was not, could never be, an absolute: and the very mind which for years probed its meaning came soon to see its incapacity for action in a time when action was imperative. Bonhoeffer's passion for involvement was equalled only by his loathing for non-involvement: and to see—as he did upon his return from America—the extent to which the German people had been led into a craving for war, made him realize that the German nation needed more than healing: it needed first an exorcism, a purging.

To identify precisely why Bonhoeffer chose tactical resistance to Hitler upon his return from America would be impossible. The choice was personally and profoundly his own; and although the conditions in Germany, critically sharpened by the War, forced upon Dietrich an entirely new challenge, was that challenge serious enough to reverse the direction of his thinking—to give, in effect, the Sermon on the Mount a totally new perspective?

Sometime after the collapse of France, Eberhard Bethge once asked Bonhoeffer whether he would, if furnished with the opportunity, assassinate the Führer. Dietrich thought a moment, and said yes, he would. The opportunity, of course, never arose, and the question was therefore a purely hypothetical one. But to reply, even hypothetically, that he *would* have used the utmost means in violence marks an incredible transition from Bonhoeffer's early position on nonviolence and peace.

Understanding this transition—as well as it can ever be understood—is important for a deeper insight into Bonhoeffer's character and, only indirectly, for interpreting some of the seemingly radical shifts in his later thought. Indeed, if the momentous letters which he wrote from prison were not actually major breakthroughs from his earlier thought but in reality a maturation of the earlier ideas in a new form of expression, then Bonhoeffer's movement to resistance marks an analogous maturation, and a similarly new form of expression. For his pacifism had been an integral part of his Christian beliefs largely *because of* the historical conditions which he recognized called for peace. Seeing peace as the greatest need in Europe, Bonhoeffer diverted much of his effort to make others aware of peace—and in doing so became something of a "pacifist." But the historical conditions had changed. There was always a great need for international understanding, and a widespread desire for peace, but now the need was sharper, more urgent. A demonic government was dragging the German people into destruction and ripping open Europe at the same time. What the world needed most now was not peace, not a quieting of the havoc, nor even primarily an effort to rescue the victims of the havoc. "The third possibility," Dietrich had written in 1932, "is not just to bandage victims under the wheel, but to put a spoke in the wheel itself." [6] The historical moment made that third alternative for Bonhoeffer an imperative.

In terms of the historical moment, then, Bonhoeffer's transition to conspiracy against the government is not a total reorientation—just as the call to a "non-religious interpretation of biblical concepts" in the prison letters is not a total reorientation. What Bonhoeffer did when he became involved in the *Abwehr* circle makes sense in terms of what he always believed and hoped in. For he believed more deeply in relating to the present, in identifying the concrete needs of the moment, than in simple pacifism.

Of course, that the situation demanded a new form of action supplies only a partial and theoretical answer. There were other motives which touch at the substance of Bonhoeffer's decision: motives which are revealing of his most fundamental values.

One motivation may well have been a disillusionment with pacifism. Bonhoeffer embraced pacifism largely because it held a tactical advantage: it answered a need. But the coming of the War made pacifism an individual (and highly risky) decision, and by obliterating the very peace which Bonhoeffer had struggled for, made his style of pacifism somewhat obsolete. And obsolescence was something which Bonhoeffer instinctively abhorred. He speaks in both the *Ethics* and the prison writings of Don Quixote, a figure who symbolized to him the appalling stupidity of fighting battles which had long been won—or lost. It is very likely that he came to see the pacifist reformer as a Don Quixote: preaching a message which—by Germany's very abandonment of it through plunging into war—made that message irrelevant and hopelessly inadequate.

Another motivation may figure in, Bonhoeffer's growing disappointment with the Confessing Church. In the late 1930's an effort had been made by Reich Church and Confessing Church leaders to consolidate the two churches. Bonhoeffer had violently opposed the effort. And though it failed, the attempt seriously weakened the Confessing Church—to a point at which its leaders were far more worried about its stability than the salvation of the people it was intended to serve. Bonhoeffer's references to the Confessing Church throughout the prison letters (generally linked to the Barthian theology which the Church drew upon) suggest its inadequacy for facing the present, and totally living in the world. Had the Confessing Church actually done what Bonhoeffer hoped it would do—sharpen consciences, stimulate critical thought about German life under the regime, identify the imperatives of discipleship to Christ in the present—then very possibly Bonhoeffer never would have had to enter the resistance. He could simply have worked with the men who themselves would make the resistance a success, trusting in their work. Once he discovered, however, that only a handful of men with the courage and vision of an Oster or a Dohnanyi were struggling to overthrow the government, Dietrich knew that he would be needed.

A third reason for entering resistance was certainly Bonhoeffer's profound love for Germany and the German people. In his 1939 letter to inform Niebuhr that he was suddenly leaving America, Bonhoeffer wrote: "I must live through this difficult period of our national history with the Christian people of Germany. I will have no right to participate in the reconstruction of Christian life in Germany after the war if I do not share the trials of this time with my people." [7] Bonhoeffer felt deeply committed to the German people, and especially the "German Christians" in a way that he was not committed to any other earthly institution, even the ecumenical movement. Throughout the War, throughout even the gloomiest of the prison letters, Bonhoeffer reveals a constant, almost obsessive faith in the reconstruction, the period which he saw as the great moment in which the Church could blossom. But his hope for restoration came not from a vivid desire to experiment with the forms of the Church, nor even from its marking an end to the War. He saw reconstruction, rather, as a period of repentance and of beginning anew, a period in which Christians would identify themselves primarily as Christians—no longer primarily as Germans. This was the goal which motivated the struggling thought of Bonhoeffer in his prison cell: to awaken Christians, the German Christians he loved.

That his love for the German people would lead Bonhoeffer to actively opposing their government shows the tragedy in which the Germans had immersed themselves. The meditation opening the prison letters, "After Ten Years," reveals the extent of Bonhoeffer's sympathy with the German people whose future had been wrecked by their Führer:

> But the German has preserved his freedom—what nation had talked so passionately of freedom as we have, from Luther to the idealists?—by seeking deliverance from his own will through service to the community. . . . The trouble was, he did not understand his world. He forgot that submissiveness and self-sacrifice could be exploited for evil ends.[8]

As much as he disagreed with their willingness to permit Hitler his atrocities and his War, Bonhoeffer still felt deeply committed to the German people, perhaps more deeply than ever, and conceived of his resistance activities as a means of helping them.

A final and related reason for Bonhoeffer's entry into the resistance would be the very terms in which he conceived resistance action. "Our action," he told Bishop George Bell in their meeting in Stockholm in 1942, "must be such that the world will understand it as an act of repentance." [9] In his meeting with W. A. Visser 't Hooft in 1941, he described resistance as a salvaging action, and an act of repentance: salvaging, in that out of the war would be plucked the foundation of a new international order of justice; repentance, meaning in his own words that "only in defeat can we atone for the terrible crimes we have committed against Europe and the world." [10]

Out of this context, out of these motivations, Bonhoeffer

took part in a conspiracy to end the Third Reich. A man who loved his country and could not bear to see it drag Europe into another holocaust; a man whose disappointment with earlier causes made him realize that the times called for action of heroic and desperate proportions; a man whose commitment to pacifism followed from a deeper commitment, which led him in time to resistance: this was Bonhoeffer.

That he could act, and did act, in the resistance movement with a tremendous certainty that he had chosen rightly only emphasizes how deeply the values that led him to this conspiracy ran. Once decided, he could see that the moral question of killing a man could well be ethically subordinated to the more urgent question of his personal responsibility to the German people and to Europe. The distinction possible earlier, between actions done (or not done) from Christian motivation and from the motivation of a citizen, was no longer possible. Bonhoeffer knew that he must act: and it was the action and what that action would achieve which counted, not delineating the origin of the action.

Bonhoeffer's work with the resistance in Germany may well be his clearest suggestion as to what "religionless Christianity," when taken to its completion, will finally mean: men of responsibility and action, making their own moral decisions and making them with a deep understanding of the world. Dietrich's movement from pacifism to active plotting for a new Reich did not come simply from a dissatisfaction with passive resistance and the desire to attack the problem more effectively. Bonhoeffer, strictly speaking, distrusted both nonviolent and active resistance. His own efforts in the movement came not as a Christian mandate, but as a tragic necessity, forced upon him by the failure of so many Christians to act responsibly at the critical moment. Bonhoeffer wanted above all to interpret Christ to the present world—not to be a chief agent in exorcising it of an antichrist. But he was forced by historical conditions to purge rather than to build—and in purging revealed how far, finally, Christ's demands could lead a Christian in a secular world.

. . . Today is Reformation Day, a feast which in our times can give one plenty to think about. One wonders how it was Luther's action led to consequences which were the exact opposite of what he intended, and which overshadowed the last years of his life and work, so that he doubted the value of everything he had achieved. He desired a real unity both for the Church and for Western Christendom, but the consequence was the ruin of both. He sought the 'Freedom of the Christian Man,' and the consequence was apathy and barbarism. . . . Kierkegaard said more than a century ago that if Luther were alive then he would have said the exact opposite of what he said in the sixteenth century. I believe he was right—cum grano salis.

Letter from Tegel prison October 31, 1943

15. *Bonhoeffer and Reunion of the Churches*

"There is still no theology of the ecumenical movement. As often as the Church has reached a new understanding of its nature it has produced a new theology, appropriate to this self-understanding." [1] Bonhoeffer wrote these words in 1932. He was well aware then, as no doubt he would be today, that the issues galvanizing the ecumenical movement are largely theological, and that worthwhile ecumenical effort is often the foremost responsibility of the Church's theologians.

Yet Bonhoeffer did not attempt a consciously ecumenical theology. Indeed, at the time of his death he would probably have been most modest in appraising the importance of his work for later theology—much less ecumenical theology. But a mighty paradox ensues: in recent years no Protestant theologian has been nearly so popular among Catholics in America, England, and numerous parts of Europe. Certainly no recent theologian has stimulated the spontaneous and highly charged theological discussions between Protestants and Catholics which Bonhoeffer has. And no theologian's ideas have been more identified with the moral impetus of the last decade's focal issues: the Negro Revolution, the world peace effort, the ecumenical movement. In effect, Bonhoeffer has achieved a fresh understanding between Protestants and Catholics and, to a lesser extent, between Christians and secular humanists. What is the nature of this understanding, and how far, in terms of Christian unity, can it be followed? What are the imperatives which Bonhoeffer's influence is giving the ecumenical movement today? What in Bonhoeffer's theology has roused this common interest, has spoken so effectively to Catholics and Protestants alike?

The answers to these questions are essential, not only for a clear appreciation of Bonhoeffer's importance for ecumenism, but for the exploratory routes his thought offers to any viable ecumenical theology. For however impressive Bonhoeffer's witness to the faith in Nazi Germany, his resistance efforts and martyrdom, he has made a powerful impact upon the groping theological mind of the generation. It is the point of impact which should be located, and the causes searched out; otherwise, Bonhoeffer is endangered by the eventual threat of having been faddish and somewhat ephemeral, "the popular theologian of a decade." He would probably have recoiled in horror at such a thought.

To pursue the question in terms of Bonhoeffer's conscious ecumenical intent in the *Ethics* and the prison writings would be slightly misleading and probably eventually futile. Although he remained in the ecumenical effort—at that time completely Protestant—until his arrest, Bonhoeffer's writings, especially the important later writings, do not reflect an explicit ecumenical effort. And indeed, if they did, Bonhoeffer would have had no occasion to approach the central ecumenical issue to arise only later: the reunion of Protestant churches with the Roman Catholic Church. Bonhoeffer's specific references to Roman Catholic theology and practice are infrequent and peripheral; they could hardly serve as guidelines for fruitful dialogue. And the one clear area which could prove most fruitful, Bonhoeffer's concern with community, has not really been explored by Catholics.

It is probably to Bonhoeffer's advantage that he did not pursue a basically ecumenical theology. He thought and wrote from the premise of a Church which he always described as one, holy, *and* catholic, despite the frequent misuse of "catholic" in German Lutheranism. For deeply imbedded in Bonhoeffer's later thought was his experience of the ecumenical movement, an experience which forged certain convictions, and was an unconscious basis to the mature thought of the *Ethics* and the prison letters.

It is difficult to assess the way in which the ecumenical movement affected Bonhoeffer; during these same years he was also involved in the struggles of the Confessing Church, struggles which made some very profound impressions upon him. And to help obscure the problem, in both his ecumenical work and the efforts to help guide the precarious Confessing Church, Bonhoeffer was not influenced so much by the ideas and doctrinal debates of this period as by the turbulent conditions which generated many of the debates.

In the 1930's the various ecumenical forces surging for several decades achieved a coalescence, and a fresh impetus to unity. The World Alliance for Promoting International Friendship through the Churches, Archbishop Söderblom's long-suffering project, was finally on its feet. The effort that the Council constantly made, to promote world peace through common understanding, could actually be no more than preliminary to the later, more sophisticated ecumenical attempts. Yet Bonhoeffer's first contact with the ecumenical movement took place at the World Alliance meetings in Cambridge late in the summer of 1931. His report on the meetings, written weeks later, is perceptive; Bonhoeffer saw the issues sharply—war guilt, the pleas for world peace, a common understanding. But he was severely critical of any efforts between the churches of different nations to proclaim abstract "Christian principles" without progressing to planned, effective action.

"Christian principles"—applied art—are most dangerous to true Christianity precisely at such conferences. . . . The fact that the churches have composed yet another resolution will simply be ignored in wide circles of this country, unless they do something now. . . .[2]

Later, especially while serving the pastorates in England, Bonhoeffer became involved in the Life and Work movement, probably the most effective effort at Christian unity in the 1930's. The motto of Life and Work, "Doctrine divides; service unites," suggests that Bonhoeffer must have felt an instinctive sympathy for this approach to ecumenism. Bonhoeffer served the Life and Work movement by providing a clear understanding to the outside world of the real dimensions of the Confessing Church struggle. During the 1930's, the Life and Work movement came to the reluctant but inevitable conclusion that doctrine could not be neglected in the intense living out of Christianity. The problems foisted upon it during these years—the main one was the Confessing Church struggle—demanded doctrinal application before action could be taken. The multiple initiatives of Faith and Order over these years, though at times misguided, gave it a tempo of excitement and a sense of promise.

The impact of these two movements upon Bonhoeffer can be seen only in the grim perspective of the German situation. For Bonhoeffer was never free of this tension which his ecumenical work and the nationalist spirit in Germany had created. Hitler had effectively transformed the humiliation of Versailles into a raging nationalism. The German spirit became the measure and goal of any effort, and into the fabric of politics, commerce, entertainment, the Church, was woven the unending thread of Teutonic superiority. At the parades, at the rallies, at restaurants and schools, frenzied Germans sang, cheered, and hailed the Führer. Nationalism was a pounding, ineluctable force during the 1930's in Germany, and most Germans welcomed it enthusiastically.

Bonhoeffer remained highly suspicious of the upsurgence of the so-called "German spirit." One of his reasons for the intense ecumenical activity and the two German pastorates in

London was his distrust of the volatile German atmosphere, and the desire to keep in contact with the Church in other countries. And the decisions—especially the decision to live in England—must have been painful for Bonhoeffer, because he loved his homeland and placed great hope in its future. The severe nationalist spirit made it especially difficult for him. Ecumenical activities were not simply looked upon askance those days; pastors who travelled to conferences abroad were labelled internationalists—implying everything from foreign sympathizers to traitors. What was demanded of Bonhoeffer, eventually, was a strong conviction in the value of ecumenical work, strong enough to overcome the stinging comments of close friends.

The effects of Bonhoeffer's ecumenical work at this time can be seen in some of the decisive directions taken after 1933. One conviction emerging from his efforts was that the ecumenical churches had the corporate responsibility to speak out on critical issues. Speaking of peace he wrote: "Only the one great Ecumenical Council of the holy Church all over the world can speak out so that the world, though it gnash its teeth, will have to hear." [3] His words to Archbishop Bell of Chichester on the ecumenical movement's recognition of the Confessing Church were even stronger:

> It seems to me that the responsibility of the ecumenic work has perhaps never been so far-reaching as in the present moment. If the ecumenical churches would keep silent during these days, I am afraid that all the trust put into it by the majority would be destroyed.[4]

Another conviction emerged from those years, one with a subtle but penetrating influence in Bonhoeffer's mature thought. The Lutheran Church in Germany had always been identified with the nation and ethos of Germany; a synthesis had always been present, and was identified by most churchmen as theologically right and necessary. However, Bonhoeffer's experience with the German Church's approval of Nazi atrocities, as well as his work with sympathetic Europeans at the same time, made him bitterly conscious of the great dangers in a national Church.

In the *Ethics* and prison writings there is no foundation for a revival of national churches; indeed, the emphasis is to do away with any constricting limits to the Church's openness before the world.

In his later writings, Bonhoeffer likewise stressed the urgency of an openness to the whole Church. In the prison letters he spoke of a "breadth of sympathy," and later of the importance of shared beliefs among the churches. In the prison outline to the book he planned but never wrote, he remarked of the conflicts between churches:

> What do we really believe? I mean, believe in such a way as to stake our whole lives upon it? The problem of the Apostles' Creed? "What must I believe?" the wrong question. Antiquated controversies, especially those between the different confessions. The Lutheran *versus* Reformed, and to some extent, the Catholic *versus* Protestant controversy. These divisions may at any time be revived with passion, but they no longer carry real conviction. Impossible to prove this, but necessary to take the bull by the horns. All we can prove is that the faith of the Bible and Christianity does not stand or fall by these issues.[5]

This outline was one of the last things which Bonhoeffer wrote and which has been preserved. He never stopped thinking about the plight of a divided Church. However, the question returns: how influential was his concern for unity in his later thought, and where is it most decisively present?

The influences probably did not take on conscious form in the major achievements of Bonhoeffer's mature thought. Yet Bonhoeffer's view of the Church, especially in the *Ethics,* is too expansive, too instinctively open, to allow any sectarian disputes.

> This space of the Church, then, is not something which exists on its own account. It is from the outset something which reaches out far beyond itself, for indeed it is not the space of some kind of cultural association as would have to fight for its own survival in the world, but it is the place where testimony is given to the foundation of all reality in Jesus Christ. . . . The only way in which the Church can

defend her own territory is by fighting not for it but for the salvation of the world.[6]

In other words, the vision of the Church to which Bonhoeffer summons Christians—a Church committed to the world and vigorously engaged in all strata of social life—is one which cannot accept a perpetual state of disunity. There is nothing dogmatic and inhibiting about the *Ethics* and the prison writings. Throughout both, Bonhoeffer is searching earnestly for a concept of the Church large enough to break from the religious, defensive attitudes so deeply imbedded in the post-Reformation Christian churches. Bonhoeffer's search was for one ineluctable principle, in the *Ethics* described as "a Church living for and in the world," in the prison letters as "religionless Christianity." The search clearly leads Bonhoeffer beyond the traditional dual principle of the reformers: "The Church is the place where the Word is preached and the sacraments are received."

Because of Bonhoeffer's background and the synthetic nature of much of his writing, Bonhoeffer's ideas encourage exploration for the churches as a basis of fresh understanding. The two opposing forces which the student Bonhoeffer met in their immensity at Berlin, liberal theology and Barth's revelation theology, continuously demanded of Bonhoeffer the effort of integration. *The Communion of Saints* and *Act and Being* are two ambitious and self-conscious attempts to fuse the major tenets of each school together in the Church. Much of Bonhoeffer's thought through the 1930's, especially on concrete revelation and proclamation, reveals the same tension. In the *Ethics* and the prison letters the effort to synthesize reaches its height: here Bonhoeffer brings a powerful, revelation-centered faith in Christ to bear on the serious problems of Church and world in which liberal theologians like Ernst Troeltsch had foundered.

What Bonhoeffer does in combining two major, and seemingly opposed, theological traditions is to arrive at a theology of the Church relevant to the followers of both schools. By describing a Church which has meaning only in terms of its self-giving to the world, Bonhoeffer is not merely lashing out at

Barth's excesses; he is bringing Barth's insights to bear upon the imminent questions of the Church's mission and witness, questions which the revelation theologians had skirted in their full complexity. Bonhoeffer's synthetic mind can be seen in almost every doctrine: Church and world; his ethics, conformation and anthropology, the critique of religion, and the "non-religious interpretation of biblical concepts."

Bonhoeffer's continuing attempt to combine two traditions has in part been responsible for his recent popularity as a theologian for an ecumenical age. Yet can this explain his popularity among Catholics? Can this account for the prophetic quality recognized in his thought? Probably not. In relating the schools of thought, Bonhoeffer has overcome some theological limitations, but in no sense has he challenged the central doctrinal differences between the churches—interpretations of justification, the use of Scripture, and the nature of faith.

Where then is the source of Bonhoeffer's influence, if not any conscious ecumenical attempt, or his synthesis of two major schools of theology? Perhaps at this point it might be questioned whether this source is, strictly speaking, theological or not. Indeed, numerous commentators on the ecumenical movement have pointed out that it is a mistake to think that the final answer to the problem of reunion can be theological. For undercutting and to some extent explaining the theological problem is a deeper and more serious difficulty: what many have called a severe language barrier.[7]

In a famous lecture given before a number of Catholic clergymen and theologians in Münster in 1927, Karl Barth suggested what might be the nature of this barrier. In substance, he said, so many of the Protestant and the Catholic ideas and definitions on the Church agree, but the distance between the two churches is enormous because everything—"everything without exception," insists Barth—is meant so differently on this side and that.

> The reality of the Church, undeniably seen as common to both Catholics and Protestants, is seen so differently or is so differently

visible on this side and on that, that neither of us can accommodate our position to the other side even with the best will on both sides.[8]

The problem as stated by Barth is essentially insoluble. Common understanding comes through communication. Yet if that communication is blocked by a language barrier—where no language barrier *seems* to exist—true common understanding is impossible; there can only be the illusion of it. In other words, Barth is suggesting that a specific theological effort to overcome disunity is finally futile. He is, moreover, suggesting the real proportions of the ecumenical problem.

Perhaps Barth overstated his case. The recent experience of many Christians attempting dialogue has borne out much of his conclusion, however. For a Roman Catholic such words as "faith," "Church," and "ethics" convey a different meaning than they do to a Protestant. Words may be defined, but the definitions convey different emphases. For the language barrier is a subtle one; it has grown from four and a half centuries of separation, when the same substantial truths were taught and preached, but within differing patterns of thought and from different points of view. Indeed, along with the whole problem of language there is the difficulty of the experience that gives support to language: an experience which for Catholics and Protestants has gone largely unshared. The religious experience of Protestants and the experience of Catholics have been, regrettably, two different things.

Inevitably the conflict is a clash between two cultures. As the historian Christopher Dawson has said in his book *The Dividing of Christendom:*

> . . . the changes that followed the Reformation are not only the work of the Churches and the theologians. They are also the work of the statesmen and the soldiers. The Catholic and Protestant worlds have been divided from one another by centuries of war and power politics, and the result has been that they no longer share a common social experience. Each has its own version of history, its own social inheritance, as well as its own religious beliefs and standards of orthodoxy.[9]

The roots of the two cultures reach back further than the Reformation, to the Middle Ages. There, the Church can be seen making a monumental effort to forge from the Gospel and the world a single Christian culture. The synthesis was constructed laboriously, though once constructed, it was admittedly tenuous. The precarious network of ecclesiastical and political power and the growth of national states gave rise to forces which shook the synthesis to its foundation, and threatened a decisive split.

The Reformation of the 16th century brought that split, with a finality and range of consequences which the reformers would have dreaded had they been able to see the effects centuries later. The impact of the Reformation eventually became clear: where one culture had unified Europe, two separate cultures, Catholic and Protestant, now split it. To worsen conditions, a deep antagonism existed between the two cultures, and that antagonism led to the bloodiest century of open warfare history has ever seen. Then came a long, tightly drawn political and religious stalemate, which eventually subsided into the "cold war" of the 19th and 20th centuries. The failure of these two religious forces, either to control the other or to ignore the common experience of Western Christendom and forge a new, more realistic cultural pattern, has led to a cultural separation and a cultural rivalry. It has also led to the emergence of a third, and totally secular culture, which over the last two hundred years has come to dominate Western civilization.

This new culture, rising to fill the vacuum left in the struggle between the two parts of the severed Christian culture, was remarkably new—new in that its very non-religious character was its source of vitality and promise. This "secular" culture, heralded by the free-thinking *libertines* in France and a lay intelligentsia throughout Europe, was slowly at work creating a hope for society kindled not by the Christian faith but by man's own prowess. The twin thrust of the Age of Enlightenment and the scientific-technological revolution of recent centuries has given this culture a self-confidence and total control over society unparalleled since the medieval Christian culture.

This "third" culture is characterized by a number of important features. Because the main impetus to its development was reaction against a jarring cultural disunity, it tended to be negative in character. As a result, its positive formation fell into the hands of men whose concern was not so much with the problem of unity or disunity, but with the validity or invalidity of Christianity. In other words, the work of giving this emerging culture a distinctive identity was left with men who came to the task with a strong anti-religious bias. That they were thinkers of intelligence and foresight enabled the modern culture they shaped to survive and, indeed, to thrive on its own religionless premises.

The rising culture made no effort to heal the split in Christendom. It attempted, though only for a while, to destroy the Catholic and Protestant religions. Eventually the secular culture came to regard these religions as irrelevant and saw the cultures these religions protected as innocuous. For as the new culture came gradually to absorb the traditional functions of the two cultures, it took from these cultures their sustenance and body. All that could be left was a language, a pattern of thinking and action, but nothing more; these were cultural residuums, robbed of their vitality and future. And the language that was left, as well as the patterns of thought and morals—these were to the secular world anachronistic and meaningless, very much out of step with the secular culture, in which the Christian cultures continued their diminished existence.

The effects are startling. This third culture, which had arisen as an expedient, temporary provision against the disunity left by the religious wars, came to demand the full development of a culture, leaving no cultural value aside. By thus becoming *the* shaping factor of civilization, it has developed its own language, its own world of ideas and aspirations. Added, then, to the languages of the two cultures is a third, which, to the man reared and nourished in the values of the secular culture, is the only language which can convey meaning.

The three cultures stand at odds, but the conflict has been so diminished it is almost ludicrous. The Protestant and Catholic worlds are less cultures than cultural residues: all of the real powers that give a culture its vitality and force have been sapped by the third culture. Yet the Protestant and Catholic cultures persist, attempting to use their impoverished resources as sightings on the world. Theological debates go on, in a language which has no meaning to the secular culture, and in a way too insulated from reality to insure that it will make any impact on the real world. The languages of the two cultures are kept alive, and men are imbued in these languages; but the power of the words to evoke deep faith has been lost.

The final outcome is a return to the condition of Babel. Men engaged in building a better world—seculars, Catholics, Protestants—have lost the ability, and in some instances the desire, to communicate. Most distressing and most obvious may be the conflict between the two Christian cultures; yet there is real tragedy in the inability of either culture to partake fluidly of the life and thought of the secular culture. The condition which Karl Barth described, in which the same words may be used but the meanings differ, is here a clear cultural reality.

The question now is inevitable: *must* these two religious cultures shelter themselves against the secular culture? Cannot in some way the Christian life draw upon a secular culture for many of its values and some of its source-of-life style? Obviously, neither of the fragmented Christian cultures can support a complete life in the modern world. If unity is to come, it must somehow come from the secular culture.

It is to Dietrich Bonhoeffer's monumental credit that he fully recognized this condition and was the first theologian to speak vigorously to the Church to admit it. For Bonhoeffer, especially in the prison writings, any attempt to restore the dwindling Christian culture was futile. That culture had been supplanted by a "godless" culture, one "radically without religion," what Bonhoeffer has termed a "world come of age." The foundations upon which the medieval synthesis stood—a cohesion of Church and state under papal supremacy; an ordered universe centered around the earth; an atmosphere of the supernatural, which thrived with superstitions and persecuted science

—these foundations had crumbled with the fissure in Christendom. And the emerging secular culture found for itself new foundations: faith in man's awakened intelligence, a sense of liberty, and a new respect for the individual.

The thrust of Bonhoeffer's mature theology can be seen as an overwhelming acceptance of the dominance and power of the secular culture, as well as its positive values. Bonhoeffer saw only one hopeful way for the Church: involvement in the secular world: not a cautious "involvement" guided by hesitations and deliberations, but the enthusiastic, full-hearted commitment of men who share intensely the agonies, loves, and hopes of that culture. The Christian, as Bonhoeffer describes him, must

> plunge himself into the life of a godless world, without attempting to gloss over its ungodliness with a veneer of religion or trying to transfigure it. He must live a 'worldly' life, and so participate in the suffering of God.[10]

What is most striking about Bonhoeffer's thought, and what has appalled so many Christians, is his uncompromising summons to the world. Nowhere in his Church-world doctrine, his anthropology, or his notion of "religionless Christianity" does he denote the limits of involvement for the Christian. This is not to say that he did not recognize dangers in imbedding the Church in a secular culture; yet he saw such a move as the only promise for Christianity, and he knew a finicky approach to the entire question would be disastrous.

Bonhoeffer has compared his effort with Paul's, when Paul had to make the decision about prescribing circumcision. "The Pauline question," Bonhoeffer wrote, "whether circumcision is a condition of justification is today, I consider, the question whether religion is a condition of salvation. Freedom from circumcision is at the same time freedom from religion." [11] As it was with St. Paul, the decision to discard religion—or the cultural accouterments of Christianity—would be momentous and costly. Yet the Christian communities of the first centuries thrived largely *because* St. Paul had been wise enough to encourage the Church to enter and assimilate the Hellenic culture of that time. Bonhoeffer's theological plea was made in the same hope, and with the same horror of a self-enclosed Church feeding on its own vitals.

Only against the background of these cultural conditions can Bonhoeffer's importance for the ecumenical movement come to light. Bonhoeffer was the first theologian to assert effectively the need for Christians to speak, no longer in their isolated languages, but in the language of the third, secular culture. "How do we speak," he asks, "in secular fashion of God? In what way are we in a religionless and secular sense Christian, in what way are we the *Ekklesia,* 'those who are called forth,' not conceiving of ourselves religiously as specially favored, but as wholly belonging to the world?" [12]

The effect is that Bonhoeffer has shown a remarkable capacity to bridge the centuries-old division between Protestant and Catholic modes of thought. While Protestants and Catholics do not share theological and religious cultures, they do possess a common culture, and thus a common language. And in the words, the patterns, and the values of this secular culture, the full meaning of the Gospel can be shared. What Bonhoeffer suggested in his "non-religious interpretation of biblical concepts" amounts, really, to an interpretation divested of the split cultural modes of thought, and therefore capable of achieving a new unity of outlook and purpose.

The venture as Bonhoeffer described it is a clear ecumenical necessity: the Church must step into the world, living passionately in and for the secular culture to which God has summoned it. As the secular culture of the Western civilization becomes the secular culture of the world, it is all the more important that Christians explore the meaning of the Gospel for that culture, and discover the secular language in which the Gospel can be spoken anew. The proportions of the task are awesome: so far most attempts to coin the biblical message in contemporary language have failed. Yet Bonhoeffer saw no alternative, and for the thrust of Christian unity, perhaps there is no alternative.

Here then may well be the source of impact in Bonhoeffer's thought, the reason why Catholics as well as Protestants have found his works so meaningful and stimulating. Here likewise is Bonhoeffer's posthumous summons to the ecumenical movement to take the most reliable path—even though that seems to be the riskiest one. As with much of his writings, a piercing criticism runs through Bonhoeffer's influence upon the ecumenical movement—that if the ecumenical movement persists in attempting to share their cultures, without attempting the new understanding which can come of speaking in a secular language, then true unity will never come nearer than illusions. Real unity lies where the Church has been called by God: in the midst of the secular world.

"Anyone who has anything to do with Dietrich Bonhoeffer today realizes again and again the amazing extent to which he provides answers to questions that only now, some twenty years later, begin to raise their heads. He anticipated solutions for problems we are only now beginning to recognize as our problems."

Hanfried Müller, "Concerning the Reception and Interpretation of Dietrich Bonhoeffer"

16. *A Catholic Looks at Bonhoeffer*

Catholics have taken to Bonhoeffer. His name appears frequently in Catholic publications, study groups, lecture series, and not simply for the radical conjectures of the prison letters; books like *The Cost of Discipleship* and *Life Together* have aroused serious interest among Catholics. From my own experience, I would say that, in general, Catholics tend to show a healthier interest in the early Bonhoeffer than Protestants. Why? What in Bonhoeffer has appealed so directly to Catholics?

The analysis of the preceding chapter may help explain Bonhoeffer's popularity in terms of a "non-religious interpretation of biblical concepts." But the question can be pursued in terms of Bonhoeffer's earlier theology and the questions he pursued there. Why a Bonhoeffer, more than a Tillich, a Bultmann, or even a Barth?

My own reflection is that a Catholic brings to a Protestant theologian a set of presuppositions and attitudes which make his understanding of that theologian fundamentally different from a Protestant's. Because a Protestant theologian is working from a tradition and a set of premises foreign to Catholics, he will tend to be, for Catholics, a "threshold theologian." That is, before he can be understood, a critical threshold must be crossed, in which the Catholic can accept—or at least recognize—the premises from which he is working. Unless a Catholic realizes, for instance, how strongly Karl Barth is reacting to an anthropological overemphasis in theology (an extreme never experienced in any similar way among Catholic theologians), Barth can be bewildering. The same is true of Tillich, Niebuhr, and even more so of Bultmann: accessibility means for a Catholic the ability to cross the threshold, to enter into the world in which wholly different attitudes toward faith and theology predominate.

What is significant and so sharply surprising about Bonhoeffer is that he does not seem to be a threshold theologian. His books speak directly to a Catholic *as* a Catholic, despite their emergence from the most vital sources in Protestant tradition. *The Cost of Discipleship* is reminiscent of the too-well-known spiritual reading books which proliferate in seminary and monastery libraries. *Life Together* has become a prized source for small groups and communities, and is recognized by many Catholics as the finest available description of living Christian community. Even the *Ethics,* probably the most Protestant theological statement of Bonhoeffer's life, speaks of a Church which Catholics can recognize and understand—often more readily than Protestants.

Again, where is the appeal; what is Bonhoeffer's secret? An important help in answering this question would be an understanding of what constitutes the distinctiveness of the Catholic mind-set, as opposed to the Protestant mind-set. What, specifically, are the *Catholic* attitudes which discourage the immediate understanding of a non-Catholic theologian?

A fundamental Catholic belief which distinguishes Catholics from Protestants is the Catholic's firm belief in the sacramental basis of the Church. The Catholic finds that God works not only with men, but through them; and the institutional and hierarchical consequences of this belief—namely the pope, the bishops, the chanceries—may at times deserve criticism, but nevertheless are critically important as symbols of a sacramental Church. The Catholic willingly accepts divine authority through a visible organization and human decisions; he could hardly think, as Luther did, that the divine element resides in the Church strictly in an invisible, almost imperceptible way. Indeed, the Catholic would find inconceivable what Luther thought perfectly natural: that at any time the traditionally established Church could betray Christ and fail to continue His presence—in other words, no longer be sacramental.

Out of this basic distinguishing belief in the sacramental nature of the Church, Catholics historically have generated several convictions which act as important assumptions whenever a Catholic approaches a non-Catholic theologian. The first of these assumptions, already mentioned, is the Catholic's commitment to divine authority in human hands. The Church, he believes, continues God's revelation and God's will through its teachings, sacraments, and laws. The process whereby the Church comes to a decision about a specific teaching may indeed be questioned; but the Church's power to come to this decision is not.

The second assumption derives from the first: a feeling (more than a specific belief) that one's commitment to the Church's teachings must be total, without individual discrepancies—at least in any major facets of belief. A third presupposition is the Catholic's high sensitivity to community. Nurtured especially by liturgy and the exclusive quality of some Catholic beliefs, the sense of community remains a very real touchstone of Catholic life and worship.

A final attitude deeply felt by Catholics would be the residual presence of the "monastic temptation." Boniface Luykx and other scholars have shown that the Church's teachings on pastoral matters have been shaped to a surprising extent by the emphasis on interiority and otherworldliness inherited from the desert monks. The result of this historical intervention has been a monastic ideal of the Christian dominating the Church's outlook on Christian life since the Middle Ages. It was against this emphasis that Luther violently reacted. Today the monastic temptation remains subtly illusive, but still an unavoidable part of the Catholic's makeup: it presents a hope which can be achieved largely through abstaining and withdrawing—refraining from the world rather than participating in shaping it.

On the basis, largely of these attitudes, all more or less coming from the sacramental conception of the Church, a Catholic will find a particular theologian near or distant, meaningful or abstruse. What then of Bonhoeffer? Unlike Barth, Bonhoeffer does not deal with the decisive points of theological friction between Protestants and Catholics. His thought, much more diffuse and exploratory than comprehensive, does not appear to be overtly ecumenical. Where, then, and how, is Bonhoeffer able to avoid being a threshold theologian?

To limit this treatment to trends of thought clearly defined in Bonhoeffer's writings, trends present much earlier than the prison letters, five distinct concerns appear: his idea of community, his search for the true nature of the Church's authority, his anthropology, his effort to forge a dynamic definition of the Church, and his struggle toward a deeply relevant Christology.

Bonhoeffer's conception of a personal community undergirds the entire development of his thought on the nature of the Church. Indeed, the one idea dominating the first two theses, *Communion of Saints* and *Act and Being,* is the identification he makes of the Church with a personal community in which Christ is present. And perhaps of all his original theological contributions, no notion had better chance for practical implementation in his lifetime.

Community fascinated Bonhoeffer from his student days: he recognized in it the possibility of a Church existing with some of the intensity and love that Christ had demanded. In his first major theological effort, *The Communion of Saints,* he wrote that "the community is constituted by the complete self-forgetfulness of love. The relationship between I and Thou is no longer essentially a demanding but a giving one." [1] And in the more theoretical, but slightly more mature *Act and Being,* he became more precise about the meaning of Christian community:

I hear another man really proclaim the gospel to me. He extends to me the sacrament: you are forgiven. He and the community pray for me, and I hear the gospel, join the prayer, and know myself in the word, sacrament and prayer of the community of Christ to be bound with the new humanity, be it now here or elsewhere, borne by it, bearing it.[2]

Only upon becoming involved in the active Church, only after seeing the intrinsic difficulties of forging a large urban parish into anything resembling a community, did Bonhoeffer see that his earlier view had been crippled by its academic tenor. "Christ existing as community" was no less true than it had been in the writing of the two treatises; but the precise meaning needed modification. Community could not be a form of monastic seclusion, but a means of living with Christian intensity in the midst of the world. In 1932 he spoke of the Church as

the congregation of the children of the earth, who refuse to separate themselves from the world and who have no special proposals to offer for its improvement. The people of this community also do not consider themselves superior to the world, but persevere together in the midst of the world, in its depths, in its trivialities and bondages.[3]

Bonhoeffer's thinking on the Church as community did not bear fruit until 1936, when he became the director of the illegal seminary at Finkenwalde. Finkenwalde was many things: possibly the only home to which Bonhoeffer ever fully belonged; the consequence of his beliefs in the way that pastors should be formed; Bonhoeffer's reaction to the political rallying cry for a "common Germany" and a "united people." Above all, though, Finkenwalde was Bonhoeffer's convictions about community become incarnate: his attempt to instill an intense and highly charged spirit of fraternal love, in which men approached Christ through their union with one another. Bonhoeffer believed that only a group of ministers who had known community, and who had discovered Christ supporting and creating that community, were capable of keeping alive the Church in Nazi-torn Germany.

Life Together, the book written after Finkenwalde, is dominated by a kernel idea: "Christianity means community through Jesus Christ and in Jesus Christ."[4] Where the early treatises theorize, *Life Together* portrays. Where the early treatises project, *Life Together* comments on what has already occurred. Yet theologically all three works gravitate around a central, sustaining belief: that the Church needs living community—more than institution, more than congregation, more even than the opportunity for social encounters. Bonhoeffer saw one purpose in community: "that Christians meet one another as bringers of the message of salvation." [5] Anything less, anything serving another purpose, could not be community, and could not be Church.

Bonhoeffer's thinking on the Church as community has not received the attention it deserves. The failure is deeply unfortunate, because Bonhoeffer's identification of the Church with personal community is surely as revolutionary as his later definition of the Church in terms of its going out to the world. For by declaring the Church as "Christ existing as community," Bonhoeffer had in effect broken from the sterile set of categories in which the Church was known: his understanding gave the Church a more human, immediate quality, and set ecclesiology into a perspective not of institutions or of explicit doctrinal beliefs, but of personal common love.

The implications for Catholics of Bonhoeffer's thought on community should be immediately noticeable. It is easy to see why *Life Together* would be more popular among Catholics (especially religious) than among Protestants; Catholics have shown a greater fascination, a more profound interest in the meaning of community as a mandate of Christ. Yet what makes Bonhoeffer's thought on community so relevant and significant to Catholics is the fact that no Catholic theologian has cut to the central issue of identifying the Church *as* community so consciously as Bonhoeffer has. By providing a new way of conceiving the Church, he has opened up a pathway for reforming it; and it is a pathway with which Catholics are already somewhat familiar.

During the mid-1930's, as Bonhoeffer struggled with the renegade Confessing Church, another problem dominated much of his concern, which again is important for a Catholic's understanding of his thought. During his studies at Berlin, the nature of authority in the Church had never especially disturbed him. But the rise of Nazi power and the failure of the national Lutheran Church to oppose such government measures as the Aryan Clauses in 1933, made Bonhoeffer grimly conscious of the Church's responsibility to clarify for Christians and non-Christians the moral intrusions of Hitler and the extent of Christian responsibility in opposing his regime.

Up until the writing of the *Ethics* (which was done in secret), Bonhoeffer's statements on authority appear guarded, kept behind a screen of carefully worded theological debate. Yet time and again in speeches made at ecumenical gatherings Bonhoeffer struggled to find a source for the Church's authority. Probably the most important discussion came in his paper presented to the Youth Peace Conference in Czechoslovakia on July 26, 1932. He entitled the paper, "A Theological Basis for the World Alliance?" The entire discussion hinges around one question: "With whose authority does the Church speak when it declares this claim of Christ to the whole?" [6] Bonhoeffer is not satisfied to claim simply that "the Church is the presence of Christ on earth. . . . For this reason alone its word has authority." [7] Someone else is needed to make the Church's word binding, truly bearing Christ's authority to the present.

> The Church must be able to say the Word of God, the word of authority, i.e., in quite concrete form. Here lies a problem of the utmost difficulty and magnitude. Can the church preach the commandment of God with the same certainty with which it preaches the Gospel? Can the Church say "We need a socialist ordering of economics," or "Do not engage in war" with the same certainty as it can say "Thy sins are forgiven thee"? [8]

Bonhoeffer recognized the problem as a vexing one, yet critical: the Church could no longer go the way it had almost always gone, by answering social problems with "evasion and turning aside to general principles." [9] Clearly the Church needed to speak, to utter the concrete command; yet how could Church leaders know they were issuing the right command? Mistakes could be made, Bonhoeffer acknowledged: the Church conceivably could insist, "Do not engage in this war," and err. Yet forgiveness is possible; and only on the basis of this forgiveness dare the Church preach the commandment concretely.

What Bonhoeffer located as the decisive point for the Church to realize was the Church's knowledge of the situation it faced. *The* great responsibility of the Church is not to command with authority, but to back up that command by an intense understanding of the crisis which made the command necessary. *"The Gospel,"* Bonhoeffer wrote in italics, *"becomes concrete in the hearers, the commandment becomes concrete in those who preach it.*" [10] If the Church really has a commandment of God, Bonhoeffer insisted, "it must proclaim it in the most definite form possible, from the fullest knowledge of the matter, and it must utter a summons to obedience." [11]

For Bonhoeffer the Church could speak only with authority when it spoke concretely, specifically. To proclaim that war is evil, that nuclear arms are intrinsically immoral, and not to challenge an actual war that threatens the unbridled use of hydrogen bombs would be to slip into the same impotence of the national Church in the 1930's.

Few of Bonhoeffer's theological efforts speak to Catholics as immediately or with fewer of the "threshold theologian" difficulties as his thought on concrete authority. Catholics accept authority. They are willing to be guided by a pope and bishop in much more binding forms than Protestants would ever permit. Yet Catholics, especially recently, can sense the critical discrepancy between a pope's command and the relevance of that command to present needs or what Bonhoeffer termed the "concrete situation." And this discrepancy can raise serious questions about the nature of authority in the Church, questions of a similar nature that Bonhoeffer was raising.

Comparing Bonhoeffer's outlook on authority with the Catholic disposition toward authority, one notes a decisive difference. Catholics accept authority in terms of sturcture, prepossessed by the Church and in the hands of the pope and the bishops. Whether the pope prefers to condemn a specific war or simply make general condemnations of war does not in any way alter the nature of his authority. Indeed, Catholics sometimes feel that it is *his* responsibility how authority is used, that the Church's authority belongs basically to the hierarchy.

Bonhoeffer's idea, however, gives responsibility precedence over authority and makes the Church's authority very much contingent upon its willingness to accept its present responsibilities to the world. No one man can "have" authority, in Bonhoeffer's view—even if he is a bishop or the head of an ecumenical council; a major claim to his authority comes in his ability to understand the concrete situation in depth, and to respond with a command which speaks in terms of that situation.

The two outlooks on authority may seem distant, and yet for a Catholic Bonhoeffer's conception of authority may offer valuable guidelines for coming to a fresh understanding of the meaning of the papacy. Obviously, neither outlook can be totally correct; nor have Bonhoeffer, in his instance, or Catholics, except for a few rare instances, believed totally in their respective interpretations of responsibility. Bonhoeffer acknowledged the need for structural leadership, and Catholics have insisted that their authorities listen to the prophetic voices of the time. But to reach an understanding of authority which makes the concrete command an *indispensable* part of the claim to authority: this is one of the challenges Bonhoeffer has presented to Catholic theologians.

It is a challenge which, if pursued, could open some important doors ecumenically. What Bonhoeffer has suggested is a conception of authority which merges the Protestant passion for the Christian commitment to an era with the Catholic awareness of authority's power to speak the command of God in the present. It could well be that here Bonhoeffer has provided an approach to solving the most delicate and critical problem in the effort for full Christian unity.

A third area in which Bonhoeffer's thought especially attracts and fascinates Catholics is his anthropology. Catholics have kept alive, for almost the entire history of the Church, a strong tradition of revering and imitating their holy men, their saints.

The list of canonized saints is incalculably long; and hagiography is itself considered a science. Bonhoeffer himself rejected the idea of consciously becoming a saint. In one of his final prison letters he wrote to Eberhard Bethge expressly disclaiming any personal efforts to "become a saint." [12]

Yet integral to Bonhoeffer's mature thought was the question of the identity of a Christian: who is a Christian, what characterizes a Chrisitan? And his thoughts, constituting what has been called his anthropology, provide a clear picture of what he believed are the most important qualities for a Christian in a secular world. Directly after criticizing the effort to make oneself a saint, Bonhoeffer went on to write about a "holy worldliness":

> This is what I mean by holy worldliness—taking life in one's stride, with all its duties and problems, its successes and failures, its experiences and helplessness. It is in such a life that we throw ourselves utterly in the arms of God and participate in his sufferings in the world and watch with Christ in Gethsemane. That is faith, that is *metanoia,* that is what makes a man and a Christian.[13]

For Bonhoeffer the Christian had to be known first and foremost as a man: energetically involved in the secular enterprises of his time, capable of a zesty and intense life, committed to the world even as he was committed to Christ. And while he discouraged the promotion of any kind of "sanctity-seeking," Bonhoeffer nevertheless kept acutely in mind the need for self-renewing effort and for a commitment to Christ which affected every reach of a man's life.

Bonhoeffer was attempting in his anthropology to illuminate the demands of living as a Christian in contemporary society. This meant, in effect, the consequences of man's being conformed to Christ, and Bonhoeffer saw these consequences strongly in human terms. Christ remained at the center of the venture in wholeness and full manhood, the "holy worldliness" Bonhoeffer spoke of; indeed, the insistence throughout the *Ethics* makes it clear that conformation is wholly Christ's work, not man's.

In terms of the Catholic sensitivity to sanctity and the conscious pursuit of holiness fostered by the monastic tradition, Bonhoeffer's anthropology offers a refreshing and modern version of full Christian discipleship. Simply because of their convictions about holiness, Catholics find it possible to frame and envision a specific form of "spirituality," an image of Christ which offers a distinct way of becoming united with Him.

Certainly it would be disastrous to interpret Bonhoeffer's anthropology as a spirituality in the traditional sense. Yet the need sensed among Catholics *for* a distinct image of sanctity—expressed recently by an outpouring of literature on "lay spirituality"—leaves open the road which Bonhoeffer's anthropology well can follow.

An acceptance of the anthropology by Catholics could be highly promising, for it conceivably could offer Catholics a deeply contemporary alternative to the monastic attitudes still embedded in life and worship. Catholics continue to live with the suspicion, if not the assuredness, that the world impedes union with Christ, that the true Christian must shun and neglect the world. Even Vatican Council II failed to offer a theology of involvement in the world integral enough to provide an image of the saint who finds Christ in partaking of the world, rather than refraining from it.

Bonhoeffer's anthropology focuses on man in the world, and will not relent by removing man from that world. Moreover, where Catholics see the need for a "spirituality," Bonhoeffer envisions a need for full manhood, and he describes this need in terms that could issue from a psychologist as much as a theologian. If Bonhoeffer's anthropology were taken seriously by Catholics searching for the terms of a lay spirituality, they would be surprised that a major assumption was shattered, that their very conception of spirituality drew on an understanding of discipleship quite monastic in origin. They would discover that what Bonhoeffer describes is not a form of sanctity in any traditional sense, but the only possible form of commitment which the Christian can make to Christ and to his age. And they would discover, above all, that the anthropology can never be forced into a system, or left on paper: that it must be a living, human quality, if by the very fact that Bonhoeffer lived it.

A fourth development in Bonhoeffer's thought which might appeal significantly to Catholics is his mature doctrine of the Church, in which he defines the Church strictly in terms of its relationship to the world. "The Church, then, bears the form which is in truth the proper form of all humanity. . . . What takes place in her takes place as an example and substitute for all men." [14] The shift in Bonhoeffer's theology at this point is a radical one: he has given up the attempt to define the Church dogmatically, even to attempt a specific description of it, isolated in a single context. The Church becomes existential: incapable of a single definition, seen from a dozen viewpoints. He presents the Church always as "Christ himself who has taken form among men,"[15] yet explores the historical and social dimensions of the Church as a human institution.

What is most significant about Bonhoeffer's later concern with the Church is the dynamic impulse which he sees in it. The very nature of the Church is such that it *cannot* be defined dogmatically, he suggests, because the Church's essence is to step into the world and work and struggle in the midst of the world. His entire *Ethics* takes up this theme: the Christian's life (and for that matter, the Church's life) cannot be understood in static terms—whether of good or bad, or of natural or supernatural. To polarize the Church's existence by playing off one theological element against its opposite is in effect to paralyze the life of the Church. In one of the book's most provocative chapters, "Thinking in Terms of Two Spheres," Bonhoeffer decisively uproots the tendency to present the Christian experience as one in which Christ and the world are set in conflict.

Thought which is conducted in terms of two spheres regards . . . secular and Christian, natural and supernatural, profane and sacred . . . as though they were ultimate static antitheses, serving to designate certain mutually exclusive entities. It fails to recognize the original unity of the opposites in the reality of Christ. . . . [In Christ] The world, the natural, the profane and reason are now all taken up into God from the outset. They do not exist "in themselves" and "on their own account." They have their reality nowhere save in the reality of God, in Christ.[16]

Not only does he attempt to give the Church a dynamic perspective: he locates at the center of this perspective, Christ. And if for Bonhoeffer the Church can exist only in mission, if its very *elan vital* is a going out to the world, the source of that self-giving lies in Christ and in Christ's Incarnation.

Here the meaning of Bonhoeffer's reorientation of thought about the Church becomes apparent. The Church is still for Bonhoeffer "Christ existing as community." What this term means has, however, changed. Bonhoeffer sees Christ as alive, dynamic, active in the world: the paradigmatic man to whom all men are conformed. Bonhoeffer's mature ecclesiology can in no way be separated from his mature Christology; indeed, the two constantly lead into one another and outward toward the world.

Before commenting on Bonhoeffer's idea of the Church and its possible meaning for Catholics, it would be best to clarify what Bonhoeffer did attempt in his Christology. Few recent theologians have made such a conscious effort to keep Christ at the center of their thought as Bonhoeffer has. Each book leads from a clear premise that the Incarnation gives reality an entirely new dimension which the theologian is best equipped to explore. Unfortunately, with one exception, Bonhoeffer never paused to clarify his Christology explicitly. His thought about Christ became an intrinsic facet of his thought about the Church, or Christian discipleship, or ethics. Christ was almost *too* present, not to merit the specific attention of a careful Christology.

The one exception—Bonhoeffer's Christology lectures of the summer, 1933—gives a clear picture of Bonhoeffer's thought on Christology at the time. Although what remains are only compiled student notes, it is clear that Bonhoeffer conceived Christology in a fundamentally different way from the traditional theology of Christ. In some incisive opening comments attempting to delineate the scope of Christology, he chastises those theologians who ask the technical—but impossible—question, "How?" The question is "Who?" and Bonhoeffer admits that any theologian stands dumb before such a question. "The ultimate question of critical thought is involved in the dilemma of having to ask 'Who?' and yet not being able to." [17]

How, then, to approach Christ? Bonhoeffer admits immediately what throughout the rest of his life he would hold, that "the christological question can be put scientifically only in the context of the Church. It can only be put where the basic presupposition, Christ's claim to be the Logos of God, has been accepted." [18] Bonhoeffer pursued his lectures in terms of "The Present Christ," "The Historical Christ," and "The Future Christ," but after his discussion of "The Present Christ," it becomes apparent that he was not in his most creative capacity. Bonhoeffer speaks most meaningfully of Christ when his terms are directed toward the Church: whether to the community in which Christ comes alive, or to the individual shaped by the Church and serving the Church.

It is dangerous, then, to presume a dividing line between ecclesiology and Christology in Bonhoeffer's thought, especially his later thought. If he merged two distinct disciplines, it was only to provide a clearer understanding of the reality which is common to both. And if in developing a radically Christ-centered idea of the Church, he refused to acknowledge the present sluggish condition of a feeble organization, Bonhoeffer threw a brilliant light on a presence that had become too habituated, too much a familiar round of cliches. Christ lived for Bonhoeffer: he wanted Christians to find him living in the source where He *should* live—the Church.

In his doctrine of a dynamic church and in his Christology, Bonhoeffer is coming closer than anywhere in his works to the Catholic mind. Indeed, here he has located the most deeply lodged and yet most sensitive nerve among Catholics. For in exploring the relationship of Christ to His Church, Bonhoeffer has revealed what for him is *the* underlying premise to all of his thought: the present meaning of the Incarnation.

Throughout the history of Christian theology a common

temptation has attracted men attempting to understand the Incarnation: to bring to it equipment, presumptions, channels of thought which inevitably obscure their understanding of this central Christian mystery. The monumental Hellenistic effort to define the process of a person taking on a human nature failed simply by the initial tendency to view God against man, God separate from man, and not begin where the New Testament begins: God *as* man. Very few theologians have had the intellectual audacity to *begin* their theology with the premise that the Incarnation *is,* that of this God and man are united, and that all else is after this fact. Too much effort has gone into the questions, Why the Incarnation? How the Incarnation? Whether or not a true Incarnation?

The most distinct recurring emphasis in Bonhoeffer's thought is his effort to see everything in the light of the Incarnation. He admits it to be a mystery he could never penetrate; he admits Christ to be a person whose power over the universe and whose presence in the Church can be known, but only through faith. But throughout all his theology, Bonhoeffer discovers and rediscovers at the source of every Christian truth the fundamental mystery of God coming to the world. And throughout his work no effort seems so strong as that of clarifying and purifying his own understanding of the Incarnation as it exists, and not as interpreted through Hegelian or Barthian categories.

Bonhoeffer's radical understanding of the Incarnation may be the key to his thought and to the developments taken in his thought. It is, I am convinced, the secret of his availability to Catholics, and the most promising avenue for pursuing his relevance for Catholic theology. Catholics are more sensitive to the Incarnation as a fundamental mystery than are Protestants, if by the simple fact that they must live with some institutional consequences of the Incarnation in a way that Protestants do not. Catholics are often able to sense whether a theologian deeply respects the total mystery of the Incarnation, or whether he has used the Incarnation as a means of solving theological puzzles. Indeed, it is perhaps on the basis of a profound sensitivity to the Incarnation that a theologian is able to communicate most meaningfully with the Catholic: for on this ground, and in terms of this mystery, the Catholic can truly listen.

What Bonhoeffer has done in all his theology has been to discover the Incarnation at the center of every Christian truth. While drawing heavily upon impressive Protestant forebears, he has yet been able to approach theology with an originality, a christological orientation, and a sensitivity to the present situation which have freed him from the necessity of being for Catholics a threshold theologian. In every aspect of his thought—most notably his sense of the urgency of community, the concrete nature of authority, his anthropology, his doctrine of the Church, and his understanding of Christ—he has shown a remarkable ability to explore with originality the meaning of the Incarnation for the twentieth century.

To say that Bonhoeffer is a theologian especially meaningful for Catholics is to understate an important truth: Bonhoeffer has discovered something of the nature of Christian existence in a secular world, and Catholics are capable of recognizing this readily. The incarnational drive of Bonhoeffer's thought provides Catholics with an opportunity to wake up and look, to listen to what someone not of their faith had to suggest about their self-understanding in the modern world.

Catholics may indeed wish to listen, and listen attentively; or they may wish to ignore. But there is something about Bonhoeffer that, once he has even briefly been touched upon, cannot be ignored. He forces questions, and remains one of the few recent thinkers to suggest some viable directions in which to look for answers.

Catholics will continue reading Bonhoeffer; they will continue seeing in the man an integrity as firm and admirable as that of a Thomas More. And as long as they read, as long as they revere the man, they will question and they will discover; and in this discovery may lie the vision to a future which need not be Catholic or Protestant, only Christian.

The common denominator is to be sought both in thought and in practical living in an integrated attitude to life. The man who allows himself to be torn into fragments by events and problems has not passed the test for the present and the future.

Letter of January 29 and 30, 1944, to Eberhard Bethge

17. *The Fragments Converge*

The sun rose and took on fresh brilliance the morning of April 9. The prisoners squinted as they faced it. One by one the prisoners were led to the ominous wooden gallows in the center of Flossenbürg's sandy courtyard. As they were quickly and efficiently taken up the platform and hanged, the S.S. guardsmen on duty did not recognize one apart from the others. Neither the bodies of Oster, Canaris, or Bonhoeffer were identified as each one was hefted into the waiting cart and hauled to the nearby crematorium. Within an hour, none could any longer be identified. The Gestapo machine had done its work smoothly, with superb timing. Only days later the American troops broke into the section where Flossenbürg was located and liberated the camp. But their arrival was too late. Dietrich Bonhoeffer, only thirty-nine and at the pinnacle of his theological career, had died a martyr to the cause for which he had so long struggled.

Reinhold Niebuhr, writing within weeks of his death, spoke

fervently of the young martyr. "The story of Bonhoeffer," he said,

> is worth recording. It belongs to the modern Acts of the Apostles . . . Bonhoeffer was a brilliant young theologian who combined a deep piety with a high degree of intellectual sophistication . . . less known than Niemöller, he will become better known. Not only his martyr's death but also his actions and precepts contain within them the hope of a revitalized Protestant faith in Germany.[1]

It is true that through the lens of martyrdom Bonhoeffer's personal integrity and courage have been seen more purely and more distinctly than they would had he lived. Yet the overwhelming tragedy of his death—its utter meaninglessness; the callous, unauthorized execution; the brutal interruption in the flow of his most exciting theological growth—gives his martyrdom a ring of the absurd. It did not have to happen, and it can rightly be seen as a stupid, clumsy intervention by some war-crazed Gestapo agents in the last futile moments. What Bonhoeffer so often lamented, wasting the most precious human resources, became in a grimly ironic way his own fate.

Bonhoeffer's stature as a watershed in contemporary theology suggests that his martyrdom has served at least to focus upon something which might otherwise have gone unnoticed: the unity Bonhoeffer maintained in living and thinking. Bonhoeffer will never be thought of simply as a Christian whose convictions carried him into hazardous political action. Nor will he be remembered only as the author of *The Cost of Discipleship, Ethics,* the prison letters. His death, occasioned by the resistance actions and terminating his thought, has forever fused these two realms for all those who would know Bonhoeffer—and has in effect made that combination the key to Bonhoeffer's importance as a theologian.

Consequently, any real understanding of Bonhoeffer means an understanding of his ideas and his life: but above all of the bonds which kept these integrally together. It is these bonds which need to be explored, for they may well constitute the most important heritage which Bonhoeffer has left to the

Church. The clearest approach would be to clarify what characterized the man Dietrich Bonhoeffer, what characterizes his theology, and then what characterizes the unity between the two.

As a man, Dietrich Bonhoeffer was muscular, and somewhat stout. He gave an initial impression of being forceful, energetic, a highly capable, though reserved man. His hands, his movements, his quick impulsive gestures all suggested an athlete, not an intellectual. And as an athlete Bonhoeffer excelled; he rarely lost at tennis, and learned other sports like skiing with a characteristic immediate deftness.

He spoke with a sustained intensity, his slightly high-pitched voice shooting out words without ever faltering for an expression. He managed discussions with skill, listening acutely to each speaker, and expressed himself in a way that gradually gave his partners greater self-confidence in what they were saying, and an ability to articulate themselves more effectively.

Dietrich worked seriously, and with long-acquired discipline. His seminarians at Finkenwalde often marvelled at the breadth of his activities, and his ability to treat everything he attempted with relish and thoroughness. Something about Bonhoeffer, his hardiness, his energetic pace, his constant demand to follow a problem through to the finish, gave everything he did a fresh significance for those who worked with him. It was as if struggling with a difficulty—whether the stormy debates of the Confessing Church, or simply relocating the seminary—Bonhoeffer would focus his resources in a way that set the problem in its proper proportions.

He lived demanding a firmness of himself which he was careful not to demand from others. Bethge has mentioned that he was often slow, sometimes too slow, in making a decision: whether it was the choice of a movie or a major life commitment. But once he had decided upon a course, he moved forward unhesitatingly, seeming never again to question whether he had chosen the right thing.

Inherited from his German aristocratic background was a passion for perfection in everything he attempted. It was not simply a matter of excelling, of overcoming his peers; Dietrich sensed in every area of human endeavor a staggering potential which was only too rarely realized. His goals were dictated by his vision of the possibilities inherent in a theological problem or a tennis match, not simply by a desire to surpass those who had gone before. Consequently, he sought constantly to purify and intensify his efforts—to make them consonant with the goals he held for them.

He brought to every effort, however, a standard which always kept the bounds clearly in sight: a penetrating sense of his own humanity. Paul Lehmann has said that he never took a theological debate with ultimate seriousness; it could be said, similarly, that he never had an encounter with someone in which the human concern was submerged by whatever business or discussion brought them together. His letters sparkle with the natural warmth and spontaneity which Bonhoeffer generated.

He relished his life, and it is clear that, as a human being, he could never have accepted the otherworldly attitude which he excoriated in his criticism of religion. He found life an exciting experience, an adventure in which even the most crippling accidents—his imprisonment, for example—were redeemed by the new types of opportunities they brought. He pitied men who could not enjoy life, who were too small, too inwardly stunted, to bring to life the enthusiasm and openness that make it worthwhile. Speaking of his enforced solitude in prison he once said, "It is a great mercy to be surrounded by thoughts and be able to follow them up. Horrid if nothing occurs to you." [2]

Bonhoeffer came very close, throughout his life, to only a few people, partly from his instinctive sense of reserve, partly because he remained incredibly close to his family until his death. Especially during the years between the dissolution of Finkenwalde and his arrest, Dietrich would visit his mother's home in the Grunewald district of Berlin. There his room was always kept waiting for him (with a separate bed for Bethge, who usually joined him), and there he would join in the family orchestra, accompanying his brother-in-law and his father on the piano. His sister Susanne lived only next door, and he used to toss chocolates to her children from the window of his room.

It is probably only due to the intervention of the Gestapo that Dietrich did not marry; he was engaged at the time of his arrest, and during his stay in prison looked forward to marriage after his release. His fiancée, Maria von Wedemeyer, was a charming, lovely girl whom he met through his good friend and Maria's grandmother, Ruth von Kleist-Retzow. Although only half his age, Maria had a naturalness and an impulsive liveliness which captivated Dietrich. He had known her since 1937, but fell in love with her only in the summer of 1942. He and Maria met together frequently during the winter of 1942-43, and became secretly engaged in January. The arrest came ten weeks later.

Despite his nearness to his friends, family, and Maria, or perhaps partly because of it, Bonhoeffer remained a Christian highly sensitive to the presence of God. He prayed frequently, and with a rare depth of belief. Dr. H. Fischer-Hullstrung, who was present at Flossenbürg the morning that Bonhoeffer was hanged, has described his final moments of prayer:

> Through the half-open door in one room of the hut I saw Pastor Bonhoeffer, before taking off his prison garb, kneeling on the floor praying fervently to his God. I was most deeply moved by the way this lovable man prayed, so devout and so certain that God heard his prayer. At the place of execution, he again said a short prayer and then climbed the steps to the gallows, brave and composed. His death ensued after a few seconds. In the almost fifty years that I worked as a doctor, I have hardly ever seen a man die so entirely submissive to the will of God.[3]

What he gave to his friends and family, what he gave to God, Dietrich likewise gave to his country. In his correspondence after the decision to return from America in 1939 and in his deeply felt meditation, "After Ten Years," Bonhoeffer describes Germany with an empathy and a sense of shame for its failure which suggest what profound bonds held him to his country. He always regarded Hitler and Hitler's Third Reich with an inner loathing, sensing in the man an abnormal capacity for evil, and a rare potential for exploiting the worst elements of the German people. What he fought for in the resistance, what he wrote for in prison, was a Germany which he desired to help revive—a Germany which would sink to its knees in atonement after the War.

As much as his life speaks of Bonhoeffer, so does his thought, albeit in a totally different way. The striking characteristics of Bonhoeffer's later theology—its sporadic, fragmentary nature, its surging movement forward, its insistent effort to locate seminal problems—have helped to identify Bonhoeffer as much as any characteristics of his life.

The most obvious characteristic of Bonhoeffer's theology, and perhaps the most important one, is its revolutionary style. By writing his most important ideas in letters of the scattered patches of his *Ethics,* and by succeeding in communicating this way, Bonhoeffer has in effect given theology a new medium: one much closer to the twentieth century than the carefully elaborated monograph so typical of earlier theology. In his final writing, especially his letters, Bonhoeffer reveals himself to be far more concerned about concept and relevance than about locating his roots in tradition and his use of language. And the ideas themselves reflect the new, exploratory style. The concepts of the prison letters are much more accessible in what Bonhoeffer criticized than in what he defined or encompassed doctrinally. Indeed, there is very little doctrinal clarification in the mature Bonhoeffer. His anthropology, for instance, provides a clear and meaningful image of Christian man, but hardly a well-wrought theological schema defining and structuring him. Bonhoeffer's theological style—probing, refusing to be limited to any specific method or discipline for formulating conclusions—may really be one of his most important contributions to the future of theological thought.

Throughout the theology there emerges an illusive but significant sense of the limitations theology inherently faces. The early treatises described the nature of Christian community, but without the smooth, mature conviction of *Life Together,* the only book of the three born out of actual experience. As much as he felt himself committed to it, Bonhoeffer nevertheless mistrusted theory and speculation, and even the conviction that he was on the right track pursuing a problem or idea would not relieve the tension inherent in all theorizing.

Another important characteristic of the theology is its dominant method—from *The Communion of Saints* to the prison letters—of pursuing questions until the core problem had been located. In every detailed theological effort Bonhoeffer is constantly careful to delineate the range and nature of the problem he faces. It was usually his major contribution in a conversation to make explicit the questions that were being discussed —often by turning a conventional question inside out, and looking at it from a radically new standpoint. Much of the success of the prison letters can be understood simply from the viewpoint that they provide one of the best articulations of the most disturbing questions posed to Christians by our age. Bonhoeffer's theology is at its best when it grapples with a question seen in a fresh, direct way.

These features of Bonhoeffer's theology, like the earlier described features of his life, give indications of the real Bonhoeffer. But the clearest, sharpest picture of Bonhoeffer comes from those features that run simultaneously through life and thought—and which can be seen best only when seen in both.

The most obvious of these features is Bonhoeffer's exuberant sense of freedom, the incredible agility and independence with which he moved, thought, and lived. The very freedom which could enable Bonhoeffer to declare himself a pacifist would later enable him to enter the movement to destroy the Third Reich. Indeed, paradoxes seem to thrive in Bonhoeffer: for example, his increasingly "religious" life during those months in prison when he was lacerating religion. In his life and in his theology Bonhoeffer set no absolute standards, or absolute limits; he remained always open, always ready to question a premise, to challenge the action which might have been effective a month ago in different conditions. Likewise, he retained throughout his life a rare ability to overcome the constricting effects of his environment, and constantly to rise above it. As a student at Berlin he kept a critical distance from the liberal theology promulgated by the professors; in the midst of the nationalist furor of the early 1930's he attempted energetically to work in the ecumenical (and by that fact, internationalist) movement. He never felt a compulsion to be different, or to conform; he simply sought his own vocation and did his best to follow it. If that vocation meant, as it often did, a radical divergence from the path of his fellow countrymen, Bonhoeffer diverged. It hurt him, but he felt his freedom and the dictates of his conscience more important than the feelings and beliefs he was urged to share.

A second characteristic apparent throughout both Bonhoeffer's life and his theology is his concern with suffering, and his actual desire for suffering. The theme of suffering runs through all of Bonhoeffer's writings, especially his Christology lectures of 1933, his biblical works, and the prison letters. For him suffering meant something substantially different from the melancholic soul-sickness of a Kierkegaard; it was rather a man's ability to live with vitality and exuberance in the midst of agonizing questions, the pain of human frailty, and the tensions imposed by a deeply original life. In his Christology lectures Bonhoeffer looked to the tortured, humiliated Christ as the real source of man's union with God. Later, in the prison letters, he wrote, "Christians range themselves with God in his suffering; that is what distinguishes them from the heathen."[4] But not simply to be humiliated: the Christian's greatest source of suffering lies in his helplessness to alleviate, in any way, that suffering. In the prison letters Bonhoeffer wrote, "Jesus does not call men to a new religion, but to life. What is the nature of that life, but participation in the powerlessness of God in the world?"[5] The kind of suffering Bonhoeffer underwent in prison was, of course, specifically this powerlessness.

A third characteristic fusing life and theology is Bonhoeffer's fierce commitment to the present: his passion for living in the moment, with relevance and significant social impact. He dreaded pastors who could only preach a gospel unaffected by the tumultuous events in which men were living. He saw, indeed, in his speeches and writings of the mid-'thirties just how critically important an understanding of the present moment was, an insurance that the Church could proclaim its message with real authority. He saw also, in his decision to enter resistance, the enormity of the German people's crime in permitting evil to choke the life of their government; he could only respond to such apathy with a radical assumption of responsibility. Few themes in all of Bonhoeffer's writings are so strikingly dominant, or so thoroughly contemporary as this constant regard for a total response to the needs of the present moment.

A final decisive characteristic of Bonhoeffer's life and thought was his constant search for the meaning of Christ for the contemporary Christian. The opening quotation of the critical section in the prison letters reads, ". . . what *is* Christianity, and indeed, what *is* Christ for us today?" [6] The concern is not ostensibly with locating Christ, or with determining whether or not he actually lived, or was God: any of these questions. Bonhoeffer began with an undaunted faith in Christ, though with many unsettling doubts about Christ's meaningfulness for contemporary men. As such, he was struggling constantly to see not only the mandates of Christ as they applied in the twentieth century (in a book such as *The Cost of Discipleship*); he was struggling above all to interpret the very meaning of who Christ is, and who, as a result, the Christian is. Bonhoeffer knew that belief, as deep as it could reach, would never surmount the difficulty of a fatal irrelevance, fostered by centuries of neglect. Identity, if it was to be true and emancipating, must emerge from the actual world—a world which Bonhoeffer came to recognize as far too mature to accept the religious stipulations with which the Church preached Christ.

Above all, in his conception of Christ, to separate (or even isolate) Bonhoeffer's theology from his deepest personal beliefs would be to dislocate and eventually miss the spiritual impetus of his thought. If what he said in his theology was not meant personally, then his theology has scant chance of resuscitating a sensitivity to Christ. But everything he said about Christ *was* meant personally, and was often enough simply the employment of theological language and concepts to externalize what Bonhoeffer personally saw and felt.

As a thinker, then, and as a deeply spiritual man, but above all as the union of both, Bonhoeffer has offered the Church a wealth of self-understanding, and the point of departure for a large-scale form of critical introspection. Indeed, it is impossible, in the final analysis, to estimate the real value of the man's integrity of thought and life. In all problems of life, he once wrote, "the common denominator is to be sought both in thought and in practical living of an integrated attitude to life." [7] Because he was a theologian with a profound faith and a rare capacity for action, Bonhoeffer met the challenge of Hitler's regime step by step in his resistance work. Because he could at one moment perceive, articulate, and live a Christian life which was based on the human potential rather than the human condition, Bonhoeffer has given the Church a vision embodied just as much in himself as in the words left on paper.

It is indeed possible that Bonhoeffer, with his life and finally with his martyrdom, has provided the epitaph to a long and ultimately sterile tradition of theology in which the theologian's personal life matters little—only the statements, the deductions, and the conclusions that form his "theology." Bonhoeffer has returned to the image of a Paul: apostle and teacher imbedded and active in the world to which he speaks. It is questionable whether theology can exist meaningfully in a world of modern, diminished men unless it takes as its theme and source of inspiration the integrity of thought and action, desire and commitment, love and suffering. And it cannot take on this theme in a vacuum of books and debates; it must search out a new relationship with the world, one which is totally sincere and which demands of the theologian that before he become a thinker, he be a man. Perhaps this conclusion is unwarranted; yet there can be little doubt that Bonhoeffer's integrity speaks as loudly as his ideas—and according to Bonhoeffer himself, only in this way can the Church truly speak to all.

Notes

CHAPTER ONE

[1] Sabine Leibholz, "Childhood and Home," in *I Knew Dietrich Bonhoeffer* (New York, 1967), p. 19 (hereafter cited as *I Knew*).

[2] *Ibid.*, pp. 23-4.

[3] From Eberhard Bethge. Unpublished.

[4] From Eberhard Bethge. Unpublished.

[5] Dietrich Bonhoeffer, *No Rusty Swords* (New York, 1965), pp. 29-30 (hereafter cited as *NRS*).

[6] Dietrich Bonhoeffer, *Letters and Papers from Prison* (New York, 1962), p. 81 (hereafter cited as *LP*).

[7] *Ibid.*, p. 168.

CHAPTER TWO

[1] Quoted in Eberhard Bethge, "The Challenge of Dietrich Bonhoeffer's Life and Theology," *The Chicago Theological Seminary Register,* LI (February, 1961), 5.

[2] Peter Berger, "The Social Character of the Question Concerning Jesus Christ: Sociology and Ecclesiology," in Martin E. Marty, ed., *The Place of Bonhoeffer* (New York, 1962), p. 57.

[3] Dietrich Bonhoeffer, *The Communion of Saints* (New York, 1963), p. 20 (hereafter cited as *CS*).

[4] John D. Godsey, *The Theology of Dietrich Bonhoeffer* (Philadelphia, 1960), p. 27.

[5] *CS,* p. 103.
[6] *Ibid.,* p. 175.
[7] *Ibid.,* p. 197.
[8] *Ibid.*
[9] *Ibid.,* p. 100.
[10] *Ibid.,* p. 178.
[11] *Ibid.,* p. 57.
[12] *Ibid.,* p. 129.
[13] *Ibid.,* p. 198.

CHAPTER THREE

[1] Dietrich Bonhoeffer, *I Loved This People* (Richmond, Va., 1965), pp. 11-12 (hereafter cited as *I Loved*).
[2] *NRS,* p. 37.
[3] *Ibid.*
[4] *Ibid.,* p. 40.
[5] Franklin Sherman, "The Methods of Asking the Question Concerning Jesus Christ: Act and Being," in Marty, ed., *op. cit.,* pp. 51-80.
[6] Dietrich Bonhoeffer, *Act and Being* (New York, 1961), p. 123 (hereafter cited as *AB*).
[7] *Ibid.*
[8] *Ibid.,* p. 121.
[9] *Ibid.,* p. 122.
[10] *Ibid.,* pp. 90-91.
[11] *Ibid.,* p. 122.
[12] *LP,* p. 23.
[13] *AB,* p. 124.

CHAPTER FOUR

[1] *NRS,* p. 68.
[2] *Ibid.,* pp. 113-14.
[3] *Ibid.,* p. 362.
[4] Reinhold Niebuhr, "The Death of a Martyr," *Christianity and Crisis,* V, (June 25, 1945), 6.
[5] Wolf-Dieter Zimmermann and Ronald Gregor Smith, *I Knew,* p. 45.
[6] Dietrich Bonhoeffer, *Gesammelte Schriften,* I (Munich, 1958-1961), 61. Author's translation (hereafter cited as *GS*).
[7] *LP,* p. 159.
[8] *Ibid.,* p. 220.
[9] *GS,* I, 61. Author's translation.
[10] *Ibid.*
[11] *NRS,* p. 120.
[12] *Ibid.,* p. 121.
[13] *Ibid.,* p. 204.
[14] *Ibid.,* p. 124.
[15] *I Knew,* p. 60.
[16] *Ibid.,* p. 61.
[17] *Ibid.,* p. 65.
[18] *NRS,* p. 140.
[19] *Ibid.*
[20] *Ibid.,* pp. 151-2.
[21] *I Knew,* p. 57.
[22] *GS,* I, 61. Author's translation.
[23] *NRS,* p. 154.
[24] Bethge, *op. cit.,* p. 11.

CHAPTER FIVE

[1] *NRS,* p. 304.
[2] Marty, *op. cit.,* p. 34.
[3] *NRS,* p. 231.
[4] *GS,* III, 24.
[5] *NRS,* p. 237.
[6] *Ibid.,* p. 283.
[7] *Ibid.,* p. 294.
[8] Quoted in J. S. Whale, *The*

Protestant Tradition (London, 1955), p. 111.

[9] *Ibid.*

[10] In John D. Godsey, *Preface to Bonhoeffer* (Philadelphia, 1965), p. 40.

[11] *Ibid.*

[12] *Ibid.*

[13] *Ibid.*, p. 43.

[14] *NRS*, p. 294.

[15] Dietrich Bonhoeffer, *Ethics* (New York, 1963), p. 68.

[16] *NRS*, p. 275.

[17] *Ibid.*, p. 216.

[18] Godsey, *op. cit.*, p. 33.

[19] Dietrich Bonhoeffer, *Christ the Center* (New York, 1966), p. 117.

[20] Godsey, *op. cit.*, p. 33.

[21] *Ibid.*, p. 32.

[22] *Ibid.*, p. 33.

[23] *Ibid.*, p. 36.

[24] *NRS*, p. 154.

[25] *Ibid.*, p. 222.

[26] *Ibid.*, p. 223.

[27] *Ibid.*, p. 226.

[28] *Ibid.*, p. 225.

[29] *Ibid.*

[30] *Ibid.*, p. 229.

CHAPTER SIX

[1] *NRS*, p. 157.

[2] *Ibid.*, p. 172.

[3] *Ibid.*, p. 138.

[4] *Ibid.*, p. 137.

[5] *Ibid.*, p. 175.

[6] Dietrich Bonhoeffer, *Life Together* (New York, 1954), p. 37 (hereafter cited as LT).

[7] *NRS*, p. 136.

[8] *Ibid.*, p. 137.

[9] *Ibid.*, pp. 137-8.

[10] *Ibid.*, p. 157.

[11] *Ibid.*, p. 158.

[12] *Ibid.*, p. 159.

[13] *Ibid.*, p. 160.

[14] *Ibid.*, p. 161.

[15] *Ibid.*

[16] *Ibid.*, pp. 161-2.

[17] *Ibid.*, p. 164.

[18] *Ibid.*, p. 162.

[19] *Ibid.*, pp. 162-3.

[20] *Ibid.*, p. 162.

[21] *Ibid.*, p. 163.

[22] *Ibid.*, p. 167.

[23] *Ibid.*, p. 291.

[24] *Ibid.*

[25] *Ibid.*, p. 334.

[26] *Ibid.*, p. 328.

[27] *Ibid.*, p. 255.

[28] *Ibid.*, p. 267.

[29] *Ibid.*, p. 287.

[30] *Ibid.*, p. 289.

[31] *Ibid.*, p. 283.

CHAPTER SEVEN

[1] Dietrich Bonhoeffer, *The Cost of Discipleship* (New York, 1963), p. 57 (hereafter cited as CD).

[2] *LP*, p. 226.

[3] *Ibid.*, p. 227.

[4] *NRS*, p. 314.

[5] *Creation and Fall.* Translated by John C. Fletcher. New York: The Macmillan Company, first

edition, 1959; paperback edition, 1965.
King David, 1936. (Untranslated)
Temptation. Translated by Kathleen Downham. New York: The Macmillan Company, 1955; paperback edition, 1965.

6 *CD,* p. 108.
7 *Ibid.,* p. 304.
8 *Ibid.,* p. 51.
9 *Ibid.,* p. 106.
10 *Ibid.,* p. 175.
11 *Ibid.,* p. 99.
12 *Ibid.,* p. 61.
13 *Ibid.,* pp. 170-171.
14 Dietrich Bonhoeffer, *The Way to Freedom* (New York, 1967), pp. 120-21 (hereafter cited as WF).
15 *CD,* p. 41.
16 *Ibid.,* p. 282.
17 Cf. Whale, *op. cit.,* p. 111.
18 Bethge, *op. cit.,* p. 20.
19 *CD,* p. 108.
20 *Ibid.,* p. 217.
21 *Ibid.,* p. 211.

CHAPTER EIGHT

1 *AB,* p. 121.
2 Godsey, *op. cit.,* p. 36.
3 Unpublished letter, from Bethge.
4 *LT,* p. 30.
5 *Ibid.,* p. 43.
6 *Ibid.,* p. 23.
7 Eberhard Bethge, "Dietrich Bonhoeffer: Champion of Freedom," *World Dominion,* XXXV (April, 1957), 77.
8 *I Knew,* pp. 132-133.
9 *GS,* III, 25. Author's translation.
10 From Bethge, unpublished.
11 *LT,* p. 25.
12 *Ibid.,* p. 23.
13 *Ibid.,* p. 105.
14 *Ibid.,* p. 17.

CHAPTER NINE

1 *LP,* p. 140.
2 Bethge, in "Challenge," p. 29.
3 *WF,* p. 244.
4 *Ibid.,* p. 246.
5 *Ibid.,* 247.
6 Quoted in Terence Prittie, *Germans against Hitler* (Boston, 1964), p. 124.
7 Ved Mehta, "The New Theologian III: Pastor Bonhoeffer," *The New Yorker,* November 27, 1965, p. 111.
8 G. K. A. Bell, *The Church and Humanity, 1939-1946* (London, 1946), p. 172.
9 Hans Rothfels, *The German Opposition to Hitler* (Hinsdale, Ill., 1948), p. 141.
10 Bell, *op. cit.,* p. 170.
11 *Ibid.*
12 *Ethics,* p. 65.
13 *LP,* p. 109.
14 *Ibid.,* p. 168.
15 *Ethics,* p. 83.
16 Bethge, preface to *Ethics,* p. 12.
17 *LP,* p. 85.

CHAPTER TEN

1 *Ethics,* p. 262.
2 *LP,* p. 168.

[3] *Ibid.*, p. 69.
[4] *Ibid.*, p. 15.
[5] *Ethics*, p. 283.
[6] *LP*, p. 189.
[7] *Ibid.*, p. 103.
[8] *Ibid.*, p. 192.
[9] *Ethics*, p. 120.
[10] *Ibid.*, p. 137.
[11] *Ibid.*, p. 126.
[12] *Ibid.*, p. 125.
[13] *Ibid.*, p. 201.
[14] *Ibid.*, p. 198.
[15] *Ibid.*, p. 143.
[16] *Ibid.*, p. 145.
[17] *Ibid.*, p. 221.
[18] *Ibid.*, p. 110.
[19] *Ibid.*, p. 51.
[20] *Ibid.*, p. 149.
[21] *Ibid.*, pp. 19-20.
[22] *Ibid.*, p. 81.
[23] *Ibid.*, p. 82.
[24] *Ibid.*, p. 80.
[25] *Ibid.*
[26] *Ibid.*, p. 212.
[27] *LP*, pp. 243-4.
[28] *Ethics*, p. 72.
[29] *Ibid.*, p. 81.
[30] *LP*, p. 175.
[31] *Ibid.*, pp. 113-14.
[32] *I Loved*, pp. 49-50.
[33] *Ethics*, p. 67.
[34] *LP*, p. 113.
[35] *Ibid.*, p. 201.
[36] *Ibid.*, p. 141, new edition, 1967.
[37] *Ibid.*, p. 147.
[38] *Ethics*, pp. 84-85.
[39] *LP*, p. 226.

CHAPTER ELEVEN

[1] *LP*, p. 172, new edition, 1967.
[2] *Ethics*, p. 119.
[3] *GS*, II, 420 (translated by Eberhard Bethge).
[4] *Ethics*, p. 54.
[5] *Ibid.*, p. 88.
[6] *Ibid.*, p. 204.
[7] *Ibid.*, p. 322.
[8] *Ibid.*, p. 202.
[9] *Ibid.*, p. 70.
[10] *Ibid.*, p. 195.
[11] *Ibid.*, pp. 199-200, new edition, 1967.
[12] *Ibid.*, p. 74.
[13] *Ibid.*, pp. 83-84.
[14] *LP*, p. 222.
[15] *Ibid.*, p. 224.
[16] *Ethics*, pp. 205-6.
[17] *CD*, p. 314.
[18] *Ethics*, p. 202.
[19] *Ibid.*, p. 206.
[20] *Ibid.*, p. 202.
[21] *Ibid.*, p. 239.
[22] *Ibid.*, p. 203.
[23] *Ibid.*
[24] *CD*, p. 298.
[25] *Ethics*, p. 206.
[26] *Ibid.*, p. 301.
[27] *Ibid.*, p. 206.
[28] *Ibid.*, p. 83.
[29] *Ibid.*, p. 354.
[30] *Ibid.*, p. 355.
[31] *Ibid.*
[32] *Ibid.*, p. 324.
[33] *Ibid.*, pp. 202-3.
[34] *Ibid.*, p. 300.

[35] *Ibid.*, p. 301.
[36] *Ibid.*, p. 111.
[37] *Ibid.*, p. 110.
[38] *Ibid.*, p. 112.
[39] *Ibid.*
[40] *Ibid.*, p. 114.
[41] *Ibid.*, p. 116.
[42] *NRS*, p. 225.
[43] *Ethics*, p. 322.
[44] *Ibid.*, p. 109.
[45] *Ibid.*, pp. 355-6.
[46] *Ibid.*, p. 356.
[47] *Ibid.*, p. 361.
[48] *Ibid.*, p. 361.
[49] *CD*, p. 303.
[50] *Ethics*, p. 302.
[51] *LP*, pp. 197-98.
[52] *Ethics*, p. 297.
[53] *Ibid.*, p. 202.
[54] *Ibid.*, p. 199.
[55] *LP*, p. 211.
[56] *Ethics*, p. 17.
[57] *Ibid.*, pp. 26-7.
[58] *Ibid.*, p. 28.
[59] *Ibid.*, p. 64.
[60] *Ibid.*, p. 265.
[61] *Ibid.*
[62] *NRS*, p. 46.
[63] *LP*, p. 17.
[64] *Ethics*, p. 58.
[65] *Ibid.*, p. 67.
[66] *Ibid.*, p. 191.
[67] *Ibid.*, p. 85.
[68] *Ibid.*, p. 285.
[69] *Ibid.*, p. 69.
[70] *Ibid.*, p. 214.
[71] *Ibid.*, p. 193.
[72] *Ibid.*, pp. 192-3.
[73] *Ibid.*, p. 85.
[74] *Ibid.*, p. 363.
[75] *Ibid.*, p. 328.
[76] *Ibid.*, p. 364.
[77] *Ibid.*, p. 31.
[78] *Ibid.*, p. 269.
[79] *Ibid.*, p. 195.
[80] *Ibid.*, pp. 200-1.

CHAPTER TWELVE

[1] *LP*, appendix to British edition.
[2] *LP*, p. 87.
[3] *Ibid.*, pp. 206-7.
[4] *Ibid.*, p. 136.
[5] *Ibid.*, p. 52.
[6] *Ibid.*, p. 112.
[7] *Ibid.*, p. 57.
[8] *Ibid.*, p. 241.
[9] *Ibid.*, p. 97.
[10] *Ibid.*, pp. 102-3.
[11] *Ibid.*, p. 87.
[12] *Ibid.*, p. 178.
[13] *Ibid.*, p. 132.
[14] *Ibid.*, p. 81.
[15] *Ibid.*, pp. 221-2.
[16] *Ibid.*, p. 108.
[17] *Ibid.*
[18] *Ibid.*, p. 84.
[19] *Ibid.*, p. 137.
[20] *Ibid.*, p. 67.
[21] *Ibid.*, pp. 95-6.
[22] S. Payne Best, *The Venlo Incident* (London, 1950), p. 180.
[23] Bethge, in "Challenge," p. 28.
[24] Gerhard Ebeling, *Word and Faith* (Philadelphia, 1963), p.

100 (referred to hereafter as *Word*).
25 *Ibid.*, p. 106.
26 *LP*, p. 104.
27 *Ibid.*, p. 162.
28 *Ibid.*, p. 159.
29 *Ibid.*, p. 162.
30 *Ibid.*
31 *Word*, p. 109.
32 *Christ the Center*, p. 62.
33 *Ethics*, pp. 298-9.
34 *Ibid.*, p. 297.
35 *LP*, p. 164.
36 *Ibid.*, pp. 238-9.
37 *Ibid.*, p. 209, new edition, 1967.
38 *Ibid.*, p. 157.
39 *Ibid.*, pp. 162-3.
40 *Ibid.*, p. 167.
41 *Ibid.*, p. 195.
42 *Word*, pp. 148ff.
43 *LP*, pp. 164-5.
44 *Ibid.*, p. 164.
45 *Ibid.*
46 In Godsey, *Preface*, p. 32.
47 *Ibid.*, pp. 28-9.
48 Karl Barth, *Church Dogmatics*, (Edinburgh, 1952), 302.
49 *LP*, p. 168.
50 *Ibid.*
51 *Word*, p. 148.
52 *LP*, p. 165.
53 *Ibid.*, p. 155, new edition, 1967.
54 *Ibid.*, p. 237.
55 *Ibid.*, p. 210, new edition, 1967.
56 *Ethics*, pp. 196-7.
57 *LP*, p. 165.
58 *Ibid.*, p. 196.
59 *Ibid.*
60 *Ibid.*, pp. 190-1.
61 *Ibid.*, pp. 211-2.
62 *Ibid.*, p. 213.
63 *Ibid.*, p. 166.
64 *Ethics*, p. 66.
65 *LP*, p. 214.

CHAPTER THIRTEEN

1 *LP*, p. 183.
2 *Ibid.*, p. 195.
3 *Ethics*, p. 98.
4 *Ibid.*, p. 99.
5 *LP*, p. 217.
6 *Ibid.*, pp. 217-8.
7 *Ibid.*, p. 218.
8 *Ibid.*
9 *Ibid.*, p. 210.
10 *Ibid.*, pp. 196-7.
11 *Ibid.*, pp. 218-9.
12 *Ibid.*, p. 195.
13 *Ibid.*, p. 165.
14 *Ibid.*, p. 196.
15 *Ibid.*, p. 209.
16 *Ibid.*, p. 212.
17 *Ibid.*, pp. 165-6.
18 *Ibid.*, pp. 163-4.
19 *Ibid.*, pp. 197-8.
20 *Ibid.*, p. 167.
21 *Ibid.*, p. 199.
22 *Ibid.*, pp. 199-200.
23 *Ibid.*, p. 200.
24 *Ethics*, p. 324.
25 *LP*, p. 162.
26 *Ibid.*, p. 172, new edition, 1967.
27 *Ibid.*, p. 167.
28 *Ibid.*, p. 164.

[29] *Ibid.*, p. 188.

[30] *Ibid.*

[31] *Ibid.*, p. 215.

[32] *Ibid.*, p. 217.

[33] *Ibid.*, p. 133.

[34] *Ibid.*, p. 168.

[35] *Ibid.*, p. 189.

[36] *Ibid.*, pp. 187-8.

[37] *Ibid.*, p. 238.

[38] *Word,* p. 135.

[39] *LP,* p. 226.

[40] Jenkins, *Beyond Religion* (Philadelphia, 1962), p. 123.

[41] *LP,* p. 228.

[42] *Ibid.*, p. 143.

[43] Leber, *op. cit.*, p. 218.

[44] *LP,* p. 189.

[45] Walter F. Otto, *The Greek Gods* (London, 1955), p. 287.

[46] *LP,* p. 231.

[47] *Ibid.*, p. 232.

[48] *Ibid.*, p. 113.

[49] *Ibid.*

[50] *Ibid.*, p. 232.

[51] *Ibid.*, p. 222.

[52] *Ibid.*, pp. 224-5.

[53] *Ibid.*, p. 222.

[54] *Ibid.*, pp. 165-6.

[55] *Ibid.*, p. 242.

[56] *Ibid.*, p. 133.

[57] *Ibid.*, pp. 222-3.

[58] *Ibid.*, pp. 195-6.

[59] *Ibid.*, p. 204.

[60] *Ibid.*, p. 224.

[61] *Ibid.*, p. 219.

[62] *Ibid.*, pp. 219-20.

[63] *Ibid.*, p. 220.

[64] *Ibid.*, p. 166.

[65] *Ibid.*, p. 233.

[66] *Ibid.*, p. 237.

[67] *Ibid.*, pp. 237-8.

[68] *Ibid.*, p. 238.

[69] *Ibid.*, p. 243.

[70] *Ibid.*, p. 184.

[71] *Ibid.*, pp. 183-4.

[72] *Ibid.*, p. 19.

[73] *Ibid.*, p. 138.

[74] *Ibid.*, p. 27.

[75] *Ibid.*, p. 22.

[76] *Ibid.*, pp. 21-2.

CHAPTER FOURTEEN

[1] Rothfels, *op. cit.*, p. 141.

[2] *LP,* p. 226.

[3] *NRS,* pp. 289 and 219.

[4] *Ibid.*, p. 289.

[5] *WF,* p. 206.

[6] *NRS,* p. 225.

[7] *WF,* p. 246.

[8] *LP,* p. 20.

[9] *I Knew,* p. 205.

[10] *Ibid.*, p. 194.

CHAPTER FIFTEEN

[1] *NRS,* p. 157.

[2] *Ibid.*, p. 137.

[3] *Ibid.*, p. 291.

[4] *Ibid.*, p. 255.

[5] *LP,* p. 238.

[6] *Ethics,* p. 202.

[7] The basis for the rest of this chapter is an address by Dr. James Nelson, "Theology and the Third Culture," presented at

the United Theological Seminary in Dayton, Ohio, May 20, 1966.

[8] Karl Barth, *Theology and Church* (New York, 1962), p. 274.

[9] Christopher Dawson, *The Dividing of Christendom* (New York, 1965), p. 3.

[10] *LP*, p. 222.

[11] *Ibid.*, p. 164.

[12] *Ibid.*

CHAPTER SIXTEEN

[1] *CS*, p. 123.

[2] *AB*, p. 131.

[3] Godsey, *Preface*, p. 36.

[4] *LT*, p. 21.

[5] *Ibid.*, p. 23.

[6] *NRS*, p. 161.

[7] *Ibid.*

[8] *Ibid.*, p. 162.

[9] *Ibid.*, p. 163.

[10] *Ibid.*, p. 162.

[11] *Ibid.*, p. 163.

[12] *LP*, p. 226.

[13] *Ibid.*, pp. 226-7.

[14] *Ethics*, p. 83.

[15] *Ibid.*

[16] *Ibid.*, p. 198.

[17] Bonhoeffer, *Christ the Center*, p. 32.

[18] *Ibid.*

CHAPTER SEVENTEEN

[1] Reinhold Niebuhr, "The Death of a Martyr," *Christianity and Crisis*, June 25, 1945, pp. 6-7.

[2] *I Knew*, p. 135.

[3] *Ibid.*, p. 232.

[4] *LP*, p. 222.

[5] *Ibid.*, p. 224.

[6] *Ibid.*, p. 162.

[7] *Ibid.*, p. 129.

A Brief Chronology of Bonhoeffer's Life

1906 *February 4.* Born in Breslau, Germany, to Karl Bonhoeffer and Paula von Hase Bonhoeffer.

1923 *Autumn.* Began studying for the winter semester at Tübingen University.

1924 *Summer.* Toured Rome and North Africa.

September. Began studies at the University of Berlin in theology.

1927 *December 27.* Successfully presented *The Communion of Saints* and defended eleven theses for the licentiate degree in theology.

1928 *February 15.* Took on a vicarage in Barcelona for a German colony.

1929 *February 18.* Returned to Berlin.

1930 *July 18.* Submitted *Act and Being* for the entrance dissertation of a beginning professor at the University of Berlin.

September 1. The Communion of Saints published.

September 5. Left for New York, as a Sloan Fellow to the Union Theological Seminary.

1931 *July.* Met and spent several days with Karl Barth in Bonn.

September. Appointed a Youth Secretary for the World Alliance for Promoting International Friendship through the Churches.

November 11. Ordination.

November. Began difficult confirmation class in Wedding, an industrial suburb in North Berlin.

1932 *April.* Attended an important Youth Commission in London.

July. National Socialists (Nazis) gained 230 seats in Parliament.

1933 *January 30.* Adolf Hitler became Chancellor of Germany.

February 1. Bonhoeffer's broadcast on the "Leadership Principle" cut short by the Gestapo.

April 7. The appearance of the Aryan Clauses, forbidding those of Jewish origin to hold office in state or Church.

September. Bonhoeffer worked with Martin Niemöller in preparing the Pastors' Emergency League.

October. Left for England to become pastor of two German-speaking congregations, St. Paul and Sydenham in London.

1934 *May 29–31.* The first synod of the Confessing Church, at Barmen.

Summer. Preparations for the Fanö Conference.
August. World Alliance Universal Christian Council Conference at Fanö, Denmark.

1935 *January.* Plans made to visit India were confirmed. Bonhoeffer was suddenly called to take over a seminary for the Confessing Church.
April 26. Bonhoeffer met with his first class of students at the seminary in Zingst, on the Baltic.
June 24. The seminary was moved to Finkenwalde.
September. Bonhoeffer established the "Brethren House" at Finkenwalde.

1936 Began work on *The Cost of Discipleship.*
Feb.-March. A visit made with students of the seminary to Denmark and Sweden.

1937 *February.* Oxford Conference in London; the Youth Commission.
October. The Gestapo closed down Finkenwalde.
November 27. The Cost of Discipleship published.

1938 *February.* Bonhoeffer introduced through his brother-in-law Hans von Dohnanyi to Sack, Oster, Canaris, and Beck, and told of the resistance.

1939 *March.* Visited London, to confer with Bishop Bell, Reinhold Niebuhr, and Visser't Hooft.
June 2. Left England for the United States, on a specially arranged lecture tour.
July 13. Returned to London, after deciding to remain in Germany.
August 25. Bonhoeffer made an agent of the *Abwehr,* thereby avoiding conscription.

1940 *March 17.* The Gestapo broke up the seminary efforts in Koslin and Gross-Schölnwitz.
Began work on the *Ethics.*

1941 *February 24*. Visited Karl Barth in Switzerland on an *Abwehr* assignment.
October. Introduced into the inner resistance circle of the *Abwehr* and made a key resistance figure.

1942 *May 30*. Flew to Stockholm to meet Bishop Bell to confer about Allied reaction to a possible political overthrow.
September. An *Abwehr* agent was apprehended for attempting to smuggle currency over the border; his comments led to evidence incriminating both von Dohnanyi and Bonhoeffer.

1943 *April 5*. Von Dohnanyi and Bonhoeffer were arrested; Bonhoeffer sent to the military prison Tegel, in Berlin.
July. Intensive and continuous interrogations.

1944 *June 6*. The Normandy landing.
July 20. The assassination attempt on Hitler by Count von Stauffenberg.
October 8. Bonhoeffer was removed from Tegel and sent to the high-security prison Prinz-Albrecht-Strase. Writings ceased.

1945 *February*. Bonhoeffer shipped to Buchenwald.
April 3. Began the final trip from Buchenwald.
April 9. To Flossenbürg: the trip completed; there, hanged alongside Oster, Sack, and Canaris.

Bibliography

I. Works by Dietrich Bonhoeffer. Available in English.

Act and Being. Translated by Bernard Noble, with an Introduction by Ernst Wolf. New York: Harper and Brothers, 1962.

Christ the Center. Translated by John Bowden. New York: Harper and Row Publishers, 1966. Bonhoeffer's important Christology lectures of the summer of 1933.

The Communion of Saints. Translated by Ronald Gregor Smith *et al*. New York: Harper and Row Publishers, 1963.

"Concerning the Christian Idea of God," *The Journal of Religion,* XII (April, 1932), 177-185.

The Cost of Discipleship. Translated by Reginald H. Fuller, with a Memoir by G. Leibholz. New York: The Macmillan

Company, first edition, abridged, 1948; second edition, unabridged and revised, 1959; paperback edition, 1963.

Creation and Fall. Translated by John C. Fletcher. New York: The Macmillan Company, first edition, 1959; paperback edition, 1965.

Ethics. Edited by Eberhard Bethge. Translated by Neville Horton Smith. New York: The Macmillan Company, 1955.

Gesammelte Schriften, Vols. I-IV. Edited by Eberhard Bethge. Munich: Christian Kaiser Verlag, 1958-1961. These volumes contain a number of writings in English.

I Loved This People: Testimonies of Responsibility. Translated by Keith R. Crim. Richmond, Va.: John Knox Press, 1965.

Letters and Papers from Prison. Edited by Eberhard Bethge. Translated by Reginald H. Fuller. London: SCM Press, first edition, 1953; second edition, revised, 1956. American edition entitled *Prisoner for God.* New York: The Macmillan Company, third edition, with revised translation, 1967; paperback edition entitled *Letters and Papers from Prison,* 1962.

Life Together. Translated, with an Introduction, by John W. Doberstein. New York: Harper and Brothers, 1954.

No Rusty Swords, Letters, Lectures, Notes: 1928-1932. Edited and introduced by Edwin H. Robinson. Translated by Edwin H. Robinson and John Bowden. New York: Harper and Row, 1965. The first translated volumes of excerpts from *Gesammelte Schriften.*

Temptation. Translated by Kathleen Downham. New York: The Macmillan Company, 1955; paperback edition, 1965.

"Thy Kingdom Come," in *Preface to Bonhoeffer,* by John Godsey. Philadelphia: Fortress Press, 1965, pp. 28-47. An important speech made by Bonhoeffer in 1932, anticipating much of his mature theology.

The Way to Freedom: Letters, Lectures and Notes from the Collected Works, vol. II. Edited by E. H. Robertson. Translation by E. H. Robertson and John Bowden. New York: Harper and Row, 1967. A more disappointing volume than *No Rusty Swords,* perhaps because of all the intermittent and unnecessary jumps, which Robertson tries to make up for with brief notations.

II. Major Works about Bonhoeffer

Bethge, Eberhard. "The Challenge of Dietrich Bonhoeffer's Life and Theology," *The Chicago Theological Seminary Register,* LI (February, 1961), 1-38. A concise but excellent treatment of the developments in Bonhoeffer's thought. An attempt to locate the kernel idea in each phase of Bonhoeffer's writings.

Godsey, John D. *Preface to Bonhoeffer*. Philadelphia: Fortress Press, 1965. A fine though brief introduction to Bonhoeffer, followed by two of the shorter writings: "Thy Kingdom Come" (1932) and "The First Table of the Ten Commandments" (1944).

———. *The Theology of Dietrich Bonhoeffer*. Philadelphia: Westminster Press, 1960. An extensive, highly scholarly treatment of Bonhoeffer's theology. The method is to focus carefully on each work and scan the ideas and development. Extremely helpful biographically.

Marty, Martin E., editor. *The Place of Bonhoeffer*. New York: Association Press, 1962. A collection of essays emphasizing Bonhoeffer's methodology. If a bit uneven, the volume contains some excellent treatments of Bonhoeffer's work. Good criticisms of the early treatises and Bonhoeffer's use of Scripture.

Mehta, Ved. *The New Theologian.* New York: Harper and Row, 1966. Contains a lively, if not totally accurate, description of Bonhoeffer and Bethge—from the *New Yorker* article.

Phillips, John. *Christ for Us in the Thought of Dietrich Bonhoeffer.* New York: Harper and Row, 1967. A carefully constructed analysis of key terms and seminal concepts in Bonhoeffer's writings.

Robertson, E. H., *Dietrich Bonhoeffer.* Richmond, Va.: John Knox Press, 1966. (Makers of Contemporary Theology series) A brief, perhaps overly brief, attempt to interpret and outline Bonhoeffer's life and theology for the layman. Robertson's grasp of Bonhoeffer's understanding is weak in spots.

Zimmermann, Wolf-Dieter and Ronald Gregor Smith (eds.). *I Knew Dietrich Bonhoeffer.* Translated from the German by Kathe Gregor Smith. New York: Harper and Row, 1967. A very readable and inspiring group of accounts about Bonhoeffer from men who knew him. Until Bethge's biography appears, this will probably remain the best glimpse available of Bonhoeffer's personality.

III. Articles and Essays on Bonhoeffer

Berger, Peter L. "Camus, Bonhoeffer and the World Come of Age," *The Christian Century,* April 8 and 15, 1959.

Bethge, Eberhard. "Dietrich Bonhoeffer," *The Student Movement,* LVI (1954), 24-26.

———. "Dietrich Bonhoeffer: Champion of Freedom," *World Dominion,* XXXV (April, 1957), 77-81. Originally a talk given on the British Broadcasting Co. network in November, 1955, and published in "German Life and Letters."

———. "Dietrich Bonhoeffer: An Account of His Life," *The Plough,* III (1955), 35-42.

———. "The Editing and Publishing of the Bonhoeffer Papers," *The Andover Newton Bulletin,* LII (December, 1959), 1-24.

Busing, Paul F. W. "Reminiscences of Finkenwalde," *The Christian Century,* September 20, 1961, pp. 1108-1111.

Cox, Harvey. "Beyond Bonhoeffer?" *Commonweal,* September 17, 1965, pp. 653-657.

De Jong, Pieter. "Camus and Bonhoeffer on the Fall," *Canadian Journal of Theology,* VII (October, 1961), 245-257.

Ebeling, Gerhard. *Word and Faith.* Translated by James W. Leitch. Philadelphia: Fortress Press, 1963. Ebeling's careful, almost exegetical analysis of Bonhoeffer's term, "nonreligious interpretation of biblical concepts," is perhaps the clearest theological work available on the meaning of "religionless Christianity." Chapters 4 and 9.

Elson, John. "A Man for Others," *Life,* May 7, 1965, pp. 108-116.

Godsey, John D. "Barth and Bonhoeffer," *The Drew Gateway,* XXXIII (Autumn, 1962), 3-20.

———. "Theology from a Prison Cell," *The Drew Gateway,* XXVII (Spring, 1957), 139-154.

Green, Clifford, "Bonhoeffer's Concept of Religion," *Union Seminary Quarterly Review,* XIX (November, 1963), 11-21.

Hamilton, William. "A Secular Theology for a World Come of Age," *Theology Today,* XVIII (January, 1962), 435-459.

Lochman, J. M. "From the Church to the World," in *New Theology No. 1,* ed. by Martin E. Marty and Dean G. Peerman, pp. 169-191. New York: The Macmillan Company, 1964.

Marty, Martin E. "Bonhoeffer: Seminarians' Theologian," *The Christian Century,* April 20, 1960, pp. 467-469.

Minthe, Eckhard. "Bonhoeffer's Influence in Germany," *The Andover Newton Quarterly,* New Series, II (September, 1961), 13-45.

Niebuhr, Reinhold. "The Death of a Martyr," *Christianity and Crisis,* V (June 25, 1945), 6-7.

Smith, Ronald Gregor. *The New Man,* especially chapter V, "This-Worldly Transcendence." New York: Harper and Brothers, 1956.

Vidler, A. R. "Religion and the National Church." In (his own edited work) *Soundings: Essays concerning Christian Understanding,* ch. 11. London: Cambridge University Press, 1962.

IV. Useful Background Reading

Altizer, Thomas J. J., and William Hamilton. *Radical Theology and the Death of God.* Indianapolis: Bobbs-Merrill Co., 1966. As good an introduction as any to the "death of

God" controversy stemming in part from Bonhoeffer's prison writings.

Barth, Karl. *Church Dogmatics.* Edinburgh: T. and T. Clark. Especially vol. I, 2, the chapter entitled, "The Revelation of God as the Abolition of Religion," pp. 280-361.

———. *The German Church Conflict.* Translated by P. T. A. Parker. Richmond, Va.: John Knox Press, 1965.

———. *The Humanity of God.* Translated by Theodore Wieser and John Newton Thomas. Richmond: John Knox Press, 1960.

———. *Theology and Church,* Shorter Writings, 1920-28. Translated by Louise Pettibone Smith. New York: Harper and Row, 1962.

Bell, G. K. A. *The Church and Humanity,* 1939-1946, especially chapters 18 and 20. London: Longmans, Green, and Co., 1946.

Berger, Peter L. *The Precarious Vision,* especially chapters 8 and 9. Garden City, New York: Doubleday and Co., 1961.

Best, S. Payne. *The Venlo Incident.* London: Hutchinson & Co., Ltd., 1950. The memoirs of a man who was very close to Bonhoeffer the last few days.

Cochrane, Arthur C. *The Church's Confession under Hitler.* Philadelphia: The Westminster Press, 1962. An excellent treatment of the early years of the Confessing Church.

Cox, Harvey. *The Secular City.* New York: The Macmillan Company, 1965. A provocative treatment of "secular theology," very much in the vein of Bonhoeffer's mature thought.

Dawson, Christopher. *The Dividing of Christendom.* New York: Sheed and Ward, 1965.

Fletcher, Joseph. *Situation Ethics.* Philadelphia: The Westminster Press, 1966. A good statement of recent thinking on situation ethics; draws strongly from Bonhoeffer and offers interesting points of comparison with Bonhoeffer's ethical thought.

Gaevernitz, Gere S. (ed.). *They Almost Killed Hitler.* New York: The Macmillan Co., 1947.

Hartwell, Herbert. *The Theology of Karl Barth.* Philadelphia: The Westminster Press, 1964. A brief but dense presentation of the major themes in Barthian thought.

Jenkins, Daniel. *Beyond Religion,* The Truth and Error in "Religionless Christianity." Philadelphia: The Westminster Press, 1962. Contains one of the best statements of Bonhoeffer's relationship to Barth, especially in the critique of religion.

Leber, Annedore (ed.). *Conscience in Revolt.* Introduced by Robert Birley and translated by Rosemary O'Neill. Westport, Conn.: Associated Booksellers, n.d. A fine presentation of the men and women who dared challenge Hitler.

Littell, Franklin H. "The Protestant Churches and Totalitarianism (in Germany 1933-1945)," in *Totalitarianism,* edited, with an introd. by Carl J. Friedrich. New York: Grosset and Dunlap, Universal Library, 1964, pp. 108-119. A brief study into the failure of the Protestant churches to fully and effectively combat the Nazi crisis; some penetrating observations about the conditions of the Church at the time.

Manvell, Roger, and Heinrich Frankel. *The Men Who Tried to Kill Hitler.* New York: Coward McCann, 1964. One of the best books on the resistance movement and on Bonhoeffer's involvement in it.

Mascall, E. L. *The Secularization of Christianity.* New York: Holt, Rinehart and Winston, 1966. An interesting, elaborate criticism of Bishop Robinson's *Honest to God* and the entire movement of secular theology.

Otto, Walter E. *The Homeric Gods,* the Spiritual Significance of Greek Religion. Translated by Moses Hadas. London: Thames and Hudson, 1955. The book which deeply impressed Bonhoeffer in his final months at Tegel prison.

Prittie, Terence. *Germans against Hitler.* Boston: Little, Brown, and Co., 1964.

Reast, Benjamin A. *Toward a Theology of Involvement: the Thought of Ernst Troeltsch.* Philadelphia: The Westminster Press, 1966.

Robinson, John A. T. *Honest to God.* Philadelphia: The Westminster Press, 1963. The explosive book which brought Bonhoeffer into such wide popularity.

———. *The New Reformation?* Philadelphia: The Westminster Press, 1965. The important sequel to *Honest to God.* Again dependent upon Bonhoeffer, though now in a slightly different way.

Rothfels, Hans. *The German Opposition to Hitler.* Hinsdale, Ill.: Henry Regnery Co., 1948. A highly perceptive study of the resistance effort and the men involved.

Rouse, Ruth, and Stephen Charles Neill (eds.). *A History of the Ecumenical Movement: 1517–1948.* Philadelphia: The Westminster Press, 1954. The classic study of the ecumenical movement: its history, the leaders, and the times.

Sanders, Thomas G. *Protestant Concepts of Church and State.* Garden City, New York: Doubleday and Co. (Anchor Books), 1964. A valuable study of the traditional concepts of Church and state in various Protestant denominations and traditions.

Schmidt, Karl T. *Rediscovering the Natural in Protestant Theology.* Minneapolis: Augsburg Publishing House, 1962. A thesis on the loss and recent rediscovery of "the natural" as a fundamental conception for theology.

Smith, Ronald Gregor. *Secular Christianity.* New York: Harper and Row, 1966. One of the best available interpretations of what Bonhoeffer suggested in his "non-religious interpretation of biblical concepts."

———. "A Theological Perspective of the Secular," *The Christian Scholar,* XLIII (March, 1960), 11.

Student World, LVI (1963). A special entire issue on "Secularization."

Tavard, George. *Two Centuries of Ecumenism,* the Search for Unity. Notre Dame, Indiana: Fides Publishers, 1960. Translated by Royce W. Hughes. A good popular treatment of the ecumenical movement and its history.

Van Buren, Paul M. *The Secular Meaning of the Gospel,* especially ch. 1, "Introduction." New York: The Macmillan Co., 1963.

von Weizsacker, C. F. *The World View of Physics.* Chicago: University of Chicago Press, 1952. A book which impressed Bonhoeffer while he was in prison.

Wheeler-Bennett, John. *The Nemesis of Power:* The German Army in Politics, 1918–1945. New York: St. Martin's

Press, Inc., 1954. One of the best treatments of Nazi Germany available in English.

Williams, Colin W. *What in The World?* New York: National Council of the Churches of Christ in the U.S.A., 1964.

———. *Where in the World?* New York: National Council of the Churches of Christ in the U.S.A., 1963. Both of these books question the Church's building itself around a "religious function" and deliberating, building, and working on that basis. Both works attempt to forge a new life for the Church, rooted in the conception of Church as "mission"; although unstated, the dependence upon Bonhoeffer is profound.

Index

To aid further research, the index includes references to the footnotes, chronology, and bibliography. The main entries offer topical surveys.

When the book refers to a major work of Bonhoeffer, but does not give its title, reference is made to the footnote for identification; for example, 84.5 refers to footnote 5 on page 84.

Index of Personal Names

Index of Subjects